TEN
YEARS
AFTER
IVAN
DENISOVICH

TEN YEARS AFTER IVAN DENISOVICH

Zhores · A · Medvedev

*Translated from the Russian
by Hilary Sternberg*

VINTAGE BOOKS
A Division of Random House
New York

FIRST VINTAGE BOOKS EDITION, July 1974
Epilogue Copyright © 1974 by Zhores A. Medvedev
Copyright © 1973 by Zhores A. Medvedev

Grateful acknowledgement is made to Harper & Row
Publishers, Inc., for permission to reprint
"Solzhenitsyn's Open Letter to the Fourth Soviet
Writers' Congress," in *Solzhenitsyn: A Documentary
Record,* edited by Leopold Labedz. Copyright
© 1970 by Leopold Labedz. Copyright © 1971
by Harper & Row Publishers, Inc.

Library of Congress Cataloging in Publication Data
Medvedev, Zhores Aleksandrovich.
Ten years after Ivan Denisovich.
Reprint of ed. published by Knopf.
Translation of Desiat' let posle Odnogo dnia Ivana
Denisovicha.
1. Salzhenitsyn, Aleksandr Isaevich, 1918–
2. Tvardovskii, Aleksandr Trifonovich, 1910–1971.
3. Russia—Intellectual life—1917–   4. Censorship
—Russia. I. Title.
[PG3488.04Z77513   1975]   891.7'8'4409   74–3433
ISBN 0–394–71112–2

Contents

Author's Note to the English Edition

THE PUBLICATION OF this book is unconnected with my arrival in England for a temporary term of research. I began working on the book in November 1971 long before I received the invitation from my British colleagues, and I completed it at the beginning of November 1972, more than a month before I learned that permission for my trip abroad had been granted.

When in December 1972 I learned of the possibility that I might be coming to work at the National Institute for Medical Research in London, my book had already been caught up by *samizdat* and I notified my English publisher that I intended to have an authorised edition brought out in order to avoid uncontrolled publication of the work. However, after my family and I had been given our foreign travel passports I decided to restrict as far as possible the *samizdat* circulation of the book and to refrain from publishing an edition abroad so as not to give the impression that my trip was in any way connected with the intention to publish the work abroad, and so as not to create unnecessary obstacles when I returned home in 1973. Our luggage was carefully searched at the Brest frontier-station and we were even subjected to the so-called 'personal examination' (body search); all our papers were scrutinised; but the search revealed that I was not trying to take any manuscripts out of the Soviet Union. The only item confiscated by the customs officials was my draft notes on the history of the ancient Russian town of Borovsk – six pages in all.

It was after I had arrived in London that my intentions altered, when one of the characters in my book, the Soviet journalist Victor Louis, published an article in the London *Evening News* on 23 February 1973 claiming that once the USSR had signed the Universal Copyright Convention, Soviet authors who published their writings abroad without the permission of Soviet state publishing houses would be prosecuted. Louis was especially careful to stress that Solzhenitsyn might find himself the victim of severe penalties – up to seven years' imprisonment with confiscation of property. Other reports emanating from the Soviet Union also indicated that adherence to the Universal Copyright Convention was to be accompanied by new laws now in preparation which would aim to ensure that state institutions had a monopoly right to make use not only of *printed* (i.e. published) works but even of unpublished manuscripts. Thus a situation had arisen where an entirely positive act – the recognition of the International Copyright Convention by the Soviet government – could be utilised by certain opponents of liberal thought to persecute a number of authors and to prosecute them for their writings. Prior to 27 May 1973 an author could only be charged on the basis of the content of a work. The *samizdat* circulation of a work, and its publication abroad, are not mentioned in the Civil or Criminal Codes of the RSFSR as punishable acts *per se*. However, all the indications are that certain officials in the (Soviet) administration intend to change this state of affairs as from 1 June 1973. According to a Decree of the Presidium of the Supreme Soviet of the RSFSR dated 21 February 1973, which 'will apply to legal relations arising after 1 June 1973 ... The procedure whereby an author who is a citizen of the USSR assigns the right for his work to be utilised on the territory of a foreign state shall be determined in accordance with the legislation of the USSR.'

This legislation does not yet exist, but (when it does come into force) it is unlikely to be particularly liberal. Prior to June 1973 not every writer has been able to publish his work in the USSR, but the state has had no legal control over publication abroad, and an author has had the right to dispose of his work as he sees fit. From June 1973 this right may disappear. Dozens of works, completed or still in preparation, may never reach their potential readers if authors' rights are to be severely restricted by Soviet laws, if direct contact between an author and a foreign publisher is to be an indictable offence. I hope that this will not be the case. But if it does happen, I do not wish to find myself an offender against Soviet law in 1974. That is why I am publishing this book before 1 June 1973.[1] I very much regret that its publication coincides in time with my stay in Great Britain, but from the standpoint of existing legislation it

[1] The Russian edition was in fact published in May.

viii

is a wholly legal step. Article 478 of the Civil Code of the RSFSR states: 'Copyright shall be deemed to belong to citizens of the RSFSR and other Union Republics whose works are first published or exist in any objective form on the territory of a foreign state.' This liberal article of the law is shortly to be altered and supplemented. And that is the reason for my haste.

Zhores A. Medvedev

Preface

IT HAS LONG been customary to publish collections of papers honouring a scientist who has made a fundamental contribution to the elaboration or solution of a particular problem. The tradition began in Germany, and the German word, *Festschrift*, is used all over the world. These collections are usually published by friends, colleagues and pupils of the scholar whose achievement is being commemorated; they record events in his career, as well as his personal qualities, explain the substance of his scientific achievement and include papers of their own connected with his ideas. The published book is presented to the scientist at a special celebration.

In the past I had occasion to participate in the compilation of a *Festschrift* dedicated to Professor Fritz Verzar, an eminent specialist in the study of the ageing process, on his eightieth birthday. The collection, to which about thirty scholars from various countries contributed, was presented to Professor Verzar in 1966 during the International Gerontology Congress in Vienna. I hope I shall also be able to contribute to a *Festschrift* for Professor Verzar's ninetieth birthday.

The present book is also a *Festschrift* in honour of an anniversary. It is not an anniversary in the life of a man but of the publication of a book. Scientific landmarks of this kind are also commonly celebrated if the publication in question is one which altered our conceptions in some sphere of knowledge. The present study is dedicated to the tenth anniversary of the publication of a work which was unquestionably significant for the development of both literature and social thought, and its significance was not confined to our country alone.

Although the events with which this book deals revolve around two men whom I regard as my friends, Solzhenitsyn and Tvardovsky, I do not see my task restricted to giving an account of their personal fortunes. I have, on the other hand, tried to give a picture of some of the social phenomena of the past decade.

None of the people mentioned in this book knew of its preparation until it had been completed.

Zh. A. M.

1. Solidarity

IN THE SUMMER of 1964, I took a marvellous holiday on the Black Sea coast of the Crimea with my wife and two sons. During that time I almost gave up reading the papers, and so on 29 August, as I waited for my connection at Moscow's Kiev Station on my way home to Obninsk, I decided to find out what was happening in the world. It was late in the day and the only paper left on the news-stands was *Selskaya Zhizn* (Agricultural Life) for which Muscovites have no great enthusiasm. In the train I opened the paper and at once noticed an article, filling almost half a page, by the President of the All-Union Academy of Agricultural Sciences, M. A. Olshansky, entitled 'Against Misinformation and Slander'. It was clear that Olshansky, who was one of T. D. Lysenko's most faithful followers, was again using the central press as a means of bludgeoning the geneticists. Reading the article I even came upon paragraphs devoted to myself. Olshansky launched into a violent attack on my typescript book on the history of the genetic debate in the USSR which, though it had not yet been published, had circulated widely in *samizdat* since 1962, and declared that the material expounded in this 'voluminous typescript' constituted crude political speculation lacking any basis in fact, and that Medvedev must be brought to trial for dissemination of slander.

The book to which Olshansky referred was already fairly well known in scientific circles. Over the two years of its circulation in *samizdat* it had been read by thousands of people. Many of my colleagues had given me new material and had encouraged me to finish it. During this time I had received a very large number of letters from scientists and writers and several Old Bolsheviks, all of them voicing total solidarity with the criticism of Lysenko and his followers contained in the book, and with my exposure of the arbitrary methods this group of pseudo-scientists had used to deal with their scientific opponents. Consequently I was not particularly worried by Olshansky's article. Let them try me then. Dozens of scientists

1

whom I knew to be resolute supporters of my work would appear as witnesses for the defence and prove that my account was indeed accurate. I did not doubt that in the next few days I would receive scores of letters from geneticists, biologists and other scientists, and from people who had corresponded with me in the past, offering the necessary assistance and expressing their determination not to yield to crude demagogy. A week passed, but there were no letters, nor even telephone calls. The unconditional support for Lysenko expressed at every Plenum of the Central Committee of the Soviet Communist Party in 1964, as well as reports of the creation of a special commission for the reorganisation of biological and agricultural institutions, had changed the climate and made people more cautious. The Obninsk town party committee instructed the administration of my institute to convene a special meeting of its party committee to discuss my actions. The only response to Olshansky's article came from the Voice of America radio station, which reported that the *New York Times* had carried a brief paragraph on the subject.

On 5 September I found the first letter in my letter-box. It was addressed in a fine but clear and expressive hand. There was no sender's address on the envelope but from the postmark the letter had been sent from Ryazan on 2 September. I knew no one in Ryazan. Reaching my flat and opening the envelope I first of all glanced at the signature. My first feelings were of pure delight. Solzhenitsyn! I read the letter, then re-read it, and afterwards returned to it again and again.

Ryazan 2.9.64

Respected Zhores Alexandrovich,

This summer I read your 'Essays'.

I cannot recall for literally years being so haunted by any book as I was by this one of yours. Its sincerity, cogency, simplicity, scrupulous construction and accuracy of tone are beyond all praise. Its relevance to the present day goes without saying.

I know that many readers have found it very exciting even though biology is remote from them. No one can remain indifferent to its future.

On 2 August, the day before Olshansky's despicable article came out, I was planning to come through Obninsk and hoped to call and see you on the offchance, but as it happened we went another way and I didn't get to Obninsk.

At a moment so crucial for you I would like to shake your hand warmly and say how proud I am for you, for your love of the truth and of science in our country. Your book contains only irrefutable facts, and if Olshansky mutters old-time imprecations about a trial, however open and above board – on his own head be it.

I wish you well; be of good cheer and have courage!

I still hope to make your acquaintance.

Solzhenitsyn.

Ryazan, 23
I-ii Kasimovskii per. 12, kv. 3

There were no initials with the surname, but that this was a letter from Alexander Isayevich Solzhenitsyn, the author of *One Day in the Life of Ivan Denisovich* which had amazed and shaken the whole world, there could be no doubt. And this letter was the only written comment I received on the article by Olshansky. But it alone was sufficient support for me not to lose my faith in the power of solidarity.

2. *Novy Mir*, a Literary Miracle, and the Party

BY SEPTEMBER 1964 I knew a great deal about Solzhenitsyn, although at that time I had not yet met him. I had a special interest, which was partly personal, in his fate, in his writings, and in all the circumstances connected with their publication, so that I was an attentive follower of all the events surrounding the appearance of his novel and his stories in *Novy Mir*.

His novel breached – for a time – the barrier in the path of a truly realistic literature which would lay bare the crimes of our Stalinist past. Its publication, it seemed, could only help to consolidate the democratic process. It encouraged hope that in its wake other writings, polemical, historical or scientific, would find their way into print, works that would not attempt to ignore the experiences of the past. *One Day in the Life of Ivan Denisovich* was therefore seen not only as marking a new stage in the development of Soviet literature but also as a sign of improvement in all aspects of intellectual life in our society. Solzhenitsyn's success aroused great hopes in other people, myself included, who had completed works which, for political reasons, had not seen publication.

It was because of my book on Lysenko and his followers that I learned of Solzhenitsyn's novel long before it was published in *Novy Mir*. In the summer of 1962 some friends of mine had told members of the staff of *Komsomolskaya Pravda* of the first version of my work. There was strong support for the typescript in the editorial office and I was commissioned by the science department to write an article on the prospects for Soviet genetics. The article was written jointly by myself and the Leningrad geneticist V. S. Kirpichnikov. To ensure its publication editors decided to acquaint some prominent scientists and writers with the work on which it was based. While I was away on holiday and without consulting me, they had typed out several copies of the book and had shown it to a number of scientists, asking them to sign a letter to the Chief Editor on the

4

need to raise the question of the fate of Soviet genetics. By the time I returned from holiday the editors' enthusiasm had abated. On 11 July 1962 the entire Presidium of the Central Committee of the Communist Party led by N. S. Khrushchev had paid a visit to 'Lenin Hills', Lysenko's Experimental Farm, and on 12 July all the papers, including *Komsomolskaya Pravda*, had carried a report on the visit. Also published was a speech by Khrushchev fully supporting all Lysenko's enterprises. I tried to track down the copies of my book that had been circulated by *Komsomolskaya Pravda* but this proved impossible: the manuscript had undergone spontaneous reproduction.

I took my article on the prospects for Soviet genetics to *Novy Mir*. It was there that I first heard about a story of labour-camp life by an unknown author from Ryazan. The story was said to be of exceptional literary merit and one of the *Novy Mir* staff put it to me that since the novel had only recently been brought to the attention of Khrushchev, it would be better if I did not further embarrass *Novy Mir* by inquiring into other questions that might irritate the party leader. On any question concerning Lysenko and 'Michurinist biology' Khrushchev was inexorable; he had personally ordered the oldest centre of learning in the country, the Timiryazev Agricultural Academy in Moscow, to be closed down because he did not agree with the position taken by the scientists there. (This was in fact the reason for my move to Obninsk.) I took my article back from *Novy Mir*, but it was soon accepted by the Leningrad journal *Neva* and published in its 1963 issue No. 3.

My curiosity was whetted by the news of a story that described life in a camp. The writer V. A. Kaverin whom I met at that time had read it and considered it an outstanding piece of writing. He also told me that Kornei Chukovsky had called it 'a literary miracle'. But I did not succeed in tracking down the manuscript. I learned in October that a decision to publish the story had been taken 'right at the top' and that it would come out in issue No. 11 of the journal. From that moment I watched carefully for the appearance of that issue by scanning the catalogues in the Lenin Library. Copies of books destined for the Lenin Library are received in the course of the obligatory 'advance distribution' whereby the first thirty or forty copies of an edition are distributed to important institutions in Moscow.

The edition proper comes out two or three weeks later. By 9 or 10 November I was reading Solzhenitsyn's *One Day in the Life of Ivan Denisovich* in the library.

I read it three times straight through; I was there all day. Never in my life had I voluntarily read the same piece of writing several times in succession.

A week later everybody was talking of Solzhenitsyn's story, and its author, and the history of the publication of this extra-ordinary work had become the subject of countless legends. Later on, when I had become more closely acquainted with Alexander Tvardovsky and the editors of *Novy Mir* (where the question of publishing a shortened version of my book on Lysenko was being discussed) I was to hear from Tvardovsky on several occasions accounts of some of the events that had preceded the publication of Solzhenitsyn's story. Comparing the details he gave me with what I learned from other persons connected with *Novy Mir*, I am confident that the following brief account is authentic.

Solzhenitsyn had written the story between 1956 and 1958 but made no attempt to have it published until the end of 1961, since he thought its chances were nil. Nor could he bring himself to tell literary friends in Moscow about it, even privately. However, after the Twenty-Second Party Congress openly condemned Stalin's crimes the situation was radically altered. The Twentieth Congress in 1956 too had heard evidence against Stalin, and this had been in the form of a 'secret' speech by Khrushchev which was never published. At the Twenty-Second Congress members of the Presidium of the Central Committee and other leading speakers related the dreadful details of Stalinist repressions, mass executions of Soviet citizens, and the rule of arbitrariness and violence. These speeches were published in the Soviet Press, which indicated that the party leadership had resolved to disclose to the people the whole truth about the crimes of the past. In the new atmosphere Solzhenitsyn decided to offer his story for publication. In a speech to the Congress Tvardovsky had called upon writers faithfully to reflect the dark sides of the 'cult of personality', and Solzhenitsyn paid close attention to this. At Solzhenitsyn's request Lev Kopelev and his wife Raisa Orlova took the typescript to *Novy Mir* at the end of December 1961 and handed it to a staff member in the prose section. At that stage it was called simply *SHCH – 845*, after the number which Ivan Denisovich Shukhov bore on his chest, his back and his hat. Nor was there any indication of the author's identity; Kopelev would only say that he lived in Ryazan. The typescript had an unusual appearance, for it was typed in single spacing, with almost no margins, and covered both sides of the paper; either the author was saving on paper or else he felt that the less paper he used the more easily his writings could be stored.

Despite the unprofessional look of the typescript it was read with great interest in the prose section. The first member of the editorial staff to read it was Anna Samoilovna Berzer. At her request it was quickly re-typed by Tvardovsky's personal secretary after which Anna Berzer passed it to Tvardovsky, recommending it to his attention. Tvardovsky took the typescript home with him; late that evening, lying in bed, he began reading it, and was so excited that he got up and dressed and sat at his desk almost till morning to read the remainder. Next day at the office he asked to be put in touch with Kopelev immediately, for the author's name and address to be tracked down and for the author to be summoned to Moscow at once. Several meetings were held at Tvardovsky's office and it was decided to request permission of the Central Committee to publish the story. No one on the editorial staff had any doubts that an editorial decision alone would not suffice to ensure the story's safe passage through the censor's office. The journal had just published N. Bondarev's novel *Silence*, in which there was a scene describing a house search and the arrest of a person following a slanderous denunciation by an informer. The scene was successfully retained, but with great difficulty, and its publication was followed by official reprimands.

The author of *SHCH – 854* came to the offices of *Novy Mir* at Tvardovsky's invitation and made a very good impression there. At a meeting to discuss the story it was decided to change the title; it was Tvardovsky who suggested *One Day in the Life of Ivan Denisovich*.

Before approaching the Central Committee of the Communist Party Tvardovsky decided to have the story reviewed by leading literary figures in Moscow. Copies of the manuscript were sent to K. Chukovsky, S. Marshak, A. Kaverin, the literary critic V. Lakshin and a number of other men of letters. Their opinions were most favourable.

Then Tvardovsky, and his deputy A. G. Dementiev, drafted a letter to Khrushchev. They cited the unanimous opinion of members of the editorial board and prominent literary figures within the Soviet Writers' Union; *Novy Mir*, they said, requested him to consider the matter of the story's publication.

Tvardovsky knew Khrushchev well. However, he rejected the idea of delivering the letter in person, deciding to send it through official channels. The letter from *Novy Mir*, and with it the copy of *Ivan Denisovich*, was handed to Khrushchev's assistant V. S. Lebedev, who dealt with cultural matters. As personal assistant to Khrushchev, Lebedev was to a certain extent independent of the literature section of the Central Committee's Ideological Commission, which was headed by D. Polikarpov, a man of extremely conservative, Stalinist views.

Lebedev displayed enormous interest in Solzhenitsyn's story and went to great lengths to ensure that it would meet with a favourable reception from Khrushchev.

Ivan Denisovich was read aloud to Khrushchev by Lebedev at Pitsunda on the Black Sea coast, where he was spending his summer holiday. It was late August or early September. Khrushchev telephoned A. I. Mikoyan, who was holidaying nearby, praised the story and asked him to read it through. Mikoyan too expressed his approval. Following this the question of publishing the work was entered on the agenda of forthcoming sessions of the Presidium of the Central Committee. *Novy Mir* received an instruction to print off twenty copies, to be marked 'proof copy', for the members of the Presidium of the Central Committee, and this was promptly done. (In addition Tvardovsky ordered five copies for the editorial staff, and he presented one of these to the author. In accordance with regulations Chief Editors and their deputies have the right to order galley proofs and then print off a run of several bound page proofs. The censor does not read the manuscript but the printers' proof which he passes 'for printing', after which the press may print the main edition.)

I have heard various theories about why Khrushchev, who

liked Solzhenitsyn's story, did not issue a personal directive regarding its publication. All these theories are based on a failure to understand that there are limitations to the powers of the First Secretary[1]; these are most strictly observed, particularly where any kind of publication is concerned. Glavlit (the censorship) is a largely secret, inter-departmental organisation operating on instructions endorsed by the Presidium of the Central Committee, the USSR Council of Ministers and the KGB. If on the basis of such instructions Glavlit bans a particular publication, its decision can be altered only by decree of the Presidium or the Secretariat of the Central Committee. A personal directive from Khrushchev would not have sufficed to lift the censor's ban (if it was an important publication). Equally, a personal directive from Khrushchev would not have been binding on a censor about to examine the question of the publication of *Ivan Denisovich*. For whatever decision is reached by the highest authorities the proof copy of the story must still carry the censor's signature; without this the printer would not accept it to go to press. The regulations regarding the press are in fact adhered to far more strictly than is the Constitution of the USSR; in particular that part of it which deals with freedom of the press, secrecy of correspondence, freedom to demonstrate, and other civil rights. In some countries the executive head of state, the President for example, is not empowered to *prohibit* the organs of the press from publishing any particular material. In the USSR the head of state has the right to *prohibit* publication and may exercise this right even after publication has been approved by Glavlit, which is why advance copies of all publications are automatically sent to the office of the First Secretary for approval. But he does *not* have the right to bypass the censor and issue direct orders for publication, just as he may not promulgate laws, edicts and decrees, or declare a state of war.

The first session of the Presidium of the Central Committee, at which the agenda included the question of the publication of Solzhenitsyn's story in *Novy Mir*, did not manage to reach a decision. Some members of the Presidium announced that they had not had time to read it. Others ventured cautious

---

[1] Khrushchev's full title was 'First Secretary of the Central Committee and Chairman of the Council of Ministers of the USSR'.

9

remarks to the effect that the camp guards ought not to have been shown in such an unfavourable light, 'after all, they were only doing their duty'. The matter was postponed until the next session, at which a motion in favour of publication, proposed by Khrushchev and seconded by Mikoyan, was carried unanimously.

There exist several versions of what happened at that session, but they are of dubious authenticity. The agenda of a session of the Presidium covers a multitude of diverse matters, and the publication of the story could not have been the chief, much less the sole item. One cannot therefore trust either legends that tell of a lengthy debate on the matter and of clashes between differing points of view, or rumours that the question was greeted with complete silence which Khrushchev then declared a 'sign of consent'. Every member of the Presidium certainly had before him a draft resolution, prepared by the Central Committee staff, which was duly passed, and this resolution of the Central Committee eventually reached the offices of *Novy Mir*. Issue No. 11 of the journal, with Solzhenitsyn's story occupying pages 8 to 74, had secured the necessary visas to 'go to press'. Tvardovsky arranged with the publishing-house *Izvestiya*, of which *Novy Mir* is part, to have the size of the edition increased by forty thousand copies. Furthermore, two thousand five hundred copies of the journal were ordered for the enlarged Plenary Session of the Central Committee of the Communist Party, which was to open in November and be devoted to the reorganisation of industrial and agricultural administration in the country, the most radical reform proposed by Khrushchev.

The Plenum opened on 19 November 1962. Tvardovsky, as a member of the Central Committee, was also in the Kremlin Palace of Congresses. Afterwards he would relate with satisfaction how, wherever he looked, he saw blue copies of *Novy Mir* in every hand.

Reviews of *One Day in the Life of Ivan Denisovich* were quick to appear in all the main papers. And they all expressed exalted and appreciative enthusiasm. Less than a week after the story's publication *Pravda* (23 November 1962) carried an article entitled 'In the Name of Truth in the Name of Life' which said among other things:

Into our literature there has come a writer gifted with a rare talent ... Solzhenitsyn's story at times calls to mind Tolstoy's artistic power in its depiction of the national character ...

... But why is it that upon reading this remarkable story not only is one's heart wrung with grief but a light penetrates one's soul? It is because of the story's profound humanity, because in it people remained people even in an atmosphere of mockery ...

The author of this article was the literary critic Vladimir Ermilov, a conservative and an opportunist who had figured in many of the pogrom-like campaigns of the Stalin era. A real breakthrough must have occurred if a man with such a reputation now published an enthusiastic review of *One Day in the Life of Ivan Denisovich*.

A few days later TASS circulated to all newspapers an article giving biographical information about Solzhenitsyn. The article, 'A New Name in our Literature', was published on 28 November 1962 in *Moskovskaya Pravda*, *Sovetskaya Rossiya* and many republican and provincial papers. It contained the following passage:

... Alexander Isayevich Solzhenitsyn was born in Kislovodsk in 1918. Having lost his father, he was brought up by his mother from an early age. He spent his childhood and youth in Rostov-on-Don, attending the grammar school there and graduating from the Faculty of Physics and Mathematics at the University in 1941.

In 1941 he was conscripted into the Soviet Army as a private. In 1942, after graduating from an artillery school, he was appointed commanding officer of an artillery battery and in this capacity he served in the front line without a break until February 1945. He was awarded two orders. In February 1945, when serving in East Prussia with the rank of Captain, Solzhenitsyn was arrested on an unfounded political charge and sentenced to eight years' imprisonment. After serving the full term he was sent into exile, from which he returned in 1956. In 1957 he was fully rehabilitated for lack of corpus delicti. He is now working as a schoolteacher of mathematics and physics.

11

Solzhenitsyn's talent was appreciated too by the USSR Union of Writers. Without waiting for Solzhenitsyn, who at that time was teaching physics in a Ryazan school, to submit an application for membership of the Writers' Union, the Union admitted him to membership on its own initiative. The Novosti Press Agency dispatched a special correspondent to Ryazan to observe Solzhenitsyn giving his lessons of the winter term.

3. The Nomination of *Ivan Denisovich* for the Lenin Prize

IT MUST BE stressed first of all that the immediate success of Solzhenitsyn's story, and the enthusiastic assistance rendered to the author by the editors of the Soviet Union's finest literary journal, were due first and foremost not to its unusual subject but to the truly outstanding artistic quality of the work. In critical articles written at the end of 1962 and in 1963 comparisons were frequently drawn between Solzhenitsyn's style and those of Dostoyevsky and Tolstoy, and they seemed to be valid. The January 1963 issue of *Novy Mir* published two new stories by Solzhenitsyn, *Matryona's Place* and *An Incident at Krechetovka Station*. The distinctive style, originality of language, depth of psychological insight and richness of observation in these stories showed that *Ivan Denisovich* was not the only highly original work by this newly discovered writer. It was not difficult to believe that he would produce many more.

Since the Twentieth Party Congress, the subject of illegal repressions had been discussed, though in a different manner, in Soviet literature. The finest pages of Dudintsev's splendid novel *Not by Bread Alone* are those which describe the hero's arrest and 'court martial', a glaring example of senseless arbitrariness. Yury Bondarev's novel *Silence* and Tvardovsky's poem *Distances* (*Za Dalyu Dal*) had touched upon the theme of illegal repressions. Just before Solzhenitsyn's story came out, *Izvestiya* (6 November 1962) had printed G. Shelest's camp tales about innocent men condemned to languish in the terrible camps of Kolyma.

The chief role in securing a favourable decision on the fate of *Ivan Denisovich* is sometimes ascribed to Alexei Adzhubei, editor of *Izvestiya* and son-in-law of Khrushchev. Stories are told of how Adzhubei and his wife Rada used their influence with Khrushchev. But there is no truth in them. In reality

Adzhubei was envious of Tvardovsky's find and attempted to seize the initiative with Shelest although his work was inferior. Shelest lived in Chita,[1] and his stories, written in 1960–61, had been rejected by *Novy Mir* a year before, on the grounds that the writing was poor and that they did not ring true. When Adzhubei learned that *Ivan Denisovich* had been passed for printing he arranged for the text of Shelest's stories to be telegraphed to him. His one aim was to get out ahead of Tvardovsky. The influence of Adzhubei and Rada on Khrushchev should not be overrated. Biologists and geneticists tried repeatedly to convey directly to Khrushchev various documents and articles concerning Lysenko and the situation in genetics. On several occasions they attempted to enlist the help of Rada, herself a biologist by training, and of Adzhubei, but they always refused to become involved for fear of provoking Khrushchev's displeasure.

Although, of course, the Presidium's approval of *One Day in the Life of Ivan Denisovich* did influence reviews, it was obvious that on the whole the reviewers were sincere in their admiration for both the form and content of the story. At the end of December 1962 there was a meeting between party and government leaders and representatives of the literary and artistic world. A speech made at this meeting by L. F. Ilichev, Chairman of the Ideological Commission and Secretary of the Central Committee, was published on 22 December in *Pravda* (and other papers). It contained a great number of quite unjust reproaches directed at artists and sculptors (for abstract painting that was 'alien to the people'). On the subject of literature, though, Ilichev had this to say:

> In recent months, with the approval of the Central Committee, works have been published that are powerful in both the artistic and the political sense in which the arbitrariness permitted during the period of the personality cult is truthfully and boldly exposed. I need only cite Alexander Solzhenitsyn's story *One Day in the Life of Ivan Denisovich*.

During 1963 a great many articles about Solzhenitsyn's work appeared in national and provincial newspapers, literary and sociological journals and even in learned philological journals.

[1] More than 3,000 miles east of Moscow.

14

It is not my intention to review them all. A list of titles is indicative enough: 'Thus It Was, Thus It Will Not Be' (N. Kruzhkov in *Ogonyok* No. 49, 1962); 'The Hero – Life – Truth' (V. Bushin in *Podyom* No. 5, pp. 112–21, 1963); 'The Daily Bread of Truth' (*Neva*, No. 3, pp. 180–5, 1963); 'Man Triumphs' (N. Gubko in *Zvezda* No. 3, pp. 213–15, 1963), and so on.

Against the general wave of favourable criticism there were isolated voices expressing displeasure, but they were promptly and vigorously rebuffed; these are discussed in V. Ya. Lakshin's excellent essay 'Ivan Denisovich, His Friends and Foes', published in the January 1964 issue of *Novy Mir* (pp. 223–45).

The person of Alexander Solzhenitsyn was an object of enormous interest in literary circles and amongst broad sections of the intelligentsia. I have already mentioned that the press agency 'Novosti' sent a special correspondent to Ryazan at the end of 1962 to do a piece on Solzhenitsyn. The piece ('Visiting Solzhenitsyn in Ryazan' by Victor Bukhanov) was published in the weekly paper *Literaturnaya Rossiya* on 25 January 1963. In itself it was of little interest. Solzhenitsyn had declined to talk about his life, his literary plans or what he had already written. For the most part Bukhanov questioned other people, but they too knew very little about Solzhenitsyn. But what alarmed readers of Bukhanov's article was one section with the rather too blunt heading 'SOLZHENITSYN ILL'. The nature of Solzhenitsyn's illness remained unclear but Bukhanov informed his readers that a few years ago Solzhenitsyn had been at the point of death. He was now undergoing regular and repeated courses of treatment with an extremely powerful drug which caused him to be bed-ridden for a month at a time. Various rumours began circulating in the wake of this article; some people said Solzhenitsyn had cancer, others thought it was tuberculosis. Some maintained that his days were numbered. All this gave rise to great anxiety.

One Day in the Life of Ivan Denisovich not only stimulated widespread discussion in the press on the problem of illegal repressions, it also high-lighted the question of honesty which is so vital to literature. Here was honest realism combined with true craftsmanship; it set a standard for socially conscious and artistic writing. Solzhenitsyn had only uncovered a tiny fragment of our past; now thinking people wanted to see the whole picture. His story was read by vast numbers of people. The entire enlarged edition of *Novy Mir* sold out within hours. In January 1963 *Ivan Denisovich* came out by itself in the 'Roman-Gazeta' series in an edition of at least 750,000 copies – perhaps more, since 'Roman-Gazeta' often make a second and third impression. In February 1963 the publishing house Sovetskii Pisatel also published the story in book form in an edition of 100,000 copies. All these editions sold out very quickly.

From December 1962 editorial offices of journals and publishers began to be flooded with typescripts of short stories, essays, diaries, novellas and novels describing life in Stalin's camps, in exile, on convict trains, and in prisons, depicting the lawlessness of the bureaucratic hierarchy, the fate of the millions who returned home from captivity, the death and sufferings of the hundreds of thousands of people deported during the years of collectivisation, and many other painful subjects. It seemed that all these years people had been writing quantities of material of the most diverse kinds about their past experiences, the fate of friends and relatives, the rule of terror, the mockery and brutality of the Stalinist regime. But they had hidden it all away until better times. The publication of Solzhenitsyn's story showed them that those better times had arrived. They were, of course, of variable literary quality, but some reached a very high standard.

However, the publishing system, under the most rigid control of the censors, did not cater for the publication of works like these. Solzhenitsyn's story had appeared by decision of the Presidium, which decision related only to that one work and did nothing to remove existing restrictions in general. If Soviet literature as a whole was to rise to the level of realism achieved in Solzhenitsyn's story, the censorship had to be abolished. Tvardovsky, to whom many of these works of fiction and memoirs were sent in late 1962 and early 1963, understood this very well. (The best known of the works he received was Evgenia Ginzburg's documentary chronicle *Into the Whirlwind*.) Tvardovsky could not appeal to the Central Committee in each individual case. He therefore decided to confront the Committee with the more general problem of relaxing censorship. Tvardovsky's first talk with Khrushchev on the subject was extremely encouraging. He had prepared his argument very carefully. His main contention was that editors, whether on journals or in publishing houses, were far more responsible and experienced than censors, since the staff of the censor's office is made up for the most part of the less successful employees of publishing houses. 'I mean, you wouldn't give them my job, would you? But why can't I, a member of the Party's Central Committee, a writer and an editor, decide whether or not to publish a particular story or a poem? After all, our entire editorial staff discusses it and makes a decision – and then some total stranger from Glavlit, some fool who understands nothing about literature, goes and blue-pencils our decisions.'

Khrushchev took a very favourable view of the suggestion that literary censorship should be abolished. He even recalled the recent lifting of censorship on articles by foreign correspondents accredited in Moscow.[2] 'We lifted the censorship on foreign correspondents,' Khrushchev remembered, 'and look what happened. Nothing. They told rather fewer lies.'

Following this conversation Tvardovsky at once informed the literature section of the Central Committee of Khrushchev's attitude and also that a question on the subject of censorship was in preparation.

About this time Tvardovsky completed his celebrated poem *Tyorkin in Paradise* which had not the slightest chance of being passed by the censor. The poem included a rather sharp, albeit satirically couched reference to censorship itself.

> All of a sweat he corrects articles,
> Nosing through them back and forth:
> Now compressing, now expanding,
> Now inserting a word of his own,
> Now striking out someone else's,
> Or conferring a tick,
> He's his own boss, both Glav and Lit,[3]
> Now he adds inverted commas,
> Now he strips words bare again.

[2] Prior to 1961, all dispatches from Moscow by foreign correspondents had to be subjected to compulsory censorship; this had made their work very difficult and led to continual clashes. (Author's note.)

[3] In Russian a play on *Glavlit*, the official name of the censorship machine, and the word *glava*, meaning head or chief.

Then he quietens, peering dully,
Mouth agape, with vacant gaze.
Takes an eyeglass to the line,
Crowing like a strutting cock.
Now the final scrutinising,
Over the same old page he goes,
Reads not only top to bottom,
But from bottom to top as well.

Once you fall into his clutches,
Sheer fantasy – he'll dig your grave!

There is a superfluity of fools,
And what arrant fools at that,
In the system, in the Party Network . . .
How can we get rid of them,
When there are such swarms of them?
We work here systematically
With fools.

We'd give anything to persuade them
To retire, but they hang on and on.
So then we steer them into censorship
With a rise in salary.
It's such a cosy little job,
They're unlikely to move on anywhere else . . .

(The poem did indeed meet with objections from Glavlit.
Tvardovsky recited it at a meeting between Khrushchev and
foreign journalists, and it was subsequently published in the
paper *Izvestiya* in 1963 as a result of an instruction issued by
Krushchev and approved by the Secretariat of the Central
Committee.)[4]

[4] Publication in *Izvestiya* rather than in a literary journal was occasioned
first and foremost by the desire to avoid intervention by the relevant section
of Glavlit. Notwithstanding Khrushchev's approval of the poem, Glavlit
could still insist on changes being made since the Central Committee had not
issued any special resolution on its publication. But material published by
newspapers is not checked by the literary department of Glavlit. The representative of Glavlit attached to the editorial board of a central newspaper
has the special assignment of controlling the publication of information

But the question of abolishing or relaxing censorship ran up against serious difficulties. Khrushchev was being energetically pushed in the opposite direction. The party hierarchy included many who did not want liberal change. It also numbered many persons guilty of acts of repression during the Stalin era, or who had been involved in one campaign or other, from the liquidation of the kulaks to the hounding of Boris Pasternak. After the Twentieth Party Congress some new blood was taken into the KGB; the most notorious perpetrators of criminal mass repressions were retired, and several were even tried. But in other departments of the state and party system there were no substantial changes. Molotov, Kaganovich, Malenkov, and some of Stalin's other most intimate accomplices were admittedly removed from power, but there still remained a great many executives who did not wish the whole truth about the past to be told. These people now prepared a counter-offensive to the movement in favour of freedom of the press. They too prepared their arguments for Khrushchev. On 7–8 March 1963 a meeting was held between party and government leaders and workers in literature and the arts, and at this meeting Khrushchev backed down decisively from that attitude which in the previous year had cleared the way for the publication of Solzhenitsyn's story. In a lengthy speech addressed to this meeting and published on 10 March in *Pravda* and *Izvestiya* and other papers, Khrushchev once again praised *One Day in the Life of Ivan Denisovich* as a work which 'truthfully reflected the reality of those years, in accordance with party positions'. But then he complained that editorial offices and journals had been flooded out with manuscripts describing life in exile, and in prisons and camps. 'Take my word for it,' said Khrushchev, 'this is a very dangerous theme. It's the kind of "stew" that'll attract flies like a carcass, enormous, fat flies, all sorts of bourgeois scum from abroad will come crawling all over it.' And so Khrushchev advised his audience to put a stop to the flood and treat the

constituting a state of military secret. For all other contents of the newspaper it is the Chief Editor, as a political figure, who bears full responsibility for publication. Only after appearing in *Izvestiya* was the poem published in *Novy Mir*. And although the text had by then already been made public, the censor made an attempt at this stage to have the extract quoted above removed. (Author's note.)

19

publication of 'prison camp' writings with extreme caution so as not to damage the work of the party.

On the subject of modern trends in the fine arts Khrushchev expressed himself even more strongly. Speaking of the work of the talented sculptor Ernst Neizvestny, which had been pointed out to him at the Manège exhibition, he declared:

> Last time we saw the nauseating concoctions of Ernst Neizvestny and we were filled with indignation that this man, who is obviously not lacking in promise, and has completed his higher education in a Soviet institution, repays the people with such black ingratitude.[5]

Immediately after his speech a rigid ban was imposed on the publication of works exposing the arbitrariness of the period of the 'personality cult'. The Leningrad journal *Neva* in its March 1963 issue (No. 3) published the first part of the novel *Face to Face* (*Odin na Odin*) by L. Semin, which told of the fate of Soviet prisoners of war who, released from Hitler's concentration camps at the end of the war, took part in the final battles against fascist Germany. After the victory, hundreds of thousands of these people were arrested and sent to Soviet camps. The beginning of the novel foreshadowed the author's intentions clearly enough and publication of the next instalment was banned, so that the novel was cut short before its main theme had developed. Other works were stopped at the editorial stage.

Solzhenitsyn's story *For the Good of the Cause* (*Novy Mir* No. 7, 1963), which exposed the arbitrariness of the present bureaucracy in a provincial town, met with a critical reception. It was reviewed unfavourably in *Literaturnaya Gazeta* on 31 August 1963 by the paper's deputy editor Yury Barabash, who pronounced it 'a failure for the writer'. *Novy Mir*, however, in its No. 10 issue of 1963, published three readers' letters which replied convincingly to Barabash's review. One of these letters said that 'Solzhenitsyn upholds our own Soviet, communist justice, the ethical norms of our moral code, the democratic bases of our life'.

[5] After Khrushchev's death in 1971, it was Neizvestny whom his family commissioned to carve a monument to his grave in the Novodevichy cemetery. At the time of writing the monument has been completed, but so far not put up. It consists simply of a relief of Khrushchev's head, squeezed between two massive blocks of black and white marble.

Literaturnaya Gazeta rallied to the support of Barabash and, in a special editorial on 12 December 1963, accused *Novy Mir* of bias in its selection of favourable responses. 'It is difficult to believe,' thought *Literaturnaya Gazeta*, 'that the editors of *Novy Mir* received only letters singing the story's praises.' In reply the editors of *Novy Mir* sent to *Literaturnaya Gazeta* a full account of the comments they had received from readers of *For the Good of the Cause*, which was published in *Literaturnaya Gazeta* on 26 December. According to this account, the editors had received 58 readers' letters, only one of which voiced criticism of the story. It was however, impossible to publish that letter because of the offensive expressions it used.

When, at the end of 1963, nominations were invited for the finest works of literature, art, science and technology for the 1964 Lenin prizes, the editors of *Novy Mir* put in Solzhenitsyn's *One Day in the Life of Ivan Denisovich* for the literature prize. The nomination was seconded only by the State Archive of Literature and Art. The boards of the USSR, RSFSR and Moscow Writers' Union, and other literary associations, proposed different works. The list of candidates for Lenin Prizes was published in *Literaturnaya Gazeta* on 28 December 1963.

4. The Lenin Prize Committee Makes its Selection

AT THE BEGINNING of 1964 many people were intently following the discussion that centred around the works nominated for the Lenin Prize in Literature. It was obvious that Solzhenitsyn had no serious rivals. Using a scientific analogy one might say that the other authors had also done good research but research concerned with detail in areas that were already known. Solzhenitsyn's work had been an original discovery which advanced fresh problems and shifted earlier problems into a new perspective. This was self-evident, and any failure to acknowledge it would be hypocrisy on the part of the Lenin Prize Committee. Moreover, all the critics so far had singled out *Ivan Denisovich* as an outstanding phenomenon; party leaders had spoken of it as a work deserving of every possible support. It was too late now to erase what had already been said.

On 15 January 1964 *Izvestiya* carried a piece by V. Pallon entitled 'Hello, Captain'. In it the author recounted a meeting he had had with one of the prototypes of Ivan Denisovich, who appears in the story under the name of Buinovsky, a Captain of the second rank, and is one of the most striking characters in the book. One feels that there is a real person behind this character, and the reader bids him farewell with an aching heart when he is taken off to the cold stone cage of the punishment cell. But now it turned out he had survived after all, had been rehabilitated and returned to the navy, and was serving in the battleship *Aurora* in Leningrad as head of a branch of the Museum of Military History. His real name was B. V. Burkovsky. He told the journalist about Solzhenitsyn, who had spent four years in the same camp barrack as himself. 'I read in the papers not long ago,' Burkovsky said, 'that Solzhenitsyn's story had been nominated for the 1964 Lenin Prize. I was very excited . . . I am no expert on literature and I shan't try to analyse the story . . . But if I were asked to say what I thought of it, I'd say it's a fine, truthful piece of writing. It's clear to

22

any reader of the story that with rare exceptions, people remained people in the camps for the very reason that they were Soviet in their hearts, and that they never identified the evil done to them with the party, or with our régime . . .'

On 30 January 1964 *Pravda* published an excellent review of *Ivan Denisovich* written by S. Marshak. Entitled 'A Truthful Tale', it expressed the conviction that the story was worthy of the Lenin Prize. The fact that two important papers were supporting the story could not be accidental. There was little mention of the other works proposed for the prize, and what there was lacked the clear assurance of Solzhenitsyn's backers.

The Committee for Lenin Prizes in art and literature carries out its task in two stages. The first stage consists of sifting the criticism in the press and the selection of five or six of the most suitable candidates for each prize from amongst the several dozen works proposed. Thus a short list of the most important works in each category (prose, poetry, cinema, etc.) goes forward to the final round in April (prizewinners are announced, of course, on Lenin's birthday),[1] and these are examined by a Plenary session of the Committee consisting of over a hundred people.

On 19 February a list of works selected for final consideration appeared in the papers. Out of the works nominated in the prose section, six had been chosen for the final round. They were as follows: A Solzhenitsyn, *One Day in the Life of Ivan Denisovich;* O. Honchar, *The Sheep-bell;* L. Pervomaisky, *Wild Honey*; G. Serebryakova, *Prometheus* (a trilogy); A. Chakovsky, *Distant Starlight;* D. Granin, *Into the Storm. The Sheepbell* and *Into the Storm* had been proposed by the Board of the USSR Writers' Union, *Prometheus* by the Board of the RSFSR Writers' Union and a number of other organisations; this trilogy on the life of Karl Marx was the work that received the largest number of nominations – even including the Directorate of Weather Bureaux for the Central Provinces. Of these short-listed works, the majority of my friends had read, apart from *Ivan Denisovich* only *Into the Storm*, a novel about physicists. It is a very good novel but not a literary milestone. The three volumes on Karl Marx under the general title of *Prometheus* were of no artistic distinction, though they did seem an impressive

[1] 22 April.

compilation. The writing was poor, the content artificial, and the dialogues with Marx pure fiction. I did try to read the first volume but I couldn't get beyond the first hundred pages. Marx's letters are far more interesting; they are more colourful, wittier, more lively.

On 11 April 1964 I noticed a big article on the back of *Pravda* headed 'High requirements'. It was devoted entirely to a survey of letters about *Ivan Denisovich* received by the paper.

> Many letters about Solzhenitsyn's story are arriving on our desk . . . [the article ran]. There are favourable ones approving the nomination of the story for the Lenin Prize . . . And there are those that express just as firmly the opposite point of view and give the story a totally negative appraisal . . . Then there is an objective, third category of letters, and it is the largest . . . whose authors point out substantial defects, thereby evidencing their high requirements and their keen interest in raising the ideological–artistic standards of our literature. They all come to the same conclusion: that Solzhenitsyn's tale deserves a positive assessment, but cannot be placed among such oustanding works as merit the Lenin Prize.
>
> The stream of letters of this kind has swollen in recent days as a result of the exaggerated opinions of reviewers.

The paper went on to give what were undoubtedly selective quotations from some of the letters, especially those which were in doubt as to the merits of the story and spoke out against it being awarded the Lenin Prize. The writers of these letters, blue- and white-collar workers in state institutions, asserted that the story was 'on an insufficiently high literary level', had a 'simplistic approach to the delineation of the character of the Soviet man and his spiritual world', that the 'inner world of the hero was rather primitive', that 'the author's creative work was not in the best traditions of Russian literary language' and so on. Also cited was the opinion of V. Golitsyn, head of the municipal department of the Krasnoyarsk Town Council Executive Committee; he felt that 'the figure of Ivan Denisovich does not reflect the radiant ideal of the popular hero'.

It was shameful to read all those primitive, stereotyped, stupid formulae passed off by *Pravda* as the opinion of the

Soviet reading public as a whole. It was clear that with the publication of this article the conservatives intended to prepare the Soviet public for the news that Solzhenitsyn would not be awarded the Lenin Prize. It was also a means of exerting pressure on the Prize Committee which was just then being convened.

The decision of the Lenin Prize Committee was announced on 22 April. The Literature Prize had been awarded to O. Honchar for his novel *The Sheep-bell*. I am unable to express an opinion on it, since I did not read it either before or after the award. Neither did any of my friends. Acquaintances of mine more knowledgeable about literary matters have told me that it is a mediocre work of no particular interest.

I later heard from Tvardovsky and M. I. Romm about the steps that had been taken to deflect the Prize Committee's consideration from *Ivan Denisovich*. Back in February Tvardovsky had been sure that it would win; he was himself a member of the Prize Committee and he was aware of the sympathies of many other Committee members. In March, though, there was an abrupt change of mood somewhere at the top. As editor of *Novy Mir*, which had recommended *Ivan Denisovich* for the prize, Tvardovsky wrote a comprehensive article in which he examined the literary virtues of the story. But permission was refused for the article to be published in the central press. Tvardovsky asked Lebedev to find out what had happened. But when Lebedev found the moment to put the question to Khrushchev, the latter replied sharply: 'Let's not bother ourselves with that, it's the business of the Prize Committee to decide.'

The Lenin Prize Committee makes its decisions by secret ballot after a full discussion. During the discussion of *Ivan Denisovich* it became obvious that most members involved with the arts were for Solzhenitsyn. (The Committee included the Ministers of Culture and Education, Secretaries of the Komsomol Central Committee, and executives of the Ideological Commission.) In the circumstances it was not possible to begin the secret ballot. Next day the Committee's Chairman N. S. Tikhonov tabled a resolution eliminating Solzhenitsyn's story from the secret ballot-list, in other words, adding it to the list of works which had been rejected at the beginning of February during the preliminary round. Rejections of this kind are normally carried out by *a show of hands*. But this resolution was against the rules, since the list of works which had been passed for secret ballot had already been made public. Tvardovsky objected strongly. Mikhail Romm was also particularly upset. 'What's going on, what's going on?' he said indignantly. 'They're twisting our arms.' The Minister of Culture, Furtseva, however, supported Tikhonov. But the majority of the Committee were not to be persuaded. It was then that S. P. Pavlov, First Secretary of the Central Committee of the Komsomol, rose to his feet. He declared that the Lenin Prize could not be awarded to Solzhenitsyn for political and legal reasons. According to Pavlov, Solzhenitsyn had surrendered to the Germans during the war and had subsequently been convicted for a criminal offence; contrary to the general beliefs he had still not been rehabilitated. Tvardovsky was on his feet in an instant. 'It's a lie,' he said. 'You will have to prove it's a lie,' replied Pavlov.

The Secretary of the Komsomol Central Committee is a responsible person, and any statement from him has to be taken seriously. Furthermore, S. P. Pavlov was considered a friend of Semichastny, the Chairman of the KGB, and might have access to information about which other people knew nothing. Solzhenitsyn's story was eliminated from the secret ballot-list, but Tvardovsky and a group of people from the film world raised their hands against the resolution all the same. During a break Romm said to Tvardovsky: 'If Solzhenitsyn doesn't get it no-one else will.'

He was right. In its secret ballot the Lenin Prize Committee successively voted against all the other works proposed for the prize. Even *The Sheep-bell*, which an 'expert group' had recommended, was rejected. But the following day N. S. Tikhonov once again had *The Sheep-bell* put to the vote. Pressure was brought to bear to force the Committee by hook or by crook to award the prize to somebody. A repeat ballot produced the desired result.

The work of the Lenin Prize Committee goes on for several days, since it has to view films, theatrical productions and works of art. The day after his altercation with Pavlov, Tvardovsky asked Solzhenitsyn to show him his certificate of rehabilitation. However, the brief wording on the certificate to the effect that 'the case was closed owing to the absence of proof of a crime', which is issued to every rehabilitated person, was not enough for Tvardovsky's purpose. He needed the full text of the court 'ruling' with the legal argument attached. Tvardovsky submitted a request to the USSR Supreme Court, and after a talk with Deputy Chief Military Prosecutor Colonel Terekhov, who had reviewed Solzhenitsyn's case in 1957, he obtained, and took to the Prize Committee, the full text of the USSR Supreme Court's 'ruling'. At the next session Tvardovsky asked for permission to speak.

'Last time we met,' he said, 'Comrade Pavlov asserted that Solzhenitsyn's military record was not irreproachable and that I must prove [my statement] that this was untrue. I have here a document issued by the supreme Court of the USSR. I shall hand it to the Secretary of our Committee and ask him to read the full text of the Supreme Court's ruling.' Whereupon Tvardovsky passed the document to the Secretary. The latter, after examining the seal and signature, read the entire text aloud.

SUPREME COURT OF THE USSR
DECISION NO. 4n–083/57

The Military Collegium of the Supreme Court of the USSR, presided over by Judicial Councillor Borisoglebsky and comprising Judicial Colonels Dolotsev and Konev, has examined at its session of 6 February 1965 THE PROTEST OF THE CHIEF MILITARY PROSECUTOR against the decree of the Special Board of the NKVD of the USSR, dated 7 July 1945, on the basis of which, under articles 58 (10), part two and 58 (11) of the RSFSR Criminal Code, a sentence of eight years imprisonment in corrective labour camps was passed on SOLZHENITSYN, Alexander Isayevich, born 1918, a native of Kislovodsk and with a higher education. Before his arrest he had held the post of battery commander, had participated in the war against the fascist German armies and was awarded the Order of the Fatherland War, class two, and the Order of the Red Star.

Having heard the report of Comrade Konev and the statement of the Deputy Chief Military Prosecutor, Judicial Colonel Terekhov, who advocated that the protest be accepted, the Collegium ESTABLISHED the following:

The charge against SOLZHENITSYN was that from 1940 until the day of his arrest he had conducted anti-Soviet propaganda among his friends and undertaken steps to establish an anti-Soviet organisation.

In his protest the Chief Military Prosecutor proposed the annulment of the Special Board's decree with regard to SOLZHENITSYN and the cancellation of the case owing to the absence of proof of a crime.

The reasons given were as follows:

It is clear from the evidence in this case that SOLZHENITSYN, in his diary and in letters to a friend, N. D. Vitkevich, although speaking of the correctness of Marxism–Leninism, the progressiveness of the socialist revolution in our country and the inevitability of its victory throughout the world, also spoke out against Stalin's cult of personality and wrote of the artistic and ideological shortcomings of the works of Soviet authors and the air of unreality that pervades many of them. He also wrote that our works of art fail to give readers in the bourgeois world a sufficiently comprehensive and versatile explanation of the inevitability of the victory of the Soviet army and people, and that our literary works are no match for the adroitly fashioned slanders of the bourgeois world against our country.

These statements by SOLZHENITSYN do not constitute proof of a crime.

In the process of verifying SOLZHENITSYN's petition the following people were questioned: Reshetovskaya, Simonyan and Simonyants, to all of whom SOLZHENITSYN is said to have made anti-Soviet allegations. These people characterised SOLZHENITSYN as a Soviet patriot and denied that he had conducted anti-Soviet conversations.

From SOLZHENITSYN's military record and a report by Captain Melnikov, who served with him, it is clear that from 1942 until the day of his arrest, that is until February 1945, SOLZHENITSYN served on several fronts of the Great Fatherland War, fought courageously for his homeland, more than once displayed personal heroism and inspired the devotion of the personnel of the section he commanded. SOLZHENITSYN's section was the best in the unit for discipline and battle effectiveness.

Basing himself on the above-mentioned evidence, the Chief Military Prosecutor considers the conviction of SOLZHENITSYN to have been incorrect and in this connection applies for the case against him to be closed on the basis of article 4, point 5 of the RSFSR Code of Criminal Procedure.

Having examined the case material and the material of the supplementary verification and concurring with the arguments expounded in the protest, while also taking into account the fact that SOLZHENITSYN's actions do not constitute a crime and his case should be closed for lack of proof, the Military Collegium of the USSR *RESOLVES* that the decree of the Special Board of the NKVD of the USSR dated 7 July 1945, concerning SOLZHENITSYN, Alexander Isayevich, shall be revoked, and his case, for lack of proof, be closed on the basis of article 4, point 5 of the RSFSR Code of Criminal Procedure.[2]

Secretary of the Komsomol Central Committee S. P. Pavlov listened in silence to the document, then rose to his feet and, in obvious confusion, uttered the words: 'I am defeated, I offer my apologies.'

However, the slanderous aspersions which Pavlov had earlier cast were not forgotten, and would be repeated in later years in different forms and places, and with numerous additional 'details'.

[2] Translation quoted *Solzhenitsyn: A Documentary Record*, edited by Leopold Labedz (Allen Lane, the Penguin Press 1970).

5. *The First Circle*

AFTER THE PATENTLY biased decision of the Lenin Prize Committee, discussion of *Ivan Denisovich* continued in the press, but in a very different key. It was clear that new directives had gone out on how the story was to be evaluated. On 12 May 1964 *Literaturnaya Gazeta* published a long article by Yury Barabash entitled 'The Leaders, the "Led", and the Proprietors of Life', in which the author raised strong objections to the theses propounded in detail by V. Ya. Lakshin in his article 'Ivan Denisovich, his Friends and Foes' on the contribution of Solzhenitsyn's novel to Soviet literature. On 29 May 1964 an article by Vs. Surganov in *Literaturnaya Rossiya* [Literary Russia], 'Noun Substantive',[1] reproached Solzhenitsyn for selecting the wrong sort of hero in his writings.

'It is not the Matryonas and Shukhovs[2] that the party looks to for support in its struggle to renew the countryside...'. On 4 June 1964 *Literaturnaya Gazeta* published an article entitled 'The Debate Goes On', in which Lakshin was given the opportunity to reply to Barabash's criticism. However, Lakshin's letter was accompanied by a reply 'from the editors' which was far more extensive than the letter itself. In the editors' opinion, many readers and critics felt strongly that Solzhenitsyn had not shown us that 'the Soviet people never abandoned their faith in the Communist Party, in Soviet power... even in the most brutal conditions of Beria's terror...' Lakshin's article was pronounced 'a relapse into demagogic criticism that conflicts with our task of rallying the forces of Soviet literature...'

Similar remarks about Solzhenitsyn's story and Lakshin's article were made by G. Brovman in his essay 'Real Life and Observance of Norms' (*Moskva*, No. 7, 1964). The discussion concluded with an article in the journal *Kommunist* (No. 12,

---

[1] In Russian a play on words. *Imya Sushchestvitelnoye* means both 'noun' and 'a name of substance'.
[2] The surname of Ivan Denisovich.

1964) entitled 'Art in a Heroic Epoch' which also condemned Lakshin's piece on *Ivan Denisovich*.

Solzhenitsyn's supporters, however, were not too disheartened by the decision of the Lenin Prize Committee. In the Soviet Union the allocation of prizes almost always depends on a multitude of political factors. *Ivan Denisovich* was, after all, the writer's first published work. Now a large-scale work was expected of him, ranging widely over the events of our lifetime. In the summer of 1964, describing *Novy Mir*'s plans for 1965, Tvardovsky had announced that a new novel by Solzhenitsyn was lying on the editor's desk. I heard this announcement on the radio – for it had not gone unnoticed by foreign correspondents. Publication of the new novel by Solzhenitsyn was announced in *Novy Mir* itself in July and August in advertisements listing works to be published in 1965. Subscriptions to periodicals are taken out in September and, with the aim of attracting more subscribers, many journals announce forthcoming publication of works by popular authors although the works may not yet have been written. Tvardovsky's statement showed that Solzhenitsyn's novel did exist, but the theme of the novel remained obscure.

It was at this juncture that I received the letter from Solzhenitsyn quoted above.[3] Naturally I replied to it at once.

On 20 September I had another letter from Solzhenitsyn, suggesting that we meet in Moscow in November; he planned to spend the whole month in the capital. Wet met in mid-November. I had expected to see a sick and sombre man, but there he was, tall, full of energy and *joie de vivre*, outwardly well, and the most genial company. He was not at all like the photograph in the edition of *Ivan Denisovich*, where he looked a little gloomy and not too well – in fact, much as a man who has spent so many years in confinement might be expected to look.

It transpired that he knew a colleague of mine at Obninsk, the eminent geneticist Nikolai Vladimirovich Timofeev-Resovsky. They had met in 1946 in a large communal cell in Butyrka Prison where they had spent about two months together. After his release and return from exile Solzhenitsyn made inquiries about the fate of Timofeev-Resovsky but did not succeed in meeting him – Timofeev-Resovsky was working

[3] See page 2.

31

in the Urals at the time. He did not come to Obninsk until the Spring of 1964, when he became head of the genetics department there.

Naturally I asked Solzhenitsyn about his new novel and when it was due to be published. His face darkened instantly. He said that the situation had altered greatly since the events of October and publication of the novel was apparently to be postponed. His allusion to the changed situation was clear.

The removal of Khrushchev in October 1964 was not directly connected with his policy of 'de-Stalinisation' and his attempts to introduce a certain measure of democracy. Those aspects of his policies had found him favour with the people. By 1964, however, his popularity with all sections of our society had sharply declined because of his inability to carry through an intelligent economic policy in the industrial and agricultural sectors, and because of his continual and ill-considered reorganisations. The chief source of discontent in the ranks of the party hierarchy had been the division, in 1962, of all regional party committees into industrial and agricultural committees. This had created a diarchy within the party and, in practice, its division into two large factions. Khrushchev's mistakes in the management of agriculture caused a serious decline in agricultural production and necessitated the outlay of huge sums of reserve gold and foreign currency on the purchase of foodstuffs from abroad. There were other reasons too for Khrushchev's fall from power. However, he had been the initiator of so-called 'de-Stalinisation', and it was clear that those who objected to the frank exposure of the crimes of the Stalin period would take advantage of Khrushchev's removal to halt the process of democratisation, intensify press censorship and bring about, if only partially, a rehabilitation of Stalin.

These people were displeased first and foremost by the publication in newspapers and journals of writings concerning the camps and violations of legality, and especially by the appearance of memoirs which referred to the men who perpetrated the criminal acts of Stalin's day by their real names. While Khrushchev was in power the influence of these conservative elements was, to a considerable extent, neutralised. Now they had more chance.

In view of this situation Tvardovsky had decided not to raise the question of the publication of Solzhenitsyn's new novel. Stalin appeared as a character in it and was of course not at all favourably portrayed.

But Solzhenitsyn promised to show me the typescript very soon.

In January 1965 Solzhenitsyn allowed a mutual friend in Moscow to read the novel and at the same time told me that if I wished, I might also read the typescript but only if I did not take it away from the apartment. At that time the great possibilities of *samizdat* had begun to be appreciated. That was why, by agreement with *Novy Mir*, Solzhenitsyn was taking the strictest possible precautions to ensure that his novel did not circulate in an uncontrolled fashion. I arrived at our friend's apartment at about ten o'clock in the morning and was given two files containing the neatly typed text of a novel entitled *The First Circle*. Late that evening I telephoned my wife in Obninsk to say that I would be spending the night in Moscow. I could not tear myself away from the novel. I read all through the night, stopping at intervals for cups of black coffee. Since it is now famous all over the world there is no need for me to discuss its literary merits. I realised just what a difficult position Tvardovsky was in. As an editor he could not publish the novel; but as a man of letters he could not fail to see that it would be impossible to conceal the work's existence for long, and that sooner or later it was bound to be discovered for Russian literature and the literature of the world.

As I later learned, Tvardovsky had officially accepted the manuscript, obtained editorial approval, drawn up a contract for publication and paid the author an advance. In so doing he wanted to indicate that the editorial board earnestly intended to publish the work.

But the more auspicious moment for which Tvardovsky was waiting failed to arrive. Early in 1965 he was summoned to an interview with the head of the Central Committee's department of literature, at which he was shown a recent issue of *Grani*, a Russian language journal published quarterly in West Germany from offices in Frankfurt-am-Main; it is devoted largely to literature and the arts. (The monthly journal *Possev*, issued by the same publishers, is a mainly political paper but also sometimes includes literary essays and reviews.) There, printed in *Grani*, were *Miniature Stories* by A. I. Solzhenitsyn, a series of short stories, none of them more than three pages in length, 'poems in prose'.

The gist of the interview with Tvardovsky was roughly the following: 'Comrade Tvardovsky, just look who it is you're supporting; see what connections your author has and who takes an interest in his writing.'

Their publication was, to use the Western publishers' term, an act of 'piracy' – that is, it was done without the knowledge or consent of the author. A similar breach of copyright would have been impossible with regard to a Western author; but Soviet writers were not protected by international copyright law since the USSR refused to sign the Universal Copyright Convention.[4] Thus the Soviet Union was able to publish and reproduce any book published in the West without informing the author or the original publisher, and without paying them royalties. But by the same token Western publishers may disregard the wishes of Soviet authors. And they may extend their powers not only to works already published inside the USSR but also to typescripts by Soviet writers which they acquire through *samizdat* or in some other way. Solzhenitsyn's *Miniature Stories* had been circulating from hand to hand for a year and a half and I had managed to read them before I met the author. They could quite well have been published in a Soviet periodical. As I discovered later, they had been considered for publication by *Novy Mir*, but had not been accepted because they were not in keeping with the journal's literary trend. They had, however, been accepted for publication by the journal *Semya i Shkola* (Family and School) and were already being set up in type. Now, of course, the initiative of *Semya i Shkola* had lost its point.

Of all the *Miniature Stories*, only one, 'Lake Segden', would not, I think, have passed the censor. Compressed in form, but teeming with images, it voiced the indignation of the writer at the attempts of high-ranking officials, 'princes of evil', to

---

[4] On 27 May 1973 the Soviet Union joined the Unesco Universal Copyright Convention. However, new domestic laws related to this act have been introduced by the Supreme Soviet which will significantly restrict the right of Soviet authors to authorise translations of their books and to make direct approaches to foreign publishers.

fence off vast tracts of land, usually in areas of the greatest natural beauty, for their country residences and *dachas*. This story would have met with Khrushchev's disapproval, for he was very fond of building picturesque 'state dachas', and had appropriated for his own residences the most beautiful stretches of coastline in the Crimea and on the Black Sea coast of the Caucasus.

It was from Tvardovsky that Solzhenitsyn first learned of the publication of his stories in *Grani*, and of the Central Committee's reaction. Tvardovsky was distressed by the turn events had taken. Soviet law expressly forbids contact with organisations such as the NTS. Therefore any dealings with *Grani* and *Possev* could be regarded as anti-Soviet activity.

The mere fact of possessing copies of these journals, may, if discovered, be grounds for prosecution under articles 70 or 190–1 of the RSFSR Criminal Code. We shall not go into the question here of how far the practical application of these articles of Soviet law conforms to the legal guarantees contained in the UN Declaration of Human Rights. We shall merely note the important fact that these articles do exist, and are a reality that has to be reckoned with. Emigré journals do not always take account of this.

I cannot deny the fact that Russian émigré organisations in West Germany, Canada or France have the right to publish their own journals or newspapers. But if certain of these organisations include among their aims the transformation of the Soviet régime, the creation of underground cells inside the USSR, the Soviet government has every reason to prohibit the publications of these organisations in the USSR. In these circumstances publication by *Grani* or *Possev* of a manuscript by a Soviet writer which has been illegally brought out of the USSR places the writer concerned in an extremely difficult position, for it renders him open to the accusation of having connections with an illegal organisation according to the Soviet legal code. And even in instances where the case cannot be brought to court, for lack of objective proof of any such connection, the mere fact of publication in an anti-Soviet journal, of a typescript not published inside the USSR, may be exploited for propaganda purposes or in order to discredit the author. I know of cases when mysterious agents have surreptitiously pushed single copies of *Grani* or *Possev* through Moscow letter-boxes, but these cowardly acts have always been regarded as provocations by the 'recipients'.

I would not even rule out the possibility that on occasions the people who pass on Soviet *samizdat* typescripts to publishers in the West are the very ones who are most interested in stamping out *samizdat*. Because of this practice, the chief danger to any Soviet author who decides to acquaint a certain circle of people with one of his works which has no chance of being approved by the censor, lies in the possibility that the work may find its way into the anti-Soviet émigré press, and appear, perhaps in an unrevised version, with commentaries of which he is unlikely to approve. Many authors are not at all pleased to see their work used in this way, and they either avoid circulation in *samizdat* or try to ensure that their rights are protected by authorising the publication of editions abroad and copyrighting their works with publishers of repute. This too is risky, and no easy matter.[5]

Tvardovsky was very disturbed to discover that the writer whom he had supported with such ardour had turned out to be one of *Grani*'s authors. He accused Solzhenitsyn of committing, at the very least, a serious imprudence. The *Miniature Stories*, thought Tvardovsky, were simply not worth the great risk involved. He could hardly have foreseen that a few years later his own excellent poem 'By Right of Memory', withdrawn from a *Novy Mir* proof by the censor, would find its way mysteriously to West Germany and be published in the same journal.

Early in 1965 more directives were issued regarding literary works that exposed the lawlessness of the Stalin period – and they were specifically directed against Solzhenitsyn's *Ivan Denisovich*. These directives were set forth in an article by N. G. Egorychev, a First Secretary of the Moscow Party Committee, which was published in the journal *Kommunist* (No. 3. p. 15, 1965).

> . . . One must take to task [wrote Egorychev] that part of our creative intelligentsia which sometimes displays an excessive fondness for describing the arbitrariness of the period of the

---

[5] This practice is one of the factors which have contributed towards the USSR signature to the Copyright Convention. It aims to stop the direct approach of Soviet writers to foreign publishers.

cult of personality, the moral sufferings and physical privations endured by the innocent people who were convicted. These are painful pages of history. Yet although the Soviet people, and especially the young, are disoriented by this prismatic view of a particular period of our history, works of this kind are being praised to the skies, at times quite unreservedly and undeservedly, and any criticism of them is regarded as inadmissible. For instance, it is obvious that one or two people still overrate Alexander Solzhenitsyn's *One Day in the Life of Ivan Denisovich*, a work which from the ideological and the artistic point of view is unquestionably suspect.

From the beginning of 1966 the name of Solzhenitsyn was no longer mentioned in articles of literary criticism, and references to *Ivan Denisovich* ceased completely in Soviet journals. This was not a voluntary precaution taken by the literary critics themselves. Tvardovsky and the editorial board of *Novy Mir* received letters from literati, critics and literary historians telling of how any favourable comment on *Ivan Denisovich* was now crossed out of their articles by editors or censors. It became known that a secret directive existed regarding Solzhenitsyn, and that it was based, among other things, on an analysis of his early writings.

Now that Solzhenitsyn's work had become the target for a campaign of silence, *Novy Mir*, No. 8, (the five hundredth issue since its first appearance in 1924) which appeared at the beginning of September 1966, published the second part of the essay by V. Ya. Lakshin entitled 'Writer, Reader, Critic'. The article gave a detailed analysis of Solzhenitsyn's story *Matryona's Place*, and showed up the flimsy arguments of critics who had taken a negative view of its subject-matter and themes.

I think that Solzhenitsyn's strength as an artist [wrote Lakshin] lies precisely in his ability to depict attractive, positive human beings without prejudicing the truthful sobriety of his portrayal; he loves people, loves his heroes, and the reader responds to this vivid feeling. But the author's conception of life, his 'ideal' is not embodied in any one particular personage or moralistic maxim, but shows rather

37

in the overall structure of the story, the disposition and illumination of characters, and the innumerable examples of artistic 'juxtaposition'.

And in this sense one is very aware of the narrator himself in *Matryona's Place*, the world of his thoughts and feelings, wide-ranging and humane, the hostility of the working man towards the petty bourgeoisie, his love for the Russian way of life and language, and his optimism engendered in suffering. And it is this that is most dear to us in the story.

In his article, Lakshin quoted extracts from the letters of many readers, all of them pointing out the artistic and moral virtues of the story.

6. The Confiscation of *The First Circle* and Solzhenitsyn's Papers

IN THE SPRING of 1965, while I was trying to overcome obstacles to a proposed trip to Czechoslovakia to attend the Mendel Memorial Symposium,[1] I had occasion to talk with a senior official of the Czechoslovak Embassy in Moscow. He spoke of the unaccountable difficulties that can crop up when a Soviet citizen wants to go abroad, and unexpectedly cited Solzhenitsyn as an example:

'He is a well-loved writer in Czechoslovakia, people call him "the Russian Fučik". He is very popular. We in the Embassy here know this, because the Embassy channels many invitations to Solzhenitsyn to visit our country. We pass them on to the Writers' Union and the Soviet-Czechoslovak Friendship Society. We usually receive a reply from the Ministry of Foreign Affairs saying that Solzhenitsyn is gravely ill – that he has cancer and cannot travel far from Ryazan. A great pity – such a talented writer ...'

I learned later from Solzhenitsyn that not one of these invitations had reached him. He had received a few invitations to various Embassy receptions through the post but they usually arrived after the date of the reception.

Following the resignation of Khrushchev the climate for biology studies took a turn for the better. Lysenko's monopoly in the field of biology and genetics came in for strong criticism in the press, and now Solzhenitsyn put a strong argument to the editorial board of *Novy Mir* that the moment had come to publish my essays on the genetic controversy.[2] The board suggested that I write a shortened version suitable for publication in a journal; I was able to do this very quickly. It was then circulated to each member of the editorial board. Since it dealt not only with the fate of biology but also with the harassment

[1] See *The Medvedev Papers* (Macmillan, London, 1971).
[2] *The Rise and Fall of T. D. Lysenko* (Columbia University Press, 1969).

of biologists, I had been keeping a close watch on current trends which sought to alter the policy adopted by the Twentieth and Twenty-second Party Congresses towards the crimes of the Stalin era. My brother Roy had been following these trends closely too, and had made a special study of the history and consequences of Stalinism. In mid-1964 he had submitted the first version of his work on the subject to Gospolitizdat (the State Publishing House for Political Literature) and to the Central Committee (in the person of Ilichev).[3]

In the first few months following the October 1964 Plenum of the Central Committee, the question of Stalinism was not raised openly, although several books criticising Stalin's activities were withdrawn before publication. Amongst them was a monograph on the history of the collectivisation of agriculture, prepared by the Academy of Sciences Institute of History. It had already been passed for printing when it was stopped by Glavlit. The monograph contained sharp criticism of Stalin's activities during the period of collectivisation.

As preparations for the celebration of the twentieth anniversary of the victory over Nazi Germany gained momentum, attempts to rehabilitate Stalin became more obvious. At first they were restricted to statements made in the course of various addresses in connection with the anniversary. But this in itself suggested the existence of some fairly clear directive. In April 1965, on the eve of the anniversary, the press started publishing eulogies of Stalin (articles by I. Bagramyan in *Literaturnaya Gazeta*, 17 April 1965; Troyanovsky in *Sovetskaya Rossiya*, 20 April; Marshal I. Konev in *Pravda*, 19 April – entitled 'To Berlin' – and a number of others). At the same time several addresses on ideological subjects referred to the exaggerated reputation of certain writers, particularly A. I. Solzhenitsyn. The 'new line' was also reflected in the way Solzhenitsyn was being treated in Ryazan. He was consistently refused any improvement in his living conditions, and continued to live in an old wooden house with none of the usual amenities. In the spring of 1965 he decided to move away from Ryazan to some quieter town nearer to Moscow. But first a job had to be found for his wife, Natalia Reshetovskaya, who is a chemist.

[3] The final version of this book was published as *Let History Judge* (Knopf, New York, 1971; Macmillan, London, 1972).

I told Timofeev-Resovsky about this. He was very keen to see his old 'cell-mate' from Butyrka Prison and suggested that Obninsk, where we lived, would be an eminently suitable place for Solzhenitsyn. The surrounding countryside was lovely, and there were a number of scientific institutions in the neighbourhood; it was only a hundred kilometres from Moscow. I passed the idea on to Solzhenitsyn. He had planned to drive around the Moscow region and the neighbouring regions of Tula, Yaroslavl, Vladimir and Kaluga, looking for possible places to move to, in the Moskvich[4] he had bought with the proceeds of the sale of *Ivan Denisovich*.

On 10 May I received a letter from him saying among other things: 'Since I spoke to you on the telephone we have sorted out our itinerary a little more, and it now looks as though it will be convenient, and a great pleasure, to call in at Obninsk. We propose to do this at the very end of May (about the 30th). I hope we shall find you there? And Nikolai Vladimirovich?[5] Sincere regards to him. My wife and I are both touched by, and interested in the hopes he has expressed of finding her a job.'

Naturally, Timofeev-Resovsky and I made sure we were there at the end of May, and received Solzhenitsyn and his wife with real delight. The meeting of the two old inmates of Butyrka was very moving. Next day we strolled around the town and went down through the park to the river to look at the beach. It is a beautiful spot; only a loudspeaker blaring out across the valley disturbed the peace. Solzhenitsyn and his wife seemed to like Obninsk more than other towns they had seen. Natalia Reshetovskaya decided to try to apply for one of the jobs in our institute. An open competition had just been announced for a new radio-isotope department and several of the vacancies were suitable for a chemist.

Shortly afterwards Natalia Reshetovskaya was almost unanimously elected as a senior scientist of the Institute of Medical Radiology. Although she had indicated on her application form that her husband was A. I. Solzhenitsyn, none of the examining commission paid any attention to this. But when the question of moving to Obninsk arose, the local party leaders for some reason or other grew extremely worried. It appeared that the

4 A mini-car.
5 Timofeev-Resovsky.

possibility of the famous writer moving into the Kaluga region had already been discussed by the Kaluga Regional Party Committee, and they were not enthusiastic about the prospect. Pressure was brought to bear upon the Director of the Institute and he delayed announcing a final decision. It was now that Solzhenitsyn was asked to go for an interview with P. Demichev, the Secretary of the Central Committee with responsibility for ideological affairs. The invitation resulted from a meeting between Demichev and Tvardovsky. Demichev had made a number of complaints about Solzhenitsyn, and Tvardovsky had advised him to have a talk with the novelist himself, since he happened to be in Moscow at the time. Solzhenitsyn went to the interview well prepared, and when Demichev started reproaching him he gave in detail examples of the unfair treatment he was subjected to, mentioning in particular the spreading of scandalous rumours about him (giving Pavlov's words at a session of the Lenin Prize Committee, and a number of other instances), the restrictions imposed upon his wife in her choice of a place of employment, and the obstacles put in the way of their move to a new town. For some reason this last instance aroused Demichev's indignation more than anything else (it had evidently not yet been reported to him), and he telephoned the Kaluga Regional Party Committee there and then ordering its members not to impede Solzhenitsyn's move to Obninsk. This was on 17 July.

Two days later the First Secretary of the Kaluga Regional Party Committee came to the Institute to talk this over with the Director. On the following day the Director summoned Natalia Reshetovskaya, and for some reason Solzhenitsyn also, to Obninsk. They had a very friendly talk and Reshetovskaya was delighted to hear that she was to start on 1 September. The move to Obninsk seemed such a reality that Solzhenitsyn even acquired a small plot of land just off the Moscow–Kiev highway near Obninsk. There, picturesquely situated beside a small stream was a tiny wooden cottage consisting of one room seven or eight metres square, and an attic. Solzhenitsyn turned the attic into his study. The cottage,[6] and the plot of land on which it stood, had not cost a great deal, and was perfectly adequate for summer accommodation.

[6] The Russian word '*dacha*' implies something rather grander than the fact!

So now Solzhenitsyn had his own summer cottage, something he had long dreamed of. The following summer he built a wooden garage alongside the house. The land was part of a dacha-housing-cooperative apparently founded in the early 'fifties when, after the death of Stalin, permission was given to city workers and office staff to set up market gardening cooperatives. At that time there were none of the restrictions which now exist; people were allotted 1000 to 1200 square metres and allowed to build small cottages. And so the estates had a pleasant, residential character. In later years more and more restrictions were imposed. The plots were cut down in size to 400, 300 or even 200 square metres per family, only one-room cottages were allowed, and no stoves or electricity. Sometimes the owner would only be allowed to erect a toolshed. As a result, towns have become surrounded by unsightly settlements, and huge areas of waste land have been fenced off into squalid little plots, thickly studded with tiny cottages resembling chicken-coops. I have one myself near Obninsk.

Solzhenitsyn called his place 'Borzovka' after its previous owner Borzov. Here he and his wife settled down to await 1 September, when Reshetovskaya had been promised work and a flat in Obninsk.

However, confirmation of Reshetovskaya's post was delayed. The Academy of Medical Sciences decided that all the vacancies be re-advertised. Once again Reshetovskaya sent in her application. The elections were to be held at the end of September, but in the second week of September there were developments that pushed Reshetovskaya's troubles into the background.

At the beginning of September I made a trip to Tbilisi. I returned home on 13 September and the next day went to Solzhenitsyn's cottage to tell him about the prospects for Natalia's job. He and his wife were sitting on the veranda. Their air of preoccupation and their reaction to my optimistic account told me that something serious had happened and the question of Natalia's job was no longer important to them. My suspicion was right. After listening to what I had to say, Solzhenitsyn told me an alarming story which he asked me to pass on to Timofeev-Resovsky and his other friends at Obninsk. He also asked me to tell them not to be surprised if

43

the business of moving to Obninsk turned out to be more complicated than had once seemed likely. He said that the typescript of his new novel, *The First Circle*, had been confiscated by the KGB.

This was indeed depressing news. The first question I wanted to ask was whether he had managed to hang on to a copy, and if so, whether it oughtn't to be reproduced quickly. I knew of a reliable photographer who had adequate equipment for this. The thought occurred naturally, for, like many others, I'd heard the sad story of V. Grossman's novel *Life and Fate* which was confiscated from the writer's flat in 1961. The fate of Grossman's novel was a terrible warning for only a very small number of people knew of its existence. I never discovered the content of the novel in detail for none of my acquaintances had read it. One day some officials arrived with a search warrant and confiscated all copies of the novel and even drafts and notes relating to it. Although in 1963 literature was temporarily allowed, thanks to Solzhenitsyn, to deal openly with the theme of repression, Grossman's manuscript never was returned to him. He died in 1964. A few years after his death it was discovered that he had spent the last two years of his life writing a new short novel *Vsyo Techyot* (Forever Flowering), also on the subject of the Stalin Terror.

After the confiscation of Grossman's novel, many authors of controversial works tried not to keep all the copies of their typescripts at home. I assumed that Solzhenitsyn had taken similar precautionary measures. I knew that he had a copy of the novel with him at the cottage and was still amending the text. Apparently he kept the original draft manuscript in Ryazan. Surely not all the copies had been seized at once? Solzhenitsyn reassured me that things were not as bad as that. He had only lost the copies at *Novy Mir*. There had been no search in Ryazan and to all appearances the KGB as yet knew nothing of the existence of his summer cottage.

The typescripts were confiscated in very strange circumstances. In the summer of 1965 Solzhenitsyn had been told frankly by *Novy Mir* that despite the contract they had signed with him, publication in the near future was unlikely. The journal kept three copies of the novel, one being the author's own, and the other two made by the editorial board for the

44

purposes of discussion and editorial processing. In September Solzhenitsyn decided to take back the copies for a time to insert the changes he had made over the last few months on his own 'working' copy. The three copies of the book were rather bulky and did not fit into a briefcase. Solzhenitsyn borrowed an old suitcase from a friend and brought it to the offices of *Novy Mir*. He collected the files containing his manuscripts from Tvardovsky, and downstairs, in a room that belonged to the editorial office, he packed them into the case. He did not take them to Ryazan at once because he had other business in Moscow, but dropped the case and its contents at the flat of his friend V. L. Teush. Solzhenitsyn had come to know Teush in Ryazan in the late 'fifties when Teush taught mathematics in an institute there. Teush was one of the first people to read Solzhenitsyn's works. He later retired and settled in Moscow.

On 11 September, three days after Solzhenitsyn's visit, Teush was confronted by a squad of KGB men armed with a search warrant looking for anti-Soviet literature. Their search was not the really thorough kind which involves wall-tapping and the checking of every possible hiding place. The men 'confiscated' a number of *samizdat* manuscripts, a few books and other material, and prepared to depart. They were on the point of leaving when one of them noticed a suitcase under the bed and asked Teush to open it. When they discovered typescript copies of a novel called *The First Circle*, they decided to seize them too. Teush tried to protest, claiming that the material was the property of *Novy Mir*, that a contract had been signed for it, that it had been removed temporarily from the offices with the editor's consent, and so on. But his protest was ignored.

On the whole Solzhenitsyn was not entirely sure that the search had been made with the express aim of seizing his novel. Therefore, as soon as he heard what had happened, he wrote a letter to P. N. Demichev, the Chairman of the Central Committee's Ideological Commission, asking him to intervene immediately in the matter and request the return of the typescript either to him or to *Novy Mir*. The Chairman of the KGB at that time was Semichastny, and Solzhenitsyn did not wish to appeal to him. Semichastny had a bad reputation among men of letters, which dated from the time when he was First Secretary of the Central Committee of the Komsomol (a

45

position he held until 1959). It was Semichastny who, in a speech made in the autumn of 1958, had uttered particularly offensive remarks about Boris Pasternak, when he had just been awarded the Nobel Prize. Semichastny had called Pasternak 'a swine' and worse ('even a swine doesn't shit where it eats'), and demanded his expulsion from the USSR. (It was the threat of expulsion which finally compelled Pasternak to turn down the Nobel Prize.) A few days later Solzhenitsyn wrote to L. I. Brezhnev, M. A. Suslov and Yu. V. Andropov, asking me to post the letters in Moscow. Andropov was then Secretary of the Central Committee concerned with international affairs in the socialist sector. He was not directly concerned with literary questions, but intellectual circles regarded him as the most educated and progressive party figure. Their assumption was based on the fact that Andropov had directed the Soviet polemic with the Chinese leadership. Documents from this polemic were published periodically in the Soviet press and met with general approval. Statements issuing from the Central Committee in the course of the dispute with China were imbued with the spirit of struggle against abuses of the cult of personality, against arbitrariness, lawlessness and dogmatism.

However, not one of Solzhenitsyn's letters elicited a reply. Nor was the confiscated novel returned to him although the KGB could certainly by then have made as many copies as it needed. V. L. Teush was several times summoned to the KGB to elucidate one or two matters. Solzhenitsyn and his wife continued to live at their cottage, putting some of their papers in order against the possibility, which could not be ruled out, of further confiscations. Foreign radio stations had recently announced the arrest of Andrei Sinyavsky and Yuli Daniel for publishing a number of their works abroad, and the situation was very disquieting. The confiscation of Solzhenitsyn's novel too was reported by foreign radio stations, but these reports were rather confused. It was reported, for example, that a search had been made in Ryazan, which had not in fact happened.

At the end of September the weather turned colder and Solzhenitsyn decided to go back to Ryazan. His hopes of moving to Obninsk had faded, and Reshetovskaya had to return to her job in the department of organic chemistry at the

Ryazan Agricultural Institute. After preparing the house and garden for winter, Solzhenitsyn and Reshetovskaya loaded their car with apples and other baggage and set off for Ryazan. Not far from Obninsk ran the concrete ring-road, and by taking this they could reach the Ryazan highway without going into Moscow. Ryazan was about 230 kilometres from the cottage. The road passed through the most picturesque country in central Russia. At this distance from Moscow there is hardly any traffic on the side-roads. All around was peace and quiet.

7. Circumstances – Known and Unknown – Behind the Confiscation

THE RAID ON Teush's flat and the confiscation of *The First Circle* marked the beginning of open conflict between the Soviet authorities and a writer who had by then acquired a well-deserved international reputation. This conflict proved to be both complex and prolonged; it became a crucial factor in the intellectual life of the USSR. It symbolised the struggle between those who believed in the need for freedom of thought and freedom to analyse reality, and certain officials who wished to impose state and ideological controls upon all forms of creative activity. In later years Solzhenitsyn repeatedly protested against the use of the confiscated material and typescripts of his novel for the purpose of bringing pressure to bear on him and discrediting him. In a number of speeches and publications of an official nature the authorities attempted to justify the confiscation in various ways and gave different reasons for searching Teush's flat. In view of this, the circumstances behind the affair merit a more detailed analysis.

In September 1965 neither I nor, apparently, Solzhenitsyn was aware that *The First Circle* was not the only item to have been confiscated from Teush. Solzhenitsyn's literary papers, which he could not bring himself to keep at home in Ryazan and had therefore given to Teush to store, had also been taken. Solzhenitsyn trusted Teush utterly. The papers included several works he had written during the period 1950–56 when he was in a camp and then in exile. These writings were naturally not intended for publication, but Solzhenitsyn had no wish to destroy them: they represented, as it were, phases in his arduous creative biography. On 16 May 1967 he sent a letter to the Fourth Soviet Writers' Congress[1] which included the following statement:

[1] See Appendix.

48

Together with this novel, my literary papers dating back fifteen to twenty years, and which were not intended for publication, were taken away from me. Now, tendentious excerpts from these papers have been privately published and are being circulated within the same circles. The play *Feast of the Victors*, which I composed in verse from memory in camp, where I went by a four-digit number – and where, condemned to death by starvation, we were forgotten by society, and NO-ONE outside the camps spoke out against such repression – this play, which I have long since left behind me, is now being ascribed to me as my very latest work . . .

On 26 June 1968 an article entitled 'The Ideological Struggle – The Writer's Responsibility' was published in *Literaturnaya Gazeta*. It gave the following, official version of the search at Teush's flat:

Bourgeois propaganda has made much play with A. Solzhenitsyn's claims that state security agencies have taken his papers and manuscripts from him. In answer to an enquiry from the Writers' Union, however, the USSR Prosecutor's Office reported that no searches had ever been conducted in A. Solzhenitsyn's flat in Ryazan and no manuscripts or papers had been taken from him. Typed copies of certain of Solzhenitsyn's manuscripts, *without his name*, were found in a search of the flat of a certain Citizen Teush in Moscow and were seized along with other compromising material, after a customs inspection of a foreign tourist's luggage had brought to light slanderous manuscript fabrications about Soviet life, and the course of the subsequent investigation led the agencies concerned to Teush . . .

In an attempt to justify the action of the security agents who made copies of *Feast of the Victors* 'for official use' in spite of the author's categorical objections, *Literaturnaya Gazeta* argued thus:

How can one pretend that such a play does not exist if A. Solzhenitsyn, having entrusted the safe-keeping of his works to a supplier of anti-Sovietism to the foreign world, thereby lost all control over them and over the play in particular?

It is hard to verify whether or not the incident of the customs inspection and the discovery of anti-Soviet writings by Teush in the possession of a foreign tourist did in fact take place. Personally I doubt it. It was established after the search, on the basis of papers belonging to Teush himself, that he was the author of an anonymous *samizdat* review of *Ivan Denisovich* written in 1964. It was a very interesting – and controversial – review, and it was only after the search that it became more widely known. I myself did not read it until 1966. It was on the grounds that he had written this review – a fact which was only proved *after the search* – that criminal proceedings were instituted against Teush. However, the case was soon dropped and Teush forgotten, and no charge of sending anti-Soviet works abroad was ever seriously made.

Teush's review of *Ivan Denisovich* was certainly outspoken; but there were many works circulating in *samizdat* at the time that were more strongly-worded and more specific – for example, original, signed writings describing the crimes of the period of the cult of personality, prison and camp conditions, the moral and ideological consequences of Stalinism, works by E. Ginzburg, V. Shalamov, G. Pomerants, M. Yakubovich and others. Some of these works did in fact find their way abroad and were published there. But no searches were ever made in this connection. The case of Sinyavsky and Daniel, which was opened in 1964, was something on its own. The visit to Teush's flat and the 'accidental' discovery of Solzhenitsyn's novel and papers might well have been the result of a large-scale campaign against *samizdat* involving a number of searches carried out simultaneously in the homes of other writers. The hypothesis, initially put forward by some of Solzhenitsyn's friends, was that the KGB were worried by his removal of the *First Circle* typescripts from *Novy Mir*, which they interpreted as signifying his intention to put them into the *samizdat* machine. The novel had been announced and had lain in the editorial office under contract; its contents might therefore be known to the sections of the party hierarchy and KGB responsible for literary affairs. Glavlit may at any time ask to be shown any typescript designated for publication, and an editor does not have the right to refuse a request for a preview of this kind, especially as in the process of publication the work will in any case be read over by Glavlit at the proof stage. Solzhenitsyn's typescript had been with *Novy Mir* for nearly a year and had been read by a number of people there, and Solzhenitsyn's own theory was that one of the staff, the inevitable informer that exists in any organisation, had reported that he was taking away a typescript. By shadowing him the KGB could have established that he had taken the suitcase to Teush's flat. Thereafter they needed only two or three days to obtain the consent of the necessary authorities to make a search.

If this hypothesis had been correct Solzhenitsyn's other papers would certainly have been a fortuitous discovery for the KGB. But the theory was soon rejected. It was *The First Circle* that was the fortuitous discovery, while the search of Teush's flat was merely carried out to supplement a second, *simultaneous* search in which Solzhenitsyn's papers were seized. They were confiscated not from Teush's flat but from the flat of a young friend of his, Z, whom Solzhenitsyn did not know. At the beginning of 1965, without asking Solzhenitsyn for his consent, Teush had given them into Z's keeping. Solzhenitsyn had known nothing about it. As it turned out later, the KGB became aware of their existence. The search parties arrived at Teush's and Z's flats simultaneously, although Teush had just returned from a long holiday and had not been to see Z. This indicates that the KGB had known about Z for a long time, and that the main object of the search had probably been to obtain Solzhenitsyn's papers and not material belonging to Teush himself. When the 'proceedings' against Teush were dropped shortly afterwards, some of the material confiscated from him was returned. To this day, however, nothing has been returned to Solzhenitsyn, although no 'proceedings' have been brought against him.

Solzhenitsyn learned of the double search a few days after news of the search at Teush's flat reached him. He stayed at his cottage, for he could not be sure that if he returned to Ryazan there would not be a search there too. However, this did not happen. In October there were indications that the consequences of the search would not be too serious. The editorial board of *Novy Mir* suggested to Solzhenitsyn that he offer them some 'acceptable' work for publication. Solzhenitsyn took this opportunity to give Tvardovsky four short stories. Only one of them, *Zakhar the Pouch*, was accepted, and it was published in the January 1966 issue of *Novy Mir*. It was a fine and patriotic tale. Another of the stories, *The Right Hand*, later circulated in *samizdat*.[2]

[2] Z left the USSR in 1971 and I have since had a long discussion with him about this affair. He told me that he thought Teush had informed Solzhenitsyn about the transfer of his papers from Teush's flat. Z is sure that the raid had no connection with *The First Circle* since subsequent investigations showed that it was planned before 11 September and was delayed because Z had returned from holiday only on 11 September. From the KGB's interrogations of Teush, Z, Yu. Stein and Veronica Turkina, it was clear that their phones had been tapped since 1965. It was also clear that Teush's room was wired. Solzhenitsyn asked Teush not to show anyone his papers, but Teush did show them to Z. In the summer of 1965 Teush was sure that his flat was under observation and had therefore decided that Solzhenitsyn's papers would be safer in Z's flat. Teush died in 1971, aged 73. [Author's Note.]

8. Solzhenitsyn and Academician P. L. Kapitsa

IN MID-OCTOBER 1965 I was told that Academician Pyotr Leonidovich Kapitsa wanted information about the position of N. V. Timofeev-Resovsky in our institute. Someone had approached Kapitsa with the request that Timofeev-Resovsky be given full membership of the Academy of Sciences in the biophysics section, and Pyotr Leonidovich needed some information about the work Timofeev-Resovsky was currently doing. Apart from that, he wanted to know something about the organisational changes that had taken place in genetics since Lysenko had been removed from his position of leadership in that field of biology. Accordingly Kapitsa invited me to come and see him at his institute. Naturally I went at once. It was my second meeting with Kapitsa. After I had told him about Timofeev-Resovsky, Obninsk and our institute I could not refrain from mentioning Solzhenitsyn's unsuccessful attempt to move to Obninsk, and the confiscation by the KGB of copies of his new novel. Kapitsa, who knew nothing of this, expressed his astonishment. He wanted to know if I could introduce him to Solzhenitsyn. I answered that it would be a pleasure, and I would try to arrange it. He then asked me to pass on to Solzhenitsyn an invitation to visit him when he was next in Moscow.

The invitation was accepted, and on 28 October Solzhenitsyn and I went to the Institute of Physics headed by Kapitsa. The Institute stands at the junction of Lenin Prospect and the Vorobyovskoye Highway. Beyond it a large garden slopes down to the Moscow River. In this garden stands a small, two-storey English-style house, which accommodates Academician Kapitsa and his family. The Institute and its grounds are guarded, though not as heavily as are some others, whose protection is both expensive and anachronistic. (The extensive grounds of the Obninsk Institute of Physical Power Engineering, for example, are still guarded by vast numbers of soldiers, two fences separated by a specially ploughed strip rather like

53

a frontier zone, a system of electrified wires, and police dogs.) At the Institute of Physics it is much more sophisticated. A system of photoelectric cells has been installed along the path leading to Kapitsa's house and the visitor passes through an invisible electric eye. But even this system appears to be a relic of bygone days; no one stopped us to ask us our business either at the entrance to the grounds or when we passed through the photoelectric device.

The meeting between Solzhenitsyn and Kapitsa was most cordial. I preferred to remain silent and listen to the conversation of these two exceptional men. I was not surprised to see Solzhenitsyn display some erudition on a number of physical and cybernetic problems. He had, after all, a higher education in physics and mathematics, and had worked for several years while a prisoner as a research worker in a special secret institute. What did surprise both Solzhenitsyn and myself was Kapitsa's extraordinary knowledge of literature – his understanding of the situation in Soviet literature, and his familiarity with contemporary works abroad.

Kapitsa read us the text of an article he had recently sent to *Pravda* discussing the question of the party's relations with the creative artists and with writers in particular. He had written it in response to some articles which had recently appeared in *Pravda*, entitled 'The Party and the Intelligentsia', under the by-line of Pravda's Editor-in-chief, Rumantsev. Kapitsa threw down an interesting, cleverly written challenge to some of the arguments advanced by Rumyantsev, and expressed his high opinion of Solzhenitsyn's published work. (Kapitsa's article was not published in *Pravda*, or anywhere else.)

Then Kapitsa outlined to us the damage done to Soviet physics by the Stalinist repressions, and also the story of the arrest and release in 1937 of the eminent physicist L. Landau, who worked with Kapitsa at his institute. Landau was released after Kapitsa sent Stalin a strongly-worded letter. But since Landau had by then been convicted as an 'enemy of the people' and a 'foreign agent', he was not simply released; a review of his case was carried out, in the course of which Kapitsa had several arguments with the USSR Prosecutor's Office concerning points in the indictment.

The conversation also inevitably touched upon the subject of the clash between Kapitsa and Lavrenti Beria that resulted from Kapitsa's refusal to participate in work on the development of the Soviet atomic bomb, begun in 1945. (Kapitsa had refused on humanitarian, not political grounds.) Beria demanded that Stalin have Kapitsa arrested, but Stalin could not bring himself to take this step. He realized that it would provoke a widespread international reaction and would lead to a deterioration in his relationships with his allies, especially Great Britain, which in 1945 were very good. Kapitsa's arrest would also have had a demoralising effect upon many Soviet physicists, for his scientific prestige stood very high. Stalin did promise Beria: 'I'll get rid of him for you – but *you're* not to lay a finger on him.' Kapitsa was sacked from his post and was unable to find a job anywhere for almost one and a half years, At the end of 1946 he was taken on as a senior scientist at the Institute of Crystallography. Only after Stalin's death was he able to return to the Institute of Physics which he had founded before the war.

Our conversation had been friendly and informal, and although no approach had been made to Kapitsa for his help, I was certain, as we left him, that he would, on his own initiative, do everything in his power to help Solzhenitsyn in his difficult situation. There was no need to ask anything of a man like Kapitsa whose stature was apparent to everyone who met him; he himself understood what he could and what he ought to do. He had already asked Solzhenitsyn if he might, at a convenient moment, read *The First Circle*.

The Institute of Physics is situated near what was formerly the Kaluga Gate and is now known as 'Gagarin Square'. Leaving the Institute, we turned left down Lenin Prospect. We had walked about two hundred metres in thoughtful silence when Solzhenitsyn suddenly stopped short on the corner in front of a tall, crescent-shaped, turreted house, built in the pompous style so typical of the last years of Stalin's rule. 'There it is, *that* house,' said Solzhenitsyn. I understood. We were standing in front of the house that Solzhenitsyn and hundreds of other prisoners had built in 1945-6. On this building site Solzhenitsyn had worked first simply as a porter, then as a stone mason and a parquet floor layer. The prison-camp had been alongside the house, fenced off from the Gorky Park of

Culture and Rest by barbed wire. Immediately after his trial Solzhenitsyn had spent more than a year there. The house with the turrets is faithfully described in *The First Circle*; two of the novel's main characters – the State Prosecutor, and Major Roitman, the engineer in charge of the laboratory at the secret MVD Institute – acquire spacious apartments there.

Opposite, on the other side of the Lenin Prospect, stands an identical house. They were built in 1946 to symbolise a 'Gateway to Moscow' on the road leading in from Vnukovo Airport.

In later years the Lenin Prospect was extended as far as the new blocks of Moscow University. This part of the University, the so-called 'Palace of Science', had also been built, for the most part, by prisoners.

9. What is to be Done with Disobedient Talent?

IN 1966 THE new leaders of Soviet ideological and cultural life made a more determined attempt to steer artists and writers into the strait-jacket denoted by the term '*partiinost*' (literally 'party-ness'). Khrushchev had in fact made a similar attempt, but he had invested the concept of '*partiinost*' with an additional meaning. In Khrushchev's day there had been conflicting interpretations of the concept, but at certain stages it included the notion of struggle against the abuses and crimes of the period of the 'personality cult'. It was precisely these political tendencies that accounted for Khrushchev's popularity in Soviet intellectual circles and with public opinion abroad. Unfortunately, Khrushchev used his popularity in traditional fashion to strengthen his personal power. He was removed by a collective initiative, out of which there grew a truly collective leadership in the country. Some foreign commentators later remarked that the 'cult of personality' had been succeeded by the 'cult of impersonality', but in reality this was not so. The increased independence, responsibility and opportunities available to individual members of the leadership resulted in a dissociation of power. For the country as a whole this was a very positive phenomenon, because it promoted more cautious and considered solutions to important political and economic problems. It meant that the Minister of Agriculture, for example, was given more opportunity to take independent decisions without fearing that he would be forced, for instance, to provide for the cultivation of maize in the Leningrad and northern, Archangel, regions, while the Minister of Foreign Affairs was better able to work towards establishing international equilibrium now that he no longer had to worry lest his Head of State should suddenly arrive at the United Nations, take off his shoe and start banging it on his desk in front of the General Assembly. But at the same time conservative leaders of culture, ideology and science, who during the Khrushchev period had been obliged to adapt to his new line, now had greater autonomy and freedom to make their own decisions. For them, the democratisation of society and the extension of creative freedom and freedom of the press were undesirable phenomena. Ideally they wished to see people engaged in creative work dutifully obeying instructions and directives from above. In the arts, this reversion to the directive as a means of control created complex problems. A similar situation, though relating to a more brutal time, had been depicted in *Ivan Denisovich*. Two camp inmates are discussing the film *Ivan the Terrible*:

> 'All show-off!' Kh-123 snapped. He was holding his spoon in front of his mouth. 'Too much art is no art at all. Like candy instead of bread! And the politics of it is utterly vile – vindication of a one-man tyranny. An insult to the memory of three generations of Russian intellectuals . . .'
>
> 'But what other treatment of the subject would have been let through . . .'
>
> 'Ha! *Let through*, you say? Then don't call him a genius! Call him a toady, say he carried out orders like a dog. A genius doesn't adapt his treatment to the taste of tyrants!'[1]

Early in 1966 there were heated discussions among philosophers, historians and writers about the attempts of certain leaders to bring about a rehabilitation – albeit a partial rehabilitation – of Stalin and Stalinist policies. Stalinist statements began to appear in the press (for example, in an article by E. Zhukov, V. Trukhanovsky and V. Shunkov entitled 'The Lofty Responsibility of Historians', published in *Pravda*, 30 January 1966). Further statements of this kind were made at various high-level meetings (in a speech by Trapeznikov, Head of the Central Party Committee Department of Science and Higher Education, and again by Sturua, a Secretary of the Central Committee of the Georgian Communist Party and by others). These speeches were vigorously denounced by a number of Soviet intellectuals: a letter from the publicist E. Genri (S. N. Rostovtsev) to the writer Ilya Ehrenburg circulated widely, as did the brilliant pamphlet 'The Moral Make-up of Historical Personality' by Grigory Pomerants, and the transcript of an article on the book *June 1941* by A. M. Nekrich, exposing the flagrant errors committed by Stalin immediately before the

[1] Translated by Max Hayward in the Praeger/Pall Mall edition.

58

war and during the first months of wartime and many other documents. A group of eminent Soviet scientists and other intellectuals (including Academicians L. A. Artsimovich, P. L. Kapitsa, M. A. Leontovich, I. E. Tamm, A. D. Sakharov, S. D. Skazkin, I. L. Knunyants, A. Kolmogorov, P. Zdrodovsky; People's Artists A. A. Popov, M. M. Plisetskaya, G. A. Tovstonogov; writers V. F. Tendryakov, K. G. Paustovsky, K. I. Chukovsky, and many more), in a gravely-worded letter to the Central Committee of the Soviet Communist Party, protested against any attempts, direct or oblique, to rehabilitate Stalin, and warned that such attempts could only provoke disillusionment with the party's ideological policy. A number of Old Bolsheviks sent letters to the Central Committee. These protests undoubtedly restrained the Stalinists from making public statements, but it was quite clear that hidden methods of suppressing creative work would continue. Editors of journals and newspapers were given strict instruction not to publish works that broached the subject of crimes during the Stalin period. When Tvardovsky told me this he asked in pretended amazement, 'But why? After all, literature is the most humane form of retribution . . .'

February saw the opening of the shameful trial of Andrei Sinyavsky and Yuli Daniel whose works had been published abroad. The case provoked a torrent of protest both inside the USSR and all over the world. The clumsily fabricated charges were based on an absurd attempt to equate the utterances of fictional characters with the attitudes of their creators. Despite the protests and despite legal proof of the groundlessness of the charges, Sinyavsky and Daniel were given very harsh sentences (seven and five years' imprisonment respectively).

The journals *Yunost* (*Youth*) and *Novy Mir* in 1966 came in for sharp criticism at ideological conferences. Since 1965 there had been no restrictions on the number of people subscribing to journals and newspapers and hence the size of a journal's edition reflected its popularity with the reading public. (This does not apply to all political journals, which are often compulsorily distributed.) Each edition of a journal comprises subscription copies for private people, subscription copies for libraries and other establishments, and a number of copies for retail sale. The number of copies destined for retail sale is determined jointly by the Committee for Press Affairs and the Press Section of the Central Committee of the Communist Party. Only the number of private subscription copies is a true index of demand. Of the 'heavy' literary-cum-political journals published in Moscow – *Oktyabr* (*October*), *Moskva*, *Znamya* (*Banner*) and *Novy Mir* – *Novy Mir* was at the top of the list for private subscribers in 1966. Its circulation had risen from 128,000 in 1965 to 141,000 in 1966, and this in spite of its comparatively high price. The Editor of *Oktyabr*, Vsevolod Kochetov, persistently tried to get his retail quota increased in order to conceal the falling-off in private subscriptions. In view of this it was decided that particularly harsh measures should be taken against *Novy Mir*. The No. 7 (1966) issue of *Novy Mir* contained a short novel by B. Mozhayev, *From the Life of Fyodor Kuzkin*, which described the hard conditions of life in the countryside. The work aroused considerable displeasure 'at the top'. The No. 8 issue of the journal published a comparatively ordinary story by A. Makarov, *Home*, which described the homecoming of a soldier on leave to his native village. The story was rather frank in its depiction of the scourge of village life – drunkenness. The Political Directorate of the Soviet Army held a special meeting on the story, and the head of the Directorate, claiming that the story smeared the soldiers of the glorious Soviet Army, issued an order forbidding military libraries and army officers to subscribe to *Novy Mir*. (The order was not revoked until after Tvardovsky was removed from his post as Editor-in-Chief in 1970.)

How did Solzhenitsyn fare during this time? Scandalous rumours were spread about him – stories about his time as prisoner-of-war and his alleged service with the German *Polizei* in occupied territory. The 'anti-Soviet' subject-matter of his play *Feast of the Victors* was quoted in certain quarters. Solzhenitsyn sent a letter to several papers denying these allegations and protesting vigorously against the publication of his old files confiscated by the KGB; but the letter was never published.

In intellectual circles his name was on everybody's lips: how was he living, had *any* copies of the confiscated novel been saved, and what could one do to help him? At the beginning of

1966 Academician Kapitsa, D. Shostakovich, and writers K. Chukovsky, S. S. Smirnov and K. Paustovsky wrote a letter to the Central Committee stating their opinion that it was essential that Solzhenitsyn be allowed a normal way of life in order to carry on his work. The letter drew attention to the writer's poor living conditions in Ryazan and requested that he be granted permission to move to Moscow and given a flat there.

Surprisingly, the letter did have some effect. Solzhenitsyn did not of course obtain permission to move to Moscow; but the Ryazan Town Soviet received a directive from Moscow to make a new flat available to him. He was called to the Soviet and offered a choice of four different flats. He declined the flats in new blocks in the town centre, fearing that they would be noisy, and chose instead quite a spacious, three-roomed flat on the ground floor of an old but solidly built house in Yablochkov Passage. It was particularly convenient because it had a garage in the courtyard.

In the spring Solzhenitsyn once again went off to his cottage, where he spent the whole summer. He loved the place: it was quiet, and he could work better there. He was writing *Cancer Ward*. Tvardovsky, who had read several chapters and knew how the story developed, hoped to be able to publish it in *Novy Mir*.

Rumours were circulating in Moscow that Solzhenitsyn was in serious financial difficulties. On the initiative of the employees of a military research institute money was collected by scientists as a housewarming present. I warned some of the people involved that Solzhenitsyn would refuse help of this kind, but they decided to see it through. An acquaintance of Solzhenitsyn's was persuaded to deliver the money in an envelope, but he soon returned with the news that Solzhenitsyn had categorically refused to accept it. The go-between had told him in vain that the money could not possibly be given back because some of the contributions had been anonymous. (It should be explained, incidentally, that Soviet intellectuals have almost always organised collections of money to help the families of political prisoners or people dismissed from their jobs.) Although Solzhenitsyn's financial position was indeed rather gloomy, his needs were modest. He bought the sturdiest shoes and clothes he could find so that they would last for years. For his morning and evening meal, especially when at the cottage, he preferred simply bread and milk. He would fetch a can of fresh milk from the next village every day. Four years in the army and twelve years in camps and exile had rid him of any idea of 'material well-being' characteristic of our modern, so-called consumer society.

Solzhenitsyn was not the only person for whom the 'new line' created difficulties. A great many writers whose works dealt with events of the past found their typescripts returned to them after being passed for press and in some cases even set up in type. This applied both to those who had written specifically of the Stalin purges (V. Shalamov, E. Ginzburg, L. Chukovskaya, G. Serebryakova, S. Gazaryan and A. Kosterin) and to those who had in one way or another given a truthful picture of bureaucratic methods, arbitrariness, the hardships of rural life and many other aspects of Soviet society at the time. A. Bek's novel *The New Appointment* was thrown out after it had been set up in type; K. Simonov's *War Diaries*, accepted by *Novy Mir* and passed by the censor, were suddenly banned when the edition of the journal was almost ready; since the diaries gave an extremely accurate picture of the first months of the war, 80,000 copies of the journal were first shredded into small pieces at the printers, and then sent for pulping. Banned publications are pre-shredded to prevent any copies from escaping while *en route* from the printer to the pulp-mill, which has a shredder of its own.)

Many other works were either withdrawn at the editorial stage or else rejected by publishers without even being properly considered.

All this made for a very tense situation which showed even in speeches at writers' party meetings, particularly in Moscow and Leningrad. In the circumstances the leadership of the USSR Writers' Union decided not to convene the Fourth Soviet Writers' Congress, the delegates to which had been elected back in 1965. It was resolved to postpone the Congress until 1967 and to hold it then in honour of the fiftieth anniversary of the October Revolution. At a jubilee Congress, criticism could be more easily suppressed.

Solzhenitsyn spent the whole summer at his cottage working twelve to fourteen hours a day. I saw him only twice during that time, and then very briefly. When he is engaged in a period of intensive work he does not like to be dragged away to meet people. He fits his social life into the periods when he is researching.

I was interested in the fate of *The First Circle* and suggested that the novel ought to be made available to a wider circle; but Solzhenitsyn for the time being rejected the idea of offering the novel to *samizdat*, fearing that pirated editions might appear abroad. He believed that the ensuing complications would destroy his peace of mind and he would be unable to work on the projects he had in hand. 'I've collected enough material for ten years', he said. He was unwilling to resort to an open conflict. His intention was still, as it had been when he decided to move to Obninsk in 1965, to remain in the background for a few years in order to finish writing the works he had already conceived in his mind.

Solzhenitsyn completed the first part of *Cancer Ward* early in the summer of 1966, and at the end of July he delivered it to *Novy Mir*. To facilitate the novel's passage through the editorial office of *Novy Mir* Solzhenitsyn decided to have it discussed at a meeting of the prose section of the Moscow branch of the Writers' Union. Surprisingly the leadership of the Moscow writers' organisation agreed to hold an open debate on the novel. Twenty copies of the typescript were ordered, to be distributed to leading Moscow critics and men of letters. In the meantime Solzhenitsyn went back to Ryazan.

On leaving to spend the summer at his cottage, Solzhenitsyn had locked his study. Upon his return he noticed at once that a small pile of mortar had fallen from the ceiling and was lying on the floor right in the middle of the room. There were no cracks in the ceiling above the spot, but a slight indentation had appeared. He discovered that the inhabitants of the flat above him had been away for a month in a holiday rest-home. A listening device could easily have been installed during their absence. The crumbling mortar and the concave patch could have been caused by the pressure of a drill working through the floor of the flat above. It was no more than hypothesis; but Solzhenitsyn's work at the institute described in *The First Circle* had taught him a thing or two about the technique of eavesdropping. There was no point in uncovering and de-activating the microphone – they would simply install another somewhere else.

As the year drew to its close Solzhenitsyn spent most of his time in Moscow. The first part of *Cancer Ward* was to be discussed on 16 November. A detailed account of the meeting compiled by several of the participants subsequently circulated in *samizdat* and was published somewhere abroad a year later. The meeting took an extremely favourable view of the work; without exception the speakers came out strongly in its support, and a resolution was passed by the prose section recommending it for publication. The hall was filled to overflowing. Speeches in support of the book (by V. Kaverin, A. Borshchagovsky, L. Slavin, B. Sarnov, Yu. Karyakin, E. Tager and many other people) were enthusiastically received by the audience. Solzhenitsyn himself was given a warm welcome by his colleagues.

But the meeting of the prose section of the Writers' Union had other important consequences. The number of typescripts continued to increase; once the 'critical mass' was reached, there began the chain reaction of *samizdat*. By the end of December the first part of *Cancer Ward* had been read by thousands of people.

During his stay in Moscow, however, Solzhenitsyn learned from his literary friends of a very disquieting event which cast a shadow even over the favourable reception of *Cancer Ward*. His files, which the KGB had confiscated in 1965, had not remained confidential. Parts of his novel *The First Circle*, and tendentious excerpts from material from his files, in particular from his long-abandoned verse-play *Feast of the Victors*, had been duplicated by the KGB, and shown to a few selected leading figures in the Writers' Union and certain party workers.

This strongly suggested blackmail; action of this kind by the KGB was manifestly against the law. By law, organs of the KGB have the right to conduct investigations when they are considering bringing a charge and to bring the accused to court; but that is the full extent of their powers. When they confiscated Solzhenitsyn's files in 1965 they had the right to open an investigation into his case if they found incriminating evidence in any of the confiscated material. If there was no incriminating evidence, all the confiscated material should have been returned, for they had no legal right to appropriate typescripts that were the property of another person. Nor was there anything incriminating about a novel which was already under contract for publication, or in draft material which was clearly in the nature of private memoranda and had never been 'put into circulation', to use the legal term. The circulation of these typescripts, even 'privately', when their author had categorically refused authorisation, was clearly illegal. Someone had decided that *Feast of the Victors* was an anti-Soviet work; but as long as it existed only in a single copy in the author's files this did not constitute a crime. It had been composed by *a prisoner* and put down on paper from memory by a person sentenced to *exile in perpetuity*. A man who has been given a *life sentence* has the right to think and write whatever he chooses; he is outside the law. In these circumstances it is only the duplication and circulation of such a work that is a criminal offence; this the KGB brought about precisely in order to put the blame on the author. In the circumstances Solzhenitsyn could no longer remain silent.

At the end of November 1966, research workers at the Kurchatov Institute of Atomic Energy invited Solzhenitsyn to 'meet his readers' at the Institute's social club. He accepted and was given an enthusiastic reception. He read extracts from his latest works, including *The First Circle* and *Cancer Ward*; then he answered questions, taking the opportunity to refute the slanderous rumours that had been circulating about him. Next day the Secretary of the Institute's Party Committee was summoned to the District Party Committee and given a severe reprimand. A few days later Solzhenitsyn was invited to a similar meeting at the Academy of Sciences Institute of Oriental Studies. Again he was given a warm reception. He read two chapters from *Cancer Ward* and several extracts from *The First Circle*. The audience's questions and Solzhenitsyn's replies were taken down in shorthand by somebody and later circulated in *samizdat*. In answer to a question about why he had abandoned his former principle of not making public statements or giving interviews, Solzhenitsyn said:

. . . if a writer's works are regularly published, he feels in touch with his audience, be it through criticism or through

65

readers' letters . . . But in recent years my things have not been published, and I have learned a lesson: it was wrong of me to opt completely out of making public appearances. I am compelled by circumstances to meet my readers. And there are three reasons why I am doing so: I need to know their reactions; I must protect my rights as author; and I must defend my name against slander.

. . . . My novel *The First Circle* has become the property of an organisation whose métier is not the custody of belles-lettres. Things of mine which I never wanted to publish have now been published in a secret, closed edition and are being passed around a certain circle of people, in particular leading figures in the creative trade-unions. These people are reading and then passing comments on manuscripts from my personal files – people like Khrennikov, Kochetov, Surkov,[2] and others.

What am I to do? If they had simply taken away my things I would have kept quiet. I complained to the Central Committee but nothing came of my petitions. . . Someone said at a meeting of the Lenin Prize Committee that Solzhenitsyn was a criminal. The same Committee heard documentary proof of the untruth of this statement. And in spite of this, speakers have been announcing from official rostrums that Solzhenitsyn was in the Polizei, Solzhenitsyn was taken prisoner. There was a meeting in Novosibirsk between representatives of *Novy Mir* and its readers, and someone asked 'Is it true that Solzhenitsyn collaborated with the Gestapo? . . .'

The Moscow intelligentsia was not alone in being perturbed by Solzhenitsyn's two appearances in public. In other quarters too certain people were worried. Once more the District Party Committee administered a reprimand, this time to the Secretary of the Party Bureau at the Institute of Oriental Studies. All party organisations in Moscow and, it appears, in other cultural centres received strict directives. Following this, several meetings between Solzhenitsyn and his readers scheduled to take place in December in Moscow and the Moscow area were cancelled. The strangest things happened. Representatives from

[2] The first a composer, the second two writers; all members of the 'establishment'.

various establishments, mainly research institutes would come to Solzhenitsyn and officially invite him to a meeting with his readers. A date and time would be agreed and Sclzhenitsyn would prepare his lecture. But on the eve of the meeting, and sometimes only a few hours before it was due to take place, the organisers would come to him in embarrassment, or simply telephone, to say that the District Committee, or the institute's party committee, had cancelled it. At one biological institute affiliated to the Academy of Sciences the organisers kept their plans secret, did not post any notices, and informed employees of the writer's impending visit only three hours before the meeting was due to begin. But an hour before Solzhenitsyn was due to arrive the director of the institute received a telephone call from the District Party Committee categorically forbidding any appearance by Solzhenitsyn. After a dozen abortive attempts he stopped accepting invitations. Someone at the top had evidently decided that he must be silenced.

10. The Appeal to the Fourth Writers' Congress

IF ANYTHING MADE the Fourth All-Union Writers' Congress a memorable event, for myself and many other lovers of literature, it was the appeal addressed to the delegates by Alexander Solzhenitsyn, who was not invited to attend the Congress even as a guest.

I learned of Solzhenitsyn's letter of appeal to the Congress about two weeks before it opened. He was staying at his cottage, and at the beginning of May arrived unannounced in Obninsk where he called on Nikolai Vladimirovich and read him the draft of his letter. Unfortunately I was away in Moscow and only learnt of the appeal the following day when I was given an account of its contents. I did not receive the text of the letter until Solzhenitsyn had begun sending it out by post. The Congress was to open on 18 May; the letters were sent out on 15 and 16 May. With the help of friends and assistants Solzhenitsyn prepared over 250 typed copies of the letter, each one signed with his own hand. All the envelopes bore the sender's name. Foreseeing the possibility of interception, Solzhenitsyn posted the letters at different times and from different districts of Moscow. Most of them went to the Presidium of the Congress and its delegates, about seventy copies to non-delegated writers and about thirty to newspapers and journals editors. On the opening day of Congress practically all the delegates knew of Solzhenitsyn's letter.

In the space of a few days *samizdat* had reproduced the letter in thousands of copies. A few days after the Congress the text of the letter was published abroad in the most important papers and in numerous weeklies, and for many days afterwards it was broadcast by various foreign radio stations.[1]

Although Solzhenitsyn's appeal, and the form it took, clearly surprised the organisers of the Congress, they had not ruled out the possibility of sharp words being spoken at the

---

[1] A translation of the text is given as an appendix, page 197.

Congress on the subject of the excessively severe pressures of censorship. The leaders of the Congress particularly feared the possibility of speeches in defence of the convicted writers Sinyavsky and Daniel, especially as letters protesting at the shameful trial and harsh sentence, signed by hundreds of writers, scientists and other intellectuals – among them many party members – had illustrated clearly enough the extent of opposition to the hard line.

Moreover this was a jubilee congress to be held in honour of the fifteenth anniversary of Soviet power, and both the leadership of the Writers' Union and the Ideological Commission intended it as a display of complete unanimity among writers and the unprecedented flowering of Soviet literature. Consequently preparations for the congress were exceptionally thorough. Lists of writers who wished to take part in debates were scrutinised beforehand, and the texts of their speeches were approved in advance, before the congress even opened. The speakers of course, had to be acquainted in advance with the contents of the main addresses that would be delivered to the various sections of the congress. A special commission assigned to check beforehand every speech prepared for each debate warned the speakers that they must not depart from their approved texts. Thus did censorship, even at a gathering of writers, strive to deaden the living, spoken language and stifle the art of genuine oratory.

It is customary to invite large numbers of guests to the opening of congresses of writers, artists, or composers. On this occasion this rule too was broken. The congress opened in the Kremlin Palace of Congresses, in a hall which can accommodate several thousand people. The delegates numbered about a thousand. But there were no guest tickets, even for members of the Writers' Union; admission was only by special invitation. The balconies in the Large Hall, which usually seat over a thousand people, were completely closed. A group of Old Bolsheviks who, ten days before it opened, requested the permission of the Writers' Union to attend the Congress were refused.

In this atmosphere Solzhenitsyn's letter to the Congress received prompt and strong support. During the first two or three days of the Congress most of the conversation in the lobbies revolved around his appeal. Many people felt that it ought to be discussed.

During the Congress a certain popular poet held a party at his house for a large number of writers. Over dinner the conversation inevitably turned upon the fate of Solzhenitsyn and his letter to the Congress. After drinking several toasts the writers began to feel a little bolder. The poet, by now rather drunk, turned to a writer from one of the national republics who was an active member of the World Peace Council and a well-known liberal.

'You're going to chair the session tomorrow morning, aren't you? Give me the chance to speak! I'll go up and read Solzhenitsyn's letter; it'll be an historic moment!'

There was a stir of eager approval among the guests. The writer from the republic, also grown a little bolder, agreed, amidst shouts of support. But somebody still doubted his good faith.

'No, don't just promise – give us your oriental word of honour, here and now, that you really will call upon him to speak.'

The prospective chairman of the Congress rose and took his oath, in the oriental manner.[2]

Now it was a serious matter. In the eyes of his people a broken word meant loss of honour. Everyone who had been at the gathering awaited the morning session of the Congress impatiently. When next day the session began the chairman's seat was occupied by an entirely different writer. It was announced that the chairman-designate had been unexpectedly taken ill.

Yet the name of Solzhenitsyn was uttered from the platform, in the course of a speech by Vera Ketlinskaya. She spoke only a few words in support of Solzhenitsyn (which were omitted from Soviet newspaper reports of the Congress proceedings), but the audience in the Kremlin Palace of Congresses greeted them with applause. While the Congress was still in session the Presidium received a statement signed by eighty writers, insisting that Solzhenitsyn's letter be discussed. (Among

---

[2] The 'oriental oath' has many forms, but they always involve the swearer in sacrificing not only himself but his close relatives, often for several generations, should he fail to comply with his oath.

the signatories were: K. Paustovsky, V. Kaverin, V. Tendryakov, Yu. Trifonov, M. Popovsky, V. Maximov, B. Mozhayev, F. Iskander, V. Aksyonov, A. Rybakov, V. Bykov, and other prominent writers.)

Some members of the Congress appealed in writing to the Presidium individually, lending cogent support to the arguments Solzhenitsyn had put forward. After the Congress these letters too were circulated in *samizdat* and published abroad. The most widely known are the letters and other statements by G. Vladimov, V. Konetsky, P. Antokolsky, S. Antonov and V. Kaverin. It was clear that, had these writers found themselves on the Congress platform or in the role of temporary chairman, the letter by Solzhenitsyn might well have been given a public reading.

11. *Cancer Ward* in *Samizdat* and in *Novy Mir*

THE FIRST PART of *Cancer Ward* was already circulating in *samizdat* when it was joined, in late May and June 1967, by the second part of the work, which in its turn was widely read. At the same time it became known that *The First Circle* too was in circulation. Obninsk was introduced to these works by a young physicist, Valery Pavlinchuk, who was an ardent admirer of Solzhenitsyn's and who helped to organise the weekly 'Scientists' Day' at the physicists' club, which was very popular in the town. At these 'Scientists' Days', writers, critics, artists, publicists, poets and scientists from other towns were invited to speak. Although he suffered from a grave and in-curable illness (chronic nephritis in both kidneys), Valery Pavlinchuk was tirelessly active in all spheres of the town's public life and commanded the love and respect of all who knew him. By the end of the summer *Cancer Ward* and *The First Circle* had been read by hundreds of people in Obninsk. In Moscow they had apparently been read by tens of thousands. Pavlinchuk also tried to have Solzhenitsyn invited to one of the 'Scientists' Days' at the club, but his attempt was unsuccessful. (An anonymous sociological poll conducted in Obninsk at the end of 1967 included the question 'who is your favourite Soviet writer?' and the name most frequently given in answer was that of Solzhenitsyn.)

It was 2 September, and summer was already drawing to its close when Solzhenitsyn finally came to Obninsk. He paid brief visits to Nikolai Vladimirovich and myself, and was very interested to hear of the circulation of *Cancer Ward* and *The First Circle*. A short while before this there had been foreign radio reports that his situation had improved consider-ably, that he had been offered a flat in Moscow, that his papers had been returned to him and that he had received guarantees that *Cancer Ward* would be published. As it turned out, this was false information supplied to some over-credulous foreign correspondent. But there was intensive discussion, in the autumn of 1967, about the possibility of publishing *Cancer Ward*. On 22 September a special session of the Secretariat of the Board of the Union of Soviet Writers examined Solzhenitsyn's letter to the Fourth Writers' Congress and discussed the fate of his writings. Solzhenitsyn attended the meeting and later compiled a shortened transcript of the proceedings. This transcript in its turn circulated in *samizdat* and was published in 1968 in several foreign journals.

Only a few members of the Board spoke in favour of *Cancer Ward*, and even they felt obliged to say that the work would certainly need some revision before it could be published. Almost all the members had read *The First Circle*, having received copies of the novel from the source that had carried out the confiscation of the original versions in 1965. They had also apparently received appropriate instructions. Consequently the attitude of the Union's leadership to the novel was sharply critical. But the KGB had not only acquainted leading members of the Writers' Union with *The First Circle*, they had also given them some of the confiscated papers, including the poem *Feast of the Victors*, to read. This indicated that the flagrant abuse of his rights against which Solzhenitsyn had protested so vigorously in his appeal to the Fourth Writers' Congress had not been halted, and had reached the proportions of blackmail. The purpose of this blackmail was clear: his adversaries were seeking to isolate him completely.

Solzhenitsyn spent the autumn of 1967 living in the country a little way from Ryazan. He did not like working in the noise of the town. When he visited Moscow he preferred to stay at Kornei Chukovsky's dacha in Peredelkino. The old writer had a great affection for Solzhenitsyn and tried to provide him with pleasant conditions in which he could work. Peredelkino is only twenty kilometres from Moscow, which made it easy for Solzhenitsyn to gather material for his new work. He became a regular visitor to the Historical Library and various other collections of archives, and talked to old men who remembered the First World War.

Cancer Ward's chances of publication unexpectedly began to sort themselves out. Tvardovsky had been trying to get the permission of the Secretariat of the Writers' Union to publish the work in *Novy Mir*. In October 1967 the Secretariat agreed that he might sign a contract with Solzhenitsyn, and shortly after this the Secretary of the Writers' Union, Voronkov, authorised Tvardovsky to send the typescript of *Cancer Ward* to the type-setters.[1] It was proposed that the first part of the story should appear in the December issue of the Journal.

I personally very much doubted that *Cancer Ward* would be published. An instruction from Voronkov was plainly insufficient. On this occasion too the question of actual publication could only be decided at Politburo or Central Committee Secretariat level. But this was 1967 and Tvardvosky was no longer a member of the Central Committee; nor had he any contacts which would allow him to repeat the experiment of 1962. By now, Solzhenitsyn's opponents had intensified their campaign of slander, especially in the form of propaganda lectures. In October 1967, at the House of the Press in Leningrad, the Deputy Editor-in-Chief of *Pravda*, M. V. Zimyanin, gave a long ideological talk. According to a transcript made by several members of the audience, Zimyanin touched upon problems of literature and said, among other things:

> ... Recently there has been a great fuss in the Western press about several of our writers whose works are bringing grist to the mill of our enemies. The campaign in the Western press in defence of Tarsis ended only when they got hold of him in the West and saw for themselves that he was a madman.
>
> At the moment Solzhenitsyn occupies an important place in the propaganda of socialist countries. He too is abnormal, a schizophrenic. He was once a prisoner-of-war, and then, with or without cause, he was subjected to repression. He expresses his grudge against the régime in his writings. The only theme he is able to write about is life in the prison-camps – he can't get away from it. It is an obsession with him. Solzhenitsyn's works are aimed against the Soviet system, in which he seeks to find only sores and cancerous tumours. He notices nothing positive in our society.
>
> In the course of my duties I have occasion to read

[1] All these 'authorisations' were given on the telephone. (Author's note).

74

unpublished writings, and I have read Solzhenitsyn's play *Feast of the Victors*. The play is concerned with the repressions heaped down upon people who returned from the front. It is an absolutely and utterly anti-Soviet work. They used to jail people for works like this. Obviously we cannot publish Solzhenitsyn. If he writes works which correspond to the interests of our society, then he will be published. Nobody is depriving him of his bread and butter. Solzhenitsyn is a teacher of physics – let him go and teach . . .

At the end of 1967 a search was suddenly carried out in the theoretical department of the Obninsk Institute of Physical Power Engineering – more precisely, in a room occupied by a team that included Valery Pavlinchuk. During the search, *samizdat* literature was confiscated including typescripts of *Cancer Ward*. The town Party Committee instituted an inquiry into the activities of staff in the theoretical departments who were Party members. Valery Pavlinchuk was expelled from the Party and dismissed from the Institute. *Cancer Ward* figured in the investigation as an 'anti-Soviet' work. But at that very moment its author was reading through proofs printed on the presses of *Izvestiya* for the twelfth issue of *Novy Mir*.

12.   The Black Market in Russian Literature

IN LATE DECEMBER 1967 a proof of an issue of *Novy Mir* was
sent to the Central Committee, The Central Committee, however, had been disqualified from corporate discussion of the
question of publishing *Cancer Ward*. An instruction was issued
to the effect that the final decision on the story was to be taken
by the Secretariat of the Writers' Union. The Secretariat
discussed the matter without the author being present. Tvardovsky passionately supported immediate publication of *Cancer
Ward*. K. Simonov wavered but on the whole came out in
favour. However, the ruling 'core' of the Secretariat – K. Fedin,
M. Sholokhov, L. Leonov, N. Tikhonov, A. Surkov, and S.
Mikhalkov – were resolutely opposed to publication. In mid-
January 1968 Tvardovsky wrote a long and explicit letter to the
Chairman of the Soviet Writers' Union, Konstantin Fedin,
which he delivered in person. In it he set forth his opinion of
Solzhenitsyn's work as a whole, recalling the story of Solzhenitsyn's arrival on the literary scene, giving a serious analysis
of his work, and, against this background, pointing out the
merits of *Cancer Ward*. 'It would be a crime to conceal this
work from the reading public,' Tvardovsky wrote. 'The first
eight chapters are already in galleys and could be published
in the January issue of *Novy Mir* . . . . Everything now depends
on you, K. A. . . .' Fedin, however, declined to reconsider the
decision he had made at the meeting of the Bureau of the
Secretariat; he answered Tvardovsky's letter by telephone and
confirmed his order to distribute the type of *Cancer Ward*.
Inasmuch as *Novy Mir* was the 'organ of the Soviet Writers'
Union' Tvardovsky was obliged to submit. (For a long time
the existence of Tvardovsky's letter to Fedin was unknown. It
began to circulate in *samizdat* only in the summer of 1968,
after a sharply worded attack on Solzhenitsyn had appeared in
Literaturnaya Gazeta. In the autumn extracts from the letter
were published abroad. It was published in its entirety in

October 1968 in the English journal *Survey*, No. 69.) The ban on *Cancer Ward*, however, provoked little or no reaction from wider literary circles – the victimisation of those who had supported Solzhenitsyn's letter to the Fourth Writers' Congress (in the form of rejection by publishers, refusal to grant visas for tourist trips abroad, or party disciplinary proceedings) was having its effect. There were few protests against the ban; the best known, Kaverin's 'Open letter to K. Fedin', circulated widely and was subsequently published abroad and broadcast repeatedly by foreign radio stations.

At the beginning of April 1968 the following telegram from Frankfurt-am-Main was delivered to the editorial offices of *Novy Mir* for Tvardovsky:

> ... This is to inform you that the Committee for State Security, acting through Victor Louis, has sent one more copy of *Cancer Ward* to the West with the aim of blocking its publication in *Novy Mir*. Accordingly we have decided to publish the work immediately.
>
> The editors of the journal Grani.

In Chapter 5 I have already discussed in some detail the position of the journal *Grani* with regard to the publishing of *samizdat* material and have explained that if any contact can be proved to exist between this journal and a Soviet citizen it may serve as grounds for criminal proceedings against him.[1]

When he learned from Tvardovsky of the telegram from *Grani*, Solzhenitsyn wrote at once to the Secretariat of the Soviet Writers' Union and to several editors of journals. After quoting the text of the telegram, Solzhenitsyn declared:

> I should like to protest against both the publication [of the work] in *Grani* and the actions of Victor Louis, but the obscure and provocative terms of the telegram make it necessary first and formost to clarify the following:
>
> 1. Whether the telegram was actually sent by the editors of *Grani* or whether it was sent by a fictitous person (this can be established through the international telegraph office, which can inquire of Frankfurt-am-Main).
>
> 2. Who is Victor Louis, what kind of person is he, of what

country is he a citizen? Did he really take a copy of *Cancer Ward* out of the Soviet Union, to whom did he give it, and where else are they threatening to publish it? And what does the Committee for State Security have to do with this?

If the Secretariat of the Writers' Union is interested in establishing the truth and stopping the threatened publication of *Cancer Ward* in Russian abroad, I believe it will help to obtain prompt answers to these questions.

This episode compels us to ponder the strange and suspicious ways in which the typescripts of Soviet writers can reach the West. It is a powerful reminder to us that literature must not be reduced to a state in which literary works become a profitable commodity for any smart operator who happens to have a travel visa. Our authors must be allowed to publish in their own country; their works must not become the plunder of foreign publishing houses.

As might be expected, no reply to this letter was ever received; furthermore no explanation of the identity of Victor Louis was forthcoming. Solzhenitsyn's letter was published in a left-wing Italian paper about a month later, and then in a number of leading Western newspapers. It was clear that somebody had realised that publication abroad was inevitable, and was taking steps to see that the first publisher of Solzhenitsyn's latest novel would be an émigré journal. *Grani* has in any case no substantial readership in the USSR, and the fact that this émigré journal had secured first publication made it seem at least feasible subsequently to accuse Solzhenitsyn of collaborating with organisations which in the eyes of Soviet law are criminal.

Suddenly Victor Louis turned up in person at Solzhenitsyn's summer cottage to explain himself. In 1968 only very few of Solzhenitsyn's friends knew where his cottage was, and none of them was acquainted with Victor Louis. Obviously, therefore, Victor Louis came by the information he needed through the same organisation that had shown an exaggerated interest in the writer's life since 1965. Louis was the first uninvited guest at Solzhenitsyn's cottage, and he it was who destroyed Solzhenitsyn's conviction – already shaken on previous occasions – that it might serve as a kind of 'hideaway' where he could work in peace. Louis found Solzhenitsyn in the garage repairing his car, and when Solzhenitsyn finally emerged they had a brief talk.

Louis claimed that he had not taken a copy of *Cancer Ward* abroad, and that the telegram from *Grani* was a provocation. But Solzhenitsyn soon cut him short and refused to listen to his detailed explanations; he felt disinclined to trust a person of Louis' character, the 'foreign correspondent' with a Soviet diplomatic passport. However, with the help of a telephoto lens, Louis did take several photographs from some distance away. They were later printed in the West German magazine *Stern* and in other Western publications. Later he wrote an article about his visit to Solzhenitsyn and the conversation he had supposedly had with him. Since there had been no real conversation, Louis' article was for the most part impressionistic. Bearing in mind the general interest in the personality of the writer, Louis realised that even an inimical report of his meeting, and one which misrepresented the facts, had some chance of publication in the West. Louis offered his article on the 'meeting' with Solzhenitsyn to several foreign journals and newspapers simultaneously, though not until many months after his visit to the writer's cottage. The reason for this delay remains obscure; evidently a need arose at a particular moment to cast some suspicion on Solzhenitsyn's character.

I know of two outlets for Louis' article: one, in the *International Herald Tribune* (17 March 1969) and the other, in the journal *Survey* (No 70/71, 1969). In both cases the article was prefaced with an editorial note explaining to the reader who he was and why he was writing so unsympathetically about Solzhenitsyn. The author of the *Herald Tribune* commentary was the Moscow correspondent of *The Washington Post*, Anatole Shub, while the commentary in *Survey* was from the journal's editor, Leopold Labedz. Shub wrote:

Victor Louis, a Soviet citizen who also serves as correspondent for the London *Evening News*, has been first to report such inside Kremlin manoeuvres as the fall of Nikita Khrushchev. He has also travelled abroad more frequently than most Soviet officials, and became a celebrity in the summer of 1967 when he carried westward carbon copies of Svetlana Alliluyeva's *Twenty Letters to a Friend* as well as intimate photos of the Stalin family.

Repeating the story of how Louis reported the ousting of Khrushchev to the West, Mr Labedz mentions some of Louis' other 'achievements':

... more recently (in November 1968), he was, as he said over a drink in Phnompenh, the 'first Soviet citizen in 19 years' to have visited Generalissimo Chiang Kai-shek's bastion on Formosa ...

The article by Victor Louis was an extremely clumsy attempt to blacken Solzhenitsyn. There is no need to quote the text of the article here in its entirety, but I feel I ought to include some excerpts to illustrate the level – which was undoubtedly approved by those who direct Victor Louis in his work. I have taken these extracts from the English text as printed in *Survey*, since the *International Herald Tribune* only published an abridged version.

... A little less modest, however, is the way he signs his letter simply with one name – Solzhenitsyn – without preceding it with 'A. I.' or 'Alexander'. This has also been the habit of many great men in the past, and this master of words, with his understanding of nuances, is obviously not doing it by accident. Of course, it is hard for any human being to resist when people around them persuade them that they are geniuses ...

So far, however, Solzhenitsyn is not a Tolstoy, but he appears to be becoming one gradually, although only in mini-form. 'I am a country man, a villager. I live and breathe real air,' he exclaims. He looks very well on it, and has started growing a beard, but it is nothing compared with Tolstoy's ...

Louis goes on to describe Solzhenitsyn's small summer cottage, trying to show it too as a mini-estate, as it were, in imitation of Tolstoy's. According to Louis, Solzhenitsyn's disagreement with the régime is also an attempt to emulate Tolstoy:

... But if, like Tolstoy, he disagrees with the régime, he will not say so openly. He uses his hard-earned knowledge of the law so that no-one can blame him. It is hard to accuse him of sending his novels abroad but he is not at all surprised that they get there ... he knows the value of having an alibi ... When the Russian émigré *Grani* publishing house, which has already printed his selected works, and claimed a copyright for some of them, learned about Solzhenitsyn's 'protest against publication', they understandably continued their plans to publish and in addition sent a 'provocative cable' saying that Victor Louis had sent another copy of *Cancer Ward* to the West ... And after all, if I am to be blamed for sending one copy, who was it who sent the others? Why are they not sharing the blame?

... in Western Germany nobody encourages novels about the horrors of Nazi concentration camps, nor in the States about murdering national leaders ... So why in the Soviet Union, where printing is in state hands, should this type of literature be stimulated, printed, distributed? Why should magazines put salt on open wounds? But the time Solzhenitsyn spent in camp and in exile shocked him so deeply that he became one-track-minded and can hardly keep off this subject in his work. Probably this is one of the reasons why for the time being his works do not appear in Russian magazines ... Russians love a martyr and Solzhenitsyn relishes the role ...

The history of Stalin's daughter Svetlana's manuscript is well known. When, after Svetlana's flight abroad, it became known that she intended to publish a book about her father, the KGB took serious measures to obstruct publication. The failure of hasty attempts to force Alliluyeva to return to the USSR by fair means or foul was one reason why Semichastny was removed from his post as Chairman of the KGB. (He was transferred to the post of Deputy-Chairman of the Council of Ministers of the Ukrainian USSR). Alliluyeva went to the United States, and it was announced that her book about Stalin would be published in several languages in November 1967, to coincide exactly with the fiftieth anniversary of Soviet power. Advance royalties to the tune of a million dollars were paid to Alliluyeva. Since the publication of her book seemed inevitable, certain

81

people in the USSR resolved to advance publication to an earlier date, so that its appearance would not coincide with the anniversary, and simultaneously to deal a financial blow to the publishing houses with whom Alliluyeva had signed a contract. A typescript copy of Alliluyeva's book was unearthed in Moscow, where she had left it with someone. A collection of rare family photographs of Stalin, and his friends and relatives, was assembled from his archives, and Victor Louis took all this material out of the country and sold it in England and in West Germany. The Russian edition of *Twenty Letters to a Friend* came out in England in July or August 1967, and at the same time *Stern* magazine began publishing the letters. Only after the event was Svetlana Alliluyeva able to restrain these pirate publications with a court injunction, while the people who had sent Victor Louis to the West had achieved their purpose: the sensation surrounding Alliluyeva's book on Stalin had broken several months before the anniversary celebrations. Long before the official publication of the book, some highly critical reviews had appeared, and taken the edge off the readers' interest. Furthermore Alliluyeva could not now make the substantial changes she had wished to make to the original text, which had many serious faults. The publishing houses with whom Alliluyeva had a contract did apparently incur losses and were disappointed by the book's comparative failure.

There exists in the West a special literature on the subject of Victor Louis, analysing his activities. He really does enjoy complete freedom to travel abroad; he conducts semi-official negotiations with influential figures in various countries, and is the first to inform the foreign press about the most sensational events in the USSR (such as the ousting of Khrushchev, the death of Khrushchev, the reasons why the three cosmonauts perished, and so on). He is, moreover, a Soviet citizen, and has never taken foreign nationality. He has even assured some people that he was in prison during the Stalin period.

But how could the manuscript of *Cancer Ward* have found its way to the pages of *Grani*? I happen to know that in 1967 *Grani* sent its agents to Moscow in quest of this typescript. A few years ago I was told an interesting story by someone in whom I have complete trust. One evening towards the end of

1967 there was a ring at the door of his flat. When he went to answer, he found there a person who by his appearance was a foreigner, and who, moreover, was unable to speak Russian. The visitor indicated by sign-language that he wanted to see the owner of the flat. The owner, whom we shall call X, asked him in and inquired, also using sign-language, what his business was, whereupon the foreigner took a letter out of his pocket which was written in Russian. The content of the letter was roughly as follows:

Esteemed . . .
The editors of the journal *Grani* know of the difficulties regarding publication of the story *Cancer Ward* by A. Solzhenitsyn. Taking into account the significance of this work for the development of Russian literature, the editors of *Grani* would like to publish it in the Russian language. We have reason to believe that you may be able to assist us in obtaining a copy of the manuscript of this work.

The letter went on to say that if X would give the manuscript of *Cancer Ward* to the visitor he would deliver it to the offices of *Grani*. It was signed by one of the editors of *Grani*.

X set about explaining to the visitor the impossibility of his acceding to a request of this kind, but the visitor did not understand what he was saying. Then X picked up the telephone to ask a friend who lived nearby and who knew French to come and interpret. The visitor jumped up in a fright and made as if to leave, probably thinking that X intended to hand him over to the KGB. However, X restrained him and explained with some difficulty that he was inviting a '*comarade*' to act as interpreter. When the French-speaking friend arrived it was explained to the visitor that there could be no question of passing on any typescript to *Grani*, and that not only could the people he visited be convicted, but he himself could be in trouble, under Soviet law, for actions of this sort, precisely because the editors of *Grani* were involved in the affair. The visitor was advised to leave for home at once. Satisfied that he was not going to be handed over to the KGB, the visitor relaxed a little and became talkative. He declared that he had to have some proof that he had in fact been to visit X, but had met with a refusal. Otherwise the people at *Grani* might not believe that he had carried out their errand. He asked X to write his answer on the back of the letter.

This immediately put X on his guard. Why should he write his reply on the back of the letter? The very existence of the letter was disagreeable enough; after all, it could have been discovered during a customs inspection when the visitor entered the USSR and would have served as grounds for subjecting X to interrogation about his possible connections with the NTS. And now the visitor wanted to take the letter back, and with his reply on it too! If it fell into the clutches of a customs official, X's contact with *Grani* would become a *fait accompli*. Accordingly X took the letter from the visitor, tore it into small pieces and asked him to tell his friends at *Grani* never again to make provocative requests of this sort to Soviet citizens.

13. Who Profits from the Literary Black Market?

THE TELEGRAM TO *Novy Mir* had, as it turned out, genuinely been sent by *Grani*. The references to Victor Louis and to certain attempts to 'block' the publication of *Cancer Ward* in the USSR were ludicrous. The ban on the publication of *Cancer Ward* had been imposed back in January, and in a rather simpler way, which did not necessitate sending Victor Louis abroad. When in April *Grani* sent its telegram to Tvardovsky, the West German journal must have known that *Novy Mir* had long since distributed the type of *Cancer Ward*. A report to this effect had been published in many West German papers, together with some considerable comment. Why, then, was there any need to send a *telegram*?

It would seem that this was *Grani*'s way of announcing its rights as first publisher of the novel. Since the Soviet Union was not at that time a signatory to any of the international copyright conventions, Solzhenitsyn's protest against pirated publication in this particular journal had no legal validity. As first publisher of *Cancer Ward*, *Grani*, on the other hand, secured, as it were, the author's rights and could sell the translation rights to other publishing houses. In this respect *Grani* really had feared competition from Victor Louis and that was why the journal had hastened to announce its intention by telegram. Had Victor Louis forestalled *Grani* by publishing a rush edition – or simply xeroxing the typescript – in a quantity of say a hundred or two hundred copies, indicating the retail market price on the cover and depositing a few copies in the libraries where newly published works are normally deposited, the 'publication rights' and all the attendant commercial benefits would have gone to whichever publishing house Louis had chosen. An energetic publisher could have done all this within a week. *Grani*'s telegram, with its allusions to machinations by the KGB, was designed to block any possible parallel Russian edition. When in 1968 translations of *Cancer Ward* were published in various languages, the publishers sometimes made special announcements to the effect that they had obtained the manuscript of the story quite independently of Victor Louis and the KGB.

It seems that there are quite a few people in our country who operate like Victor Louis. The active sale of unpublished typescripts from the Soviet Union to the West is also promoted by organisations like 'Mezhdunarodnaya Kniga' (International Book) and APN (Novosti Press Agency). Likewise, differing versions are sold abroad of books published in the USSR in abridged form – for example, *The Master and Margarita* by M. Bulgakov, or the *Memoirs of Marshal Zhukov*, and others. News items are sold too, through 'foreign correspondents' such as Victor Louis.

Most countries are parties to international agreements protecting authors' rights. The best known of these are the Berne Convention, and the Universal Copyright Convention, adopted on the initiative, and under the guidance of UNESCO. (The texts of these Conventions and also of a number of regional agreements were published in Russian in 1958 in a translation of the book *Droit d'Auteur Ou Copyright* by D. Sidjanski and S. Castanos – Lausanne, 1954. However, the extensive Preface to the Russian translation does not explain why the USSR had refused to become a signatory to these conventions. The editor of the translation, who is also the author of the Preface, notes that the conventions reflect a capitalist approach to authors' rights. He believed that in the USSR a 'Soviet concept of authors' rights' prevails, which also protects the rights of organisations which make use of the author's works. It must be emphasised that when referring to 'organisations', the editor had in mind not *the publishing houses which publish* the author's works, but precisely the organisations *which make use of them.*)

But if a writer whose country was not a party to the international conventions had his work *first* published in one of the countries which was a signatory, then all existing measures for the international protection of authors' rights applied to this work. The original publisher obtained the copyright, that is, full legal control over the distribution of the work. It is an excellent thing when the author himself possesses this right and can select his publisher. But far more often the right is in the possession of 'Mezhdunarodnaya Kniga' or special departments of the Novosti Press Agency, or other such people.

There are members of staff at 'Novosti' and 'Mezhdunarodnaya Kniga' who make a special study of the publishing plans of scientific, sociological and general publishers, and of articles scheduled to appear in journals, to decide which works, *with the censor's approval*, might be saleable to Western publishers prior to publication in the USSR. They then sell manuscripts, or proof-copies, or sometimes even bound books which have already been published – but with additional material.

It is not only scientific works and belles-lettres which are commercially viable in this trade. Foreign newspapers and news agencies will buy news stories, particularly sensational ones, which are then disseminated all over the world. But news of this kind can only be sold for hard currency *before* it has been announced by, say, TASS or Soviet radio. It is the monetary value of such news items that forms the commercial basis for the activities of Moscow correspondents of foreign newspapers like Victor Louis. The world learns of many of the most important domestic events in the Soviet Union not from TASS announcements or Soviet radio reports, which usually 'lag behind', but from Victor Louis and his friends. For his sensational communiqués Louis naturally receives a generous remuneration, and part of this must obviously go into his own pocket. Foreign correspondents who have visited Louis in Moscow have remarked in the Western press on the uncommon luxury of his large apartments which are made up of two three-roomed flats. Louis' country residence outside Moscow is even more luxurious. I shall restrict myself to a quotation from an article by Jay Axelbank, chief of the Moscow Bureau of the American magazine *Newsweek*. In this article, which appeared in *Newsweek* on 12 July 1971 (page 12), Axelbank described his impressions of a visit to Louis' dacha:

> The Soviet Union's most conspicuous consumer, Louis[1] maintains a mansion 15 miles outside Moscow where he dazzles newsmen, diplomats and assorted VIPs with his hospitality. While most ordinary Russians are lucky to live in a two-room apartment, Louis has six or seven rooms. . . .

[1] Victor Louis is a pseudonym.

A reputed millionaire, he also has a swimming pool, tennis court, a garage containing a fleet of cars and a refrigerator stacked with serried ranks of bottled Coke.

Louis, who received me in a black silk Japanese robe, takes gleeful pride in his wealth. He points out the Florentine tiles on the dining-room floor, the carved wooden icons and the heavy, sea-shell-shaped patio furniture (which he says is the same as Helena Rubinstein's). He proudly displays his electric shish kebab maker, a Hammacher Schlemmer water spigot with a metallic squirrel on top, a new $800 record player and tape recorder. 'It's just something I brought back from Israel,' he says matter-of-factly. . . .

As he bids his visitor good-by, Louis points with relish to a map of the world that is studded with red pins indicating the places he has visited 'Ha!' he says, 'people say I am a government agent and I get my money from the government. That's a laugh. My wife is English and she's rich. Besides, would the Soviet Union send anybody to places like Tahiti?'

The article is accompanied by a photograph of Louis with the telephone receiver at his ear. The caption is: Louis in his study: Six rooms plus a pine-wood sauna?

People like Louis have the full approval of 'Novosti', 'Mezh-dunarodnaya Kniga' and other state organisations, for trading in information of all and every kind. Eminent scientists are commissioned to write articles on topics which have difficulty in finding a publisher in the USSR, and then, a selection of their typescripts under the title of 'Scientific Thought', is offered to journals anywhere from Portugal to Japan. Foreign newspapers paid a high price for the right to interview Khrushchev when he was living in solitude and disgrace at his dacha near Moscow. When Sinyavsky and Daniel were on trial, West German journals, through 'Novosti' or Victor Louis, acquired photographs taken in the courtroom and extracts from the trial proceedings. A family photograph album of Stalin's was also sold. Sometimes 'unknown' persons trade in forgeries too on the black market. On one occasion my brother R. A. Medvedev had to publish a statement to the effect that an article published in *Possev* under the title of 'The Truth about the Present Times' and signed by R. Medvedev was a forgery.

Academician Andrei Sakharov also had occasion to issue a statement about a counterfeit anti-Soviet letter that somebody had composed in his name and passed on to Western newspapers. But sometimes this black market exists for the purchase as well as the sale of information, which is then printed in Soviet papers as a reflection of 'public opinion' in other countries. That is how articles criticising Alexander Solzhenitsyn's work later came to be commissioned through the black market.

14. The Open Campaign Against Solzhenitsyn Begins

ON 25 APRIL 1968 Solzhenitsyn sent letters to *Literaturnaya Gazeta*, *Le Monde* and *L'Unità* protesting that fragments from *Cancer Ward* had been printed in various Western countries and that some publishers claimed that they had copyright. Solzhenitsyn asked *Literaturnaya Gazeta* and the other papers to publish his protest immediately. '... I declare,' he wrote, 'that *no* foreign publisher has received a manuscript of this novel from me, nor any authorisation to publish it. Therefore I do not recognise as legal *any* publication of this novel, present or future, undertaken without permission, and I do not grant the publishing rights to anyone ... I already know from experience that all the translations of *One Day in the Life of Ivan Denisovich* were spoiled by haste. Evidently the same fate awaits *Cancer Ward*. But beyond money, there is literature.'

Attached to these protests were accounts of the discussion in the Soviet Writers' Union on the question of publishing *Cancer Ward*; also an account of a debate held at a session of the Secretariat of the Soviet Writers' Union devoted to 'a critique of letters from the writer Solzhenitsyn'.

Solzhenitsyn's protest was published in the West by the Italian Communist Party paper *L'Unità*. For a long time there was no response to Solzhenitsyn's letter from *Literaturnaya Gazeta*, but eventually it was published in that paper on 26 June 1968. However, the letter was accompanied by a full page editorial entitled 'The Ideological Struggle – The Writer's Responsibility'.

This article was written in an uncouth, demagogic style and advanced a number of crude arguments and analogies. After making some dogmatic generalisations the anonymous author described different instances of treachery and venality:

'... Some ne'er-do-well speculator is lured by nylon rags or drawn into currency manipulations...' '...Some circus acrobat fails to return to his motherland from a foreign tour ...' '... the graphomaniac and schizophrenic V. Tarsis is promptly made into a writer when he scribbles vast outpourings of untalented but openly anti-Soviet writings ...' '... Svetlana Alliluyeva and her memoirs are eulogised...' and so on.

Then, after this artistic introduction, came the announcement that the paper was publishing a letter by A. Solzhenitsyn. This was followed by a discussion of Solzhenitsyn's activities, although common sense required that the paper support the writer's protest. Had it done so, the protest might have had some effect, but instead of taking the intelligent view, *Literaturnaya Gazeta* alleged that Solzhenitsyn's name had been '... taken into the arsenal of Western propaganda and is being widely used for provocatorial, anti-Soviet purposes'.

In defiance of ordinary decency and Solzhenitsyn's oft-repeated warnings that he would not tolerate publication of *Feast of the Victors* in any form, nor comment on this typescript, the article gave a tendentious exposition of the theme and quoted from the play, which had been written when the author was a convict, deprived of his civil rights. The paper went on to mock at the ban imposed by the author. What right had Solzhenitsyn to ban the publication and analysis of his play after entrusting the manuscript to a person as unreliable as Teush? The story of the fate of *Cancer Ward* was related in a similarly irrelevant manner. *The First Circle* was described simply as 'containing malicious slander on our social system'.

For *Literaturnaya Gazeta* to make use of material from a writer's papers in this way, after he had categorically forbidden it, was not merely immoral but a gross infringement of Soviet laws on authors' rights. Article 475 of the RSFSR Civil Code stipulates that author's copyright applies not only to published works but also to works not yet published. Article 479 of the same Code establishes that the author is invested with the 'inviolability of his work'. Article 480 – 'Protection of the inviolability of works and of the author's name during his lifetime' – quite clearly indicates that the inviolability of a work means that it is forbidden to publish the work in any form which deviates from that chosen by the author himself, 'without the author's consent'. The same article notes that '... It is also forbidden, when publishing a work, to supply it with any prefaces, postscripts, commentaries or explanatory notes of any kind whatsoever without the author's consent.'

The principle of the 'inviolability of a work' is even more clearly defined in article 6 bis (1) of the Berne Convention:

> ... the author shall have the right, DURING HIS LIFE-TIME, to claim authorship of the work AND to object to any distortion, mutilation or other alteration THEREOF, OR ANY OTHER ACTION IN RELATION TO THE SAID WORK which would be prejudicial to his honour or reputation.

But that is precisely what *Literaturnaya Gazeta* was doing. By quoting out of context a corrupt text of *Feast of the Victors* in defiance of the author's wishes, and by making tendentious comments on it, *Literaturnaya Gazeta* demonstrated that not only had the Soviet press failed to respect the law, but that laws had also been violated by the organs of state security.

The only existing copy of the manuscript of *Feast of the Victors* had been confiscated at Teush's friend's flat. In accordance with the articles of the RSFSR Code of Criminal Procedure, material bearing no relation to a case must be returned after it is closed. The only articles that need not necessarily be returned are those 'unsuitable for circulation'. The definition of what is 'unsuitable for circulation' is vague and includes, for example, arms, forged money, and also, apparently, undesirable books and manuscripts. Evidently all Solzhenitsyn's papers, including the manuscript of *The First Circle*, were put in this category. How else can one explain the fact that they were not returned to him after the closure of the case against Teush? However, the same Code of Criminal Procedure, and the official handbook to it, quite clearly define the restricted circle of persons who may have access to materials of the kind *during the course of an investigation*. Material confiscated during a search or a seizure, or interception of correspondence, may be placed at the disposal of the investigator, the prosecutor, any expert involved in the investigation, the defence counsel, and the court. But in no circumstances may it be shown to persons unconnected with the investigations or the court, particularly if no criminal proceedings have been instituted on the basis of this material. Hence, by confiscating the personal papers of a writer and placing them at the disposal of members of the Secretariat of the Writers' Union and representatives of the mass media, the organs of state security committed a gross infringement of regulations laid down by the Procedural Code.

This article provoked a strong reaction from Soviet intellectuals, and one quite different from what the anonymous authors had apparently expected. *Literaturnaya Gazeta* received dozens of letters from people who felt rather differently about Solzhenitsyn's writings – who held a high opinion of *Cancer Ward* and *The First Circle* – and supported the stand taken by Solzhenitsyn in his letter to the Fourth Writers' Congress. The paper was unable to print a single reader's letter supporting its own allegations. Nor, of course, did it publish any letters in defence of the writer. If there *were* any letters that agreed with the line the paper had taken they remained unknown, whereas several letters of the opposite kind soon became the property of *samizdat* and passed into the field of uncensored political journalism. Some of them, such as Lydia Chukovskaya's brilliant letter 'The Writer's Responsibility and the Irresponsibility of *Literaturnaya Gazeta*', were published in newspapers abroad. I have in my own file copies of ten different letters written to *Literaturnaya Gazeta* in reply to the article. They all have these things in common – they express indignation at the base polemic initiated by the paper, indignation at the distorted version of Solzhenitsyn's life, at the publication of excerpts of *Feast of the Victors*, which looked very much like attempted blackmail, and at the negative appraisal of *Cancer Ward* and *The First Circle*, without accompanying analysis of these works. The majority of these letters came from scientists and men of letters. I will not go into them in detail; in the main they deal with the same questions as Lydia Chukovskaya's letter. I shall merely cite an extract from the letter from Valentine Turchin, Doctor of Physics and Mathematics, addressed to the Editor-in-Chief of *Literaturnaya Gazeta*, Alexander Chakovsky.

. . . For some time now I have had connections with *Literaturnaya Gazeta*, and my name has even appeared in its pages. Now I am ashamed of this. I hereby declare that as long as you remain editor-in-chief of *Literaturnaya Gazeta* I will not engage in any form of cooperation with the paper; I will not subscribe to it or buy it. I believe that, for any man sharing my views on the article on Solzhenitsyn, this is the only possible course of action.

According to Valery Pavlinchuk, for whom the summer of 1968 was to be his last (he died of uraemia and pneumonia at the end of July), about ten research scientists in Obninsk responded to his call; they cancelled their subscriptions to *Literaturnaya Gazeta*, and mailed their postal receipts and the July issues of the paper back to Chakovsky.[1]

---

[1] In the USSR subscriptions for newspapers and magazines have to be paid for in advance. Immediate cancellation is impossible and papers continue to arrive for some time after the cancellation has been made. [Author's note.]

15. The Publication of *Cancer Ward* and *The First Circle* Abroad in the Autumn of 1968

FROM MAY UNTIL the end of September 1968 Solzhenitsyn stayed at his cottage. Here 'on the soil' he found it easier to bear the difficult situation which had arisen, of unavoidable and uncontrolled publication, in many countries, of two of his most important works, in hasty and unauthorised translations. Russian language broadcasts from foreign radio stations gave conflicting information as to where and in what form they were being published. At the end of 1962 and in early 1963, in the USA alone, *One Day in the Life of Ivan Denisovich* had been published in several independent translations, all hastily done, and some of them very poor. It was reported that in one publishing house the translator worked virtually non-stop without leaving the premises and the translated pages went straight into type. The book was ready in two weeks. In *Ivan Denisovich*, the author had paid particular attention to style, taking great pains to create a sense of the unusual environment, a particular atmosphere. This was destroyed by the hasty translations which ceased to be works of art, in the way that direct copies of the paintings of great artists are not masterpieces.

Now it was all happening again. Solzhenitsyn had no knowledge of the publishers nor of the names and reputations of the translators.

His protest, which *Literaturnaya Gazeta* had published on 26 June 1968, had become known in the West some time earlier and had stimulated widespread discussion in the foreign press. In the American magazine *Publisher's Weekly*, which I sometimes glance through in the reference room of the Moscow Lenin Library, I came across a report that four publishers (Dutton, Praeger, Farrar Straus and Dial Press) were preparing to publish *Cancer Ward*, quite independently of one another, in the USA. After Solzhenitsyn's protest became known in the West, Dutton and Praeger cancelled their plans for publication.

95

Farrar, Straus claimed, apparently in good faith, that they had signed a contract with a 'representative' of the author. The 'representative' was of course an impostor. From the bibliographical index *Forthcoming Books*, which lists books that have gone to press several months in advance of their publication, I discovered that *The First Circle* was to be published by Harper and Row and was scheduled to appear in September.

Solzhenitsyn visited Obninsk on 19 June 1968, shortly before the article in *Literaturnaya Gazeta* came out. He said that forthcoming publications of his books had been announced in five countries.

On 1 September 1968 Solzhenitsyn came to Obninsk again. He called on me and we went together to pay a visit to Timofeev-Resovsky. Conversation naturally focused upon the recent events in Czechoslovakia. Solzhenitsyn had earlier been very glad to hear of the abolition of censorship in Czechoslovakia; it was in Czechoslovakia that his letter to the Fourth Writers' Congress in 1967 had been greeted with the greatest enthusiasm. Novotny was still in power at the time. In the summer of 1967 Solzhenitsyn's letter to the Fourth Soviet Writers' Congress was given an official reading from the platform of a Congress of Czechoslovak Writers, where it received warm support. This led to a clash between the writers and representatives of the party leadership, and one party leader registered his protest by leaving the conference hall. The Union of Czechoslovak Writers issued many invitations to Solzhenitsyn to visit Czechoslovakia, but each time he failed to get permission for the trip from the Soviet Writers' Union. Now, when the abolition of censorship in Czechoslovakia had proved one of the major pretexts for the suppression of liberalism in the country, he was deeply affected by the turn of events. He was prepared to help with the compilation of a collective protest, and to this end he had had a talk with Academician Andrei Sakharov at the end of August. However, a draft document composed by a small group of scientists failed to gain any general support from prominent figures in the world of science and the arts who had actively supported many important public statements in the past. Their caution stemmed from the realisation that it was useless to protest against a *fait accompli*.

On 22 September Solzhenitsyn paid yet another visit to

Obninsk. By then an English translation of *The First Circle* had been published in the United States. It had come out on 11 September 1968 and, according to reports in *Publisher's Weekly* which I read later, had become an immediate best-seller.

On 23 October two friends and I visited Solzhenitsyn at his cottage. The autumn frosts had already arrived and Solzhenitsyn planned to leave for Ryazan the following day. We spent about an hour in conversation. Solzhenitsyn told us that the cottage now appeared to be under constant surveillance. On 24 September Victor Louis had for some reason been to see him again, accompanied by a man with a camera. They had found him out; he had gone to the small nearby town of Narofominsk just a half an hour before. Louis had chatted with Solzhenitsyn's neighbours in the village and wanted to know if there was a cottage to be let. Louis' companion had taken several photographs of Solzhenitsyn's cottage and its surroundings. Solzhenitsyn's neighbours later told him that they had seen two strangers at the time of Louis' visit. The purpose of this visit remained a mystery. We all noticed a particular phrase that came up in the course of conversation.

'I've retired from the present now,' he said in answer to a question, 'I'm working on history.'

When we expressed our fear of possible legal action following the publication of *Cancer Ward* and *The First Circle* abroad, Solzhenitsyn confidently replied: 'No, I think that's unlikely. They've already exhausted themselves in that direction with the trials of Sinyavsky, Daniel and the rest. There'll be no repetition on those lines. Now they've got to think up something new.'

16. The Pseudo-Solzhenitsyn and 'Solzhenitser'

11 DECEMBER WAS Solzhenitsyn's fiftieth birthday; he had reached an age which is traditionally treated as a landmark. *Literturnaya Gazeta* usually congratulates members of the Soviet Writers' Union on such occasions, varying the nature of the congratulations according to the writers' standing and seriousness. To some are devoted several articles together with a large picture, to others a single article with picture; others receive a small notice with small picture, and still others a small notice and no picture. Sometimes the congratulations are confined to a simple, brief message. Of Solzhenitsyn's fiftieth birthday there was no mention at all either in *Literaturnaya Gazeta* or in any other literary publication in the Soviet Union. But although the public at large knew nothing about it, and only a few people knew the writer's address in Ryazan, Solzhenitsyn received there about five hundred congratulatory telegrams and almost one hundred letters. About one hundred telegrams for Solzhenitsyn came to *Novy Mir*. He received some official congratulations too, from the editorial board of *Novy Mir*, from the Ryazan and Voronezh branches of the Writers' Union, from several Moscow theatres, and from the Czechoslovak Writers' Union. This flow of messages indicated that, despite the diverse charges levelled against him in the press, and despite secret briefings, Solzhenitsyn enjoyed the widespread and firm support of large numbers of intellectuals and lovers of literature.

The *First Circle* and *Cancer Ward* were given a great deal of attention by literary critics abroad. Solzhenitsyn was elected an honorary member of the American Academy of Arts and Letters in New York and a member of the American Academy of Arts and Sciences in Boston. At the beginning of 1969 he was awarded a special literary prize in France for 'the best translated work of the year'. In March 1969 *The First Circle* was still on the best-seller list in *Publisher's Weekly*. In April the novel was no longer on the list, but seven months as a best-seller, for a hard-cover book, is considered a great success (in America, as in Britain, paperback editions cannot normally appear until eighteen months or two years after the hard-cover publication). It means that several hundred thousand copies in hard covers must have been sold. Consequently, when the cheap edition came out, the total number sold might run into millions.

The writer's growing international reputation inevitably irritated his enemies. New measures were devised to isolate Solzhenitsyn from society and blacken his reputation. This led to a series of improvisations on the anti-Solzhenitsyn theme. I shall confine myself to describing two of them.

Solzhenitsyn usually makes the best possible use of his time, reducing all unavoidable unproductive tasks to the bare minimum. He turns down many invitations and often refuses to meet people; frequently he sets himself a minimal time to talk to people, allots the briefest possible space of time to a particular conversation. His most productive working period is the morning and therefore he keeps to a strict regimen in the evenings, avoiding invitations to supper or dinner-parties, especially if they mean going out to restaurants. Solzhenitsyn's way of life is well known and so his friends do not burden him with visits or invitations to family celebrations and parties. Consequently, when rumours began to circulate that Solzhenitsyn had 'taken to drink' they were met with astonishment. But there were people, some claiming to be eye-witnesses, who described how Solzhenitsyn had become a habitué of the Slavyanskii Bazar, a Moscow restaurant, threw big impromptu parties there at his own expense, and ordered sumptuous dinners and extravagant quantities of drink. From time to time he would send a request to the band enclosing large banknotes and asking it to play a tune for him personally – usually an old Russian song. When the bandleader announced the song he would say that it was being played at Solzhenitsyn's request. The rumours also told of how he shouted drunkenly that he was the greatest Russian writer, the 'salt of the earth', and pestered the ladies.

His Moscow friends guessed that something was wrong, especially since Solzhenitsyn was rarely in Moscow at that time. When the restaurant staff were questioned they confirmed the rumours. But Solzhenitsyn's banquets at the Slavyanskii

Bazar ceased for a while, only to crop up again in other places. Some time after this Solzhenitsyn's friend Lev Kopelev had a visit from an actress from one of the Moscow theatres who told him a curious story. Solzhenitsyn had telephoned the Chief Director of the theatre, who was an admirer of Solzhenitsyn but had never met him. Solzhenitsyn told him on the telephone that he was working on a play and would like to become acquainted, for professional reasons, with a certain type of actress. He described the qualities he was looking for and asked the Director to arrange for him to meet two candidates. It was agreed that they should meet at a certain table at a Moscow restaurant. At the meeting, he was very jovial and talked a lot about his work. After they had eaten he decided on one of the two actresses and made an appointment to see her the next day in the 'Bega' restaurant. However, the actress had begun to have doubts about the authenticity of this 'Solzhenitsyn', and decided to go to one of the writer's close friends for advice. She was given Kopelev's name. At the appointed hour Kopelev and some other Moscow friends also went to the rendezvous. As expected, the actress-fancier turned out to be an impostor. When he found himself surrounded, he became very frightened, thinking that he was about to be beaten up. However, the friends restrained themselves. The false Solzhenitsyn was conveyed to the nearest police station for elucidation of his identity. The papers he produced identified him as one Alexander Fyodorovich Shalagin, former deputy director of a drama or choreography school. From the scars and tattoo marks on his arm it appeared that he had once been imprisoned on a criminal charge. In his statement to the police, Shalagin admitted having staged the drunken parties in the Slavyanskii Bazar, but they nevertheless allowed him to leave and no one was ever summonsed. No further proceedings were brought against Shalagin, although he had in fact committed offences under articles 130 and 131 of the RSFSR Criminal Code (defamation and insult).

Another incident was of a quite different kind. At an ideological lecture given in a Moscow publishing house, the speaker criticised Solzhenitsyn and referred to him continually as 'Solzhenitser'. A note was passed to him from the audience pointing out that he was mispronouncing the writer's surname.

The lecturer replied to the note by saying: 'No, it's not a mistake. The person known to you as Solzhenitsyn is really Solzhenitser and he's a Jew.'

It was later discovered that similar attempts to distort Solzhenitsyn's name had been made in several other places.

17.   Expulsion of Solzhenitsyn from the Soviet Writers' Union

IN THE SUMMER of 1969 Solzhenitsyn was working intensively on his novel *August 1914*. In late summer I called briefly to see him at his summer cottage and found him surrounded by piles of photograph albums of the First World War. They were mainly German albums; with characteristic thoroughness the Germans had recorded battle scenes and the most important political events of the period. Solzhenitsyn had learnt German and English; his mother, who had received a good classical education, was an excellent linguist. I noticed that Solzhenitsyn had compiled a vocabulary of Russian words and terms in use in 1914, especially in the army, but which have since become obsolete. His characters, after all, had to think and speak in the language of the times. Solzhenitsyn told me that he had conceived the idea of a novel about the rout of the Russian army in East Prussia a long time ago, while he was a student in Rostov-on-Don before the Second World War, and it was then that he had begun collecting material for it even though writing was as yet no more than a dream. During the war Solzhenitsyn had found himself in East Prussia as a captain and commander of an artillery unit; despite the fact that he was in the front line, he began collecting 'captured' documents and photographs relating to the First World War, and also writing down his observations in diaries. In February 1945, still in East Prussia, Solzhenitsyn was arrested. The grounds for his arrest were certain letters he had written to an old school-friend who was fighting on another front at the time. Military censorship of mail had existed since 1941 and everyone knew about it. But some people might have thought that the sole purpose of this censorship was to prevent the spread of military information and not to monitor people's thoughts and opinions. It was this naïveté that led to the arrest of Captain Solzhenitsyn, although as an army officer he was far more useful to the country fighting in the field than languishing in an NKVD[1] prison. When Solzhenitsyn was arrested his personal files containing over three hundred photographs, collected from various 'captured' albums, of events dating from the First World War were confiscated. In one of the photographs the investigator identified Trotsky. And although this photograph dated from 1917 and was connected, I think, with the Treaty of Brest-Litovsk – Trotsky had been head of the Soviet delegation negotiating with the Germans, and was by no means the only person in the photograph – the investigator made even this the basis for a charge. The indictment recorded, among other incriminating evidence, the fact that Solzhenitsyn had collected and harboured photographs of persons who had been unmasked as enemies of the people.[2]

Rumours had been circulating for a long time that Solzhenitsyn might be expelled from the Soviet Writers' Union. There had been allusions to the possibility in the June 1968 article in *Literaturnaya Gazeta*, and in May 1969 Solzhenitsyn told me information had reached him that some scheme of the kind was being discussed by the Union leadership. Some people thought it extremely unlikely, for, even allowing for the variety of approaches to Solzhenitsyn's creative thought, the fact that he was without any doubt a talented writer was universally acknowledged. However, I took these rumours very seriously. The Writers' Union had long since ceased to be simply a professional trade union. It was also a political union, an organisation representing so-called 'socialist' realism, that is, 'party' realism, the literature of which conforms strictly to all instructions emanating from party and state leadership. Solzhenitsyn had clearly taken the path of 'classical' realism, that is the critical realism traditionally found in Russian writers, from

[1] NKVD = People's Commissariat for Internal Affairs.
[2] As part of the preparations for the centenary of Lenin's birth, hundreds of display stands were produced showing photographs and documents relating to Lenin's life. These were mounted in the streets and in various institutions. Many of the photographs dating from the Revolution and Civil War periods showed Trotsky in the groups of people clustering around Lenin. Usually the figure of Trotsky was skilfully removed. But on one of the photographs which appeared on every stand – 'Lenin inspects Red Army detachments on Red Square' – the figure of Trotsky was retained. I still see this photograph today on many display stands commemorating Lenin. (Author's note.)

Radishchev and Pushkin to Tolstoy. Expulsion from the Writers' Union could therefore be equated with expulsion from the Communist Party, which, of course, happens quite frequently and often when there are considerably fewer points of disagreement between the party member and the leadership than in Solzhenitsyn's case. Moreover, there had been a precedent in the expulsion of Boris Pasternak from the Writers' Union in 1958 for the publication abroad of *Doctor Zhivago*.

There can be no doubt that the question of expelling Solzhenitsyn from the Writers' Union was discussed many times over by the Union leadership. It is clear that the leadership realised both the complications that such an act would entail and the need for careful stage-management in order to avoid an uproar. In accordance with the Statutes of the Writers' Union, expulsion from the Union is effected at a session of the Regional Organisation and endorsed by the Board of the Republican Organisation (RSFSR Writers' Union) in the presence of the writer to whom the measure is being applied. But the Ryazan Organisation was extremely weak; its members numbered no more than six or seven. In the summer of 1969, the decision was finally taken at what was evidently a very high level, to effect Solzhenitsyn's expulsion from the Union. He was living at his cottage at the time and it was impossible to summon him from there, because cottages in cooperative garden estates have no postal adress. (Local post offices sometimes do serve these settlements in the summer months but only in exceptional cases, when the cooperative will pay a fee by special arrangement.) At the end of October the writer Kornei Chukovsky died. He was 87. According to my information, immediately after the funeral of this doyen of Soviet writers on 31 October – that very evening in fact – the Secretariat of the RSFSR Writers' Union discussed the final procedural details of Solzhenitsyn's expulsion. As soon as he returned to Ryazan he was informed that there would be a session of the Ryazan branch of the Writers' Union on 4 November. The session was rehearsed at a meeting of the Ryazan Regional Party Committee. Each of the six members of the Ryazan Writers' organisation was summoned beforehand to have the matter explained to him and was subjected to a special 'working-over', sometimes including threats, so that there would be no deviations from the planned programme. The Committee exacted a pledge from each writer that he would vote in favour of the expulsion. A Secretary of the Board of the RSFSR Writers' Union, F. Taurin, came specially from Moscow to deliver a report on Solzhenitsyn's 'behaviour'. The Ryazan writers would naturally be unacquainted with those works of Solzhenitsyn which had been published abroad, and so someone 'from above' had to provide a critical evaluation of them. Also present at the session was A. Kozhevnikov, Secretary for Ideology in the Ryazan Regional Party Committee. Afterwards Solzhenitsyn set down a résumé of the debate that ensued. It circulated in *samizdat* and was later published in the foreign press and in several documentary works on Solzhenitsyn. It was also broadcast by several foreign radio stations. According to this report, only one of the writers present at the session, the poet Evgeny Markin, expressed doubts as to the wisdom of expelling Solzhenitsyn. The others mouthed the usual stereotyped jumble of 'condemnatory' phrases, citing for the most part the appreciation of Solzhenitsyn's work by the Western press. But when it came to the vote, even Markin had not the courage to dissent and raised his hand with the rest. Subsequently Markin was profoundly and painfully aware of the lack of principle he had shown. He came to Solzhenitsyn and apologised. In 1970 he wrote a poem which described Solzhenitsyn's expulsion in allegorical form. Thanks to an oversight on the part of the new editorial board of *Novy Mir*, the poem, entitled 'Weightlessness', was accidentally published in the issue for October 1971 (No. 10). Describing different kinds of weightlessness, Markin included in his poem an example of 'social weightlessness':

> . . . But I know weightlessness of another sort:
> You stand there –
>   and a mirthless little man
> Unties the tapes and ribbons of his file,
> And fishes out of it – a document.
> Denunciation!
>   Slander on a friend.
> You're thrusting for my signature, you swine?
> A friend may suffer, but we'll overcome!

A pity that I'm weightless for the moment.
But still we'll sail on limpid rivers bright!
. . . .
Splintering the jaws of dishonourable men.

But when this poem was published somebody guessed that the 'mirthless little man' Markin had in mind was in fact Taurin. Another poem of Markin's published in the same issue of *Novy Mir*, 'The Buoy-tender', also contained an allusion to those writers who had turned aside from 'Isaich'.[3] Markin himself did not deny that these poems were dedicated to Solzhenitsyn. When the story became widely known he too was summoned to a session of the Ryazan branch of the Writers' Union and expelled. But whereas the discussion which effected Solzhenitsyn's expulsion had lasted about ninety minutes, Markin was expelled in a third of the time.

A meeting of the Secretariat of the RSFSR Writers' Union to endorse the resolution passed by the Ryazan branch was fixed for 5 November. Solzhenitsyn was invited to the meeting by telephone, regardless of whether he could travel from Ryazan to Moscow in time. Moreover, the discussion of this matter on 5 November went against the strict Soviet tradition of not effecting dismissals or expulsions, or holding trials or executions, on the eve of the country's most important public celebrations – 7 November, the anniversary of the October Revolution.[4]

Solzhenitsyn told the representatives of the RSFSR Writers' Union who telephoned him that he could not come to Moscow so soon. That doubtless was precisely why the organisers had arranged the meeting at such short notice – to prevent Solzhenitsyn from being present and speaking, and to conceal from every one the details of the debate that took place. Equally they were in a hurry to endorse the decision of the Ryazan branch before the possibility of any protest arose. Even so, news of the expulsion spread throughout Moscow on 5 November and reached several Western correspondents. How-

[3] A form of 'Isayevich', Solzhenitsyn's patronymic.
[4] According to information at the disposal of R. A. Medvedev, in 1937 at the height of the Stalin terror death sentences passed on the eve of the twentieth anniversary of the October Revolution were not put into effect immediately. Executions were resumed only on 17 November.

ever, when correspondents asked the Board of the Writers' Union to officially confirm the reports, they were denied by a member of the staff. This was a false denial, designed to forestall any possible protest until the Secretariat had made the expulsion irreversible.

Very little is known about what happened at this session. Not one vote was cast against expulsion. But Daniel Granin, a member of the Secretariat and Secretary of the Leningrad branch of the Union, thought that the question ought to be discussed in the presence of Solzhenitsyn, and when the proposal to expel Solzhenitsyn was put to the vote Granin abstained. Upon his return to Leningrad Granin was summoned at once to the Regional Party Committee for a personal interview with First Secretary Tolstikov, and shortly afterwards dismissed from his position of leadership in the Leningrad branch.

On 12 November 1969 an announcement about Solzhenitsyn's expulsion was published in *Literaturnaya Gazeta*. Solzhenitsyn reacted to the decision very strongly by circulating a particularly sharply-worded statement. Some expressions the statement contained were criticised by writers who were party members and had previously supported Solzhenitsyn fully. Even Tvardovsky's initial reaction was one of disapproval. 'He shouldn't have done it,' he said to me when we met on 13 or 14 November. 'After all, it's the disobedient ones they like least of all in our country.'

On 8 or 9 November, just before circulating his statement, Solzhenitsyn had come back from Ryazan to Rostropovich's dacha near Moscow, where he had been living since September. Rostropovich had that summer issued an invitation to Solzhenitsyn to come and live and work in his dacha, after the two men had made each other's acquaintance when the famous cellist gave a concert in Ryazan. Rostropovich suddenly decided, when the concert was over, to seek out Solzhenitsyn and pay him a visit, and Solzhenitsyn, who happened to be at home, was delighted to meet the celebrated musician. A kindly and warm-hearted man, Rostropovich was immediately drawn to Solzhenitsyn and wanted to help him. Solzhenitsyn moved into a two-roomed extension at Rostropovich's dacha.

Solzhenitsyn's expulsion from the Writer's Union called

forth very little open protest from Soviet writers and scientists; considerably more protests were forthcoming from literary people abroad. Rumours circulated that a group of writers led by Tvardovsky had demanded an immediate extraordinary session of the Board of the USSR Writers' Union to revoke the decision taken by the secretariat of the RSFSR Writers' Union. Reports published abroad spoke of scores or even hundreds of protests from Soviet intellectuals, but these were not true – or no one ever saw them.

The relatively restrained reaction, quite unlike that which had followed Solzhenitsyn's letter to the Fourth Soviet Writers' Congress, or even that provoked by the article in *Literaturnaya Gazeta* on 26 June 1968, can be explained in various ways. Many people believe it had to do with the publication of Solzhenitsyn's own sharply-worded statement, and also with the fact that public activity among Soviet intellectuals had declined sharply after the armies of the Warsaw Pact went into Czechoslovakia. Prior to August 1968 the abolition of censorship in Czechoslovakia and the general democratisation of society under Dubček had served as an attractive model for many intellectuals in the USSR, and had stimulated many speeches in favour of reform. Now all those reforms took on the appearance of a Utopian dream, a thing of the distant future, so that many liberal-minded people in the Soviet Union switched to a cautious wait-and-see position. Besides, one has to bear in mind also that in a country whose people remember so well the brutal, merciless repressions of the past, expulsion from an organisation like the Writers' Union does not seem all that serious. Expulsion from Communist Party membership, which many people fear far more than dismissal from their jobs, is a fairly common occurrence for intellectuals (many were expelled in 1967–8 for signing protests), and evokes no particular response. Expulsion from a trade union (which is what the Writers' Union really is) tends to go unnoticed.

The expulsion of Solzhenitsyn from the Writers' Union, however, could not go unnoticed, because he was a writer whose talent was acknowledged not only in the USSR but throughout the world. His expulsion proved that the Soviet Writers' Union was a political, not a professional organisation.

On 26 November *Literaturnaya Gazeta* published a long editorial commenting on the expulsion. The article overflowed with the usual propaganda nonsense:

> ... In his actions and statements he [Solzhenitsyn] has virtually joined hands with those who speak out against the Soviet social system ... A series of letters, statements, manuscripts and other material by Solzhenitsyn have found their way abroad by illegal channels ... This stream of publications has been organised and steered by a practised hand ... The enemies of our country have elevated him to the rank of 'leader' of 'political opposition in the USSR' invented by them ... A report in *The Times* states that royalties from Solzhenitsyn's works are being credited to his account and also systematically transferred by some bourgeois publishers to the so-called 'International Rescue Committee', whose main task is the organisation of hostile acts against the Soviet Union and countries of the socialist commonwealth.

The editorial concluded with a clear hint that no one would restrain Solzhenitsyn – 'even if he were to desire to go where his anti-Soviet works and letters are received with such delight every time'.

Upon reading this end-piece Solzhenitsyn is reported to have said: 'I'm here at home and I have no intention of going anywhere. They'd sooner take it into their heads to go to China.'

At the end of December 1969 I paid a visit to *Novy Mir*. I had heard that Tvardovsky had been inquiring after me, and in any case I wanted to talk to him about the position of *Novy Mir* in the light of Solzhenitsyn's expulsion from the Writers' Union. Tvardovsky was still very much affected by the event and had been reflecting on the behaviour of those writers who had declined to protest publicly against the arbitrary action of an organisation to which they themselves belonged.

'There are two kinds of birds,' he said thoughtfully, 'those which courageously protect their young when they are attacked by a more powerful bird of prey and those which don't, which fly away to save their own skins – after all, they can always give birth to more fledglings. It's the same with the writers, they're saving themselves ... Many of them were even relieved when they saw Solzhenitsyn's letter, thinking that they didn't have to defend him now that he'd said things like *that*. But one should judge the man not by his hot-tempered letters, but by his work. Think how many letters like that Gorky wrote after the October Revolution, and even more scathing, and he sent them straight to Lenin or to émigré papers. And Lenin didn't stand on ceremony either in his replies; those letters of Lenin's to Gorky have never been printed, they've been locked away in such well-hidden archives that no scholar can gain access to them . . .

'But Solzhenitsyn is a man of extraordinary talent, perhaps even more so than Gorky. I'm in the middle of reading some chapters from his new novel about the First World War. Prussia, the defeat of Samsonov's army. Fascinating prose, an entirely new key.'

18. An Alibi for One of the Accusations

OF ALL THE accusations made in the *Literaturnaya Gazeta* article of 26 November 1969, written in defence of the Secretariat of the RSFSR Writers' Union, the only really serious one was that Solzhenitsyn's royalties were being transferred to some 'International Rescue Committee' for 'the organisation of hostile acts against the Soviet Union and countries of the socialist commonwealth'. This, as *Literaturnaya Gazeta* indicated, had been reported by *The Times*, but there was no mention of the date of the report. *The Times* is available for reading in the 'special holdings' of some libraries, and then only with special permission. The public catalogues of the Moscow Lenin State Library refer only to issues of *The Times* up to 1936–7, which have been included to answer the needs of historians studying the pre-war period. And even they have to have permits. Consequently it was some time before I succeeded in finding out what report *The Times* did publish. The issue for 20 November 1969 contained a brief article discussing the fate of Solzhenitsyn's royalties. It looked as if *The Times* had asked a number of publishers what they had done with the royalties accruing from Solzhenitsyn's books, and their replies had formed the basis of the article. The publishers all said that they would be glad to pay the author his royalties but so far they had not done so because they thought it impossible. The President of a leading American publishing house said his firm had paid the first year's royalties from his company's translation of *One Day in the Life of Ivan Denisovich* to the International Rescue Committee, a body which had helped refugees from Nazi and Soviet terror in the past. Remaining royalties since 1964 have been held in New York. . . .

We would be the happiest people if we could pay royalties to Solzhenitsyn [this executive said], but while that is impossible he has sought to provide Solzhenitsyn and his family

111

with much-needed medical aid. He tried to arrange for an American doctor to treat the writer for cancer of the spine, but failed ...

There was considerable confusion in this statement. There had indeed been an attempt in 1968 to make use of the royalties to meet the cost of procuring a special medicine, but this had been for the treatment of cancer of the bone-marrow (leukemia), not cancer of the spine, and moreover the patient had been not the writer but the daughter of friends of his in Ryazan. But the attempt was a failure because the publishing house was in no hurry to pay the bill presented by the laboratory which manufactured the drug. At Solzhenitsyn's request, I conducted all the correspondence with them on this matter, but during that time their representatives did not so much as hint that the main bulk of the royalties out of which it was proposed to pay the cost of the medical preparation had been earlier transferred to this 'Rescue Committee'. In the United States a book may remain on the best-seller lists for a considerable time, but after that the market becomes saturated and sales fall sharply. Since royalties are calculated on the basis of sales, those from the first year (*Ivan Denisovich* came out in the United States in 1963) obviously came to a considerable sum while royalties accruing in subsequent years are comparatively small. In the light of their statement it becomes clear why the publishing house reacted so sluggishly to the request that they would pay the bill for an urgently needed drug. Solzhenitsyn's account evidently did not contain the necessary amount. Supplying this drug would have been very expensive and the head of the firm delayed his decision at least until his assistance was no longer required. In case of any possible objection to these remarks I feel I should give a brief account of the circumstances of the affair.

At the beginning of June 1968 Solzhenitsyn approached me with a request to find out about the possibility of procuring a new medical preparation from the United States, which American doctors had begun using for the treatment of leukemia. Alla, the ten or eleven-year-old daughter of some friends of his in Ryazan, had developed acute leukemia and the doctors said there was no hope of curing her. The girl's mother was doing everything in her power to procure information about new drugs; she read specialised articles in scientific journals about methods of treating leukemia and the latest drugs in use against the disease, and she had obtained several preparations from abroad for the doctors treating her daughter. In this way her daughter was being kept alive. Leukemia can prove fatal within a few months since the malignant cells become immune to the medicinal preparations used. Life can be prolonged only by constantly changing the drugs and combinations of drugs. In 1968 there were reports of a radically new drug for the treatment of leukemia – the enzyme *asparaginase* secreted by certain bacteria. *Za Rubezhom* (Abroad) reprinted a newspaper report which claimed that asparaginase, if systematically introduced into the bloodstream, destroyed only the leukemia cells and might prove to be a radical break-through in the treatment of leukemia. However, the preparation was still only in the experimental stages and was practically impossible to obtain.

Knowing that I had many friends in the United States (and the effect of asparaginase had been discovered by American biochemists), Solzhenitsyn had approached me. I at once wrote to a number of friends and was soon able to inform Solzhenitsyn that asparaginase was being manufactured commercially in the United States by only one firm, which was selling it at the exceptionally high price of between twenty and seventy-five dollars per hundred International Units depending on the size of the order (large orders receiving the discount that private firms usually give). At that time I did not know how much was needed for the treatment, but the cost might run to well over a thousand dollars. This being so, one could not simply ask someone to send the preparation.

Solzhenitsyn told me he was willing to meet the cost of the medicine from his royalties on the American editions of *One Day in the Life of Ivan Denisovich*.[1] Although foreign publishers need not necessarily pay the author royalties for their translations, in view of the Soviet Union's refusal (until very recently) to subscribe to international copyright agreements, Solzhenitsyn had been informed nevertheless that certain publishing houses had been crediting the royalties on *Ivan*

---

[1] There were of course several publishers of *Ivan Denisovich* in America.

113

Denisovich to an account in his name. Apart from my desire to help friends of Solzhenitsyn, I was interested in the scientific side of the matter, particularly since the Institute of Medical Radiology where I worked had a special department for patients suffering from leukemia, which was also frequently a result of irradiation. Consequently I set about the problems of purchasing asparaginase from the United States with all speed. One of my friends in America asked a literary scholar of his acquaintance to find out if it would be possible for Solzhenitsyn now to receive his royalties for *Ivan Denisovich*. The literary critic approached the publisher mentioned above, since he knew him personally.

The publisher replied on 2 July 1968 with a very positive letter. He said that his firm would pay royalties to a writer of Solzhenitsyn's stature irrespective of whether the USSR was a party to the international conventions. He believed, though, that to send the money directly to Solzhenitsyn from the United States might well be dangerous for the recipient. On hearing the contents of this letter, Solzhenitsyn charged me, this time officially, to take the necessary steps towards the purchase of the requisite quantity of asparaginase in the United States. I wrote several letters – to the publisher informing him of Solzhenitsyn's intention to purchase the preparation, to the firm responsible for its commercial manufacture, and also to a number of specialists in the application of asparaginase to obtain the necessary information about methods, dosage, literature concerning clinical use, etc. I also gave the publisher the names of some eminently respectable people who could if in doubt, confirm that Solzhenitsyn intended to pay the cost of the drug out of his royalties for *Ivan Denisovich*.

The publisher's reply was favourable. He sympathised with Solzhenitsyn's intention and said that he had asked his own doctor to find out whether it would be possible to buy the asparaginase. I also received a letter from the Director of the research laboratory manufacturing asparaginase (Dr Jim Boston of the Truett Laboratory, Dallas, Texas) and an index of prices for consignments of different quantities. Dr Boston wrote that the laboratory would agree to dispatch the necessary quantity on condition that the publishing houses guaranteed to pay the bill. By that time I had accumulated a certain amount of literature sent by various scientists, and all the indications were that a clinical course of treatment lasting four weeks would require a minimum supply of approximately 200,000 International Units of the preparation, at a cost of $6,000. I informed the publisher of this and also asked him whether his firm would be willing to pay a bill of that size if they received written authorisation from Solzhenitsyn to do so. After a long delay I received a very courteous reply from his secretary dated 4 November 1968.

We were very glad to get your letters and regret that we have been so long in informing you of their receipt. Mr [X] has not answered because he was in Mexico City at the Olympic games, and immediately after his return went away on another short business trip. He will write you as soon as he comes back.[2]

I waited a little while before writing him another letter. Again, however, the reply came from his secretary, this time written on his personal notepaper. The letter was dated 26 November 1968, and I shall quote it in full:

Dear Dr Medvedev:

I am sorry that once again I have to tell you that Mr [X] is away on a trip. He had, however, already made several inquiries regarding your medical questions. But he has had no luck so far.

When he gets back around 10 December, he still intends to try further. As soon as he has something definite to report, I am sure he will write you. In the meantime please bear with him a little longer.

There was no point in conducting any further correspondence with the publishing house, for in December the girl was admitted to hospital with the usual development of advanced leukemia. On the recommendation of Dr. J. D. Broome, the discoverer of the anti-leukemic action of asparaginase, I approached the Director of the Squibb Institute for Medical Research in New Brunswick, Arnold D. Welch. This Institute was manufacturing asparaginase not for commercial purposes but for clinical tests, at the request of the National Cancer

[2] Re-translated from the Russian in the absence of the English original.

115

Institute. Welch hastily consulted Professor C. Gordon Zubrod of the National Cancer Institute and at the beginning of January 1969 an airmail consignment of 150,000 Units of asparaginase was rushed to me. *The preparation was sent free of charge.* Professor Zubrod included Alla's case in his programme of clinical trials and sent detailed instructions on methods of using the drug. The treatment with asparaginase was carried out in Moscow by Doctor A. I. Vorobyov, and this was the first instance of the application of asparaginase in the USSR in the treatment of leukemia. Unfortunately by that time it had become known that asparaginase was not a radical remedy but merely caused a remission after which the disease resumed its progress. In 1970, after two more remissions, Alla died.

One wonders, though, what induced this publishing house to transfer royalties for *Ivan Denisovich* to the 'Rescue Committee', and if the publishers were aware of the consequences an act like this might have for the author. Did they realise that, even if they had done this in 1964, there was no need to publicise the fact in 1969? By way of an answer to these questions it might be appropriate to give another example.

In October 1968 at about the same time, I was also making approaches to another publisher of *Ivan Denisovich*. A few years earlier Academician Kapitsa had shown me a paperback edition of *Ivan Denisovich* published by this particular firm. The highly-coloured cover depicted Ivan Denisovich against a background of barbed wire, while the verso of the title page carried a special announcement to the effect that royalties would be set aside in the author's name for a period of ten years, and that they would be given to the author if during that time he should come to the USA to collect the money. If he did not come to America within ten years the 'royalties would be turned over to a worthy anti-communist cause'.

My inquiry was answered first by a letter dated 28 October 1968, and then by another dated 31 October 1968. However, when I wrote back explaining my business in detail there was no reply. I repeated my request three times, sending my letter by 'Advice of Receipt'. The receipt cards came back with the publisher's stamp and signed evidently by a secretary, but there were no replies to my letters.

1968 was still a long way away from the expiry of the ten-year term, but the publishing house was refusing to conduct a correspondence that might deprive the organisers of anti-Soviet funds of any money.

It is my belief that publishers do not provide provocation of this kind on their own initiative. These 'Rescue Committees', the NTS, and similar organisations evidently rely to some extent on editions of Soviet authors published abroad for a definite part of their income; it may be from translations of Solzhenitsyn, or translations of Sholokhov, or Kochetov. Outside the Soviet Union an important part of an organisation's activity is the raising of funds to keep it in existence. There are two further aspects to the receipt of such funds from publishing houses. In the first place, they could at that time take the money without worrying about the legal consequences since Soviet authors had no legal rights abroad and the USSR was not a party to International Copyright Conventions. In the second place, an author who has been robbed in this manner may always be accused of complicity. And I am not at all sure that there are not some people who might secretly find this as useful a handle as does *Literaturnaya Gazeta*.

Literaturnaya Gazeta and the Writers' Union Secretariat, while commenting on the reference in *The Times* article to the fate of Solzhenitsyn's royalties, refrained from expressing an opinion on the concluding paragraph of the article, which was as follows:

> Victor Gollancz, who brought out a separate translation of *One Day* (published also by Penguin and by Dutton in America) signed an official agreement with the Russian trade delegation in Highgate West Hill, London, and paid advance and full royalties to them. There is, however, no reason to suppose that the unfortunate Solzhenitsyn has received a penny from these payments.

This money – and no one knows exactly how much was involved – was accepted by the Mezhdunarodnaya Kniga (International Book) agency which operates under the auspices of the USSR Ministry of Foreign Trade. I have not found out what happened to this particular payment. However, my files

117

contain material relating to another, similar case. Acting 'on behalf of' a certain Soviet author, Mezhdunarodnaya Kniga, through the mediation of a French agency, Agence Littéraire et Artistique Parisienne, received large payments of royalties from six European publishers. No one informed the author of these transactions. It was not until nine years later that he happened to find out about the payments.

As a result of intensive inquiries during which I assisted with some of the correspondence, the Director of the French agency, Georges Soria, wrote to me on 6 July 1967 and the Chairman of Mezhdunarodnaya Kniga wrote to the author; both letters informed us that the royalties had indeed been paid to the author. However, under the terms of the general agreement existing between Mezhdunarodnaya Kniga and the French agency, the latter had received 75 per cent of the royalties as commission for its services. Of the remaining 25 per cent, about one half had been spent on bringing legal action against publishers in Italy who had refused to pay out royalties. (The cases were lost.) Of the remaining 12 per cent Mezhdunarodnaya Kniga has the right to deduct 25 per cent commission. Of the balance, 35 per cent goes to Vneshposyltorg's Department of the Bank for Foreign Trade. All the remainder (about 4 per cent of the initial sum) may be paid to the author. Bearing in mind that M. Soria's agency is one of the institutions of the French Communist Party, and that M. Soria himself is a member of the Central Committee of the French Communist Party, one need go no further to calculate who in particular has received the largest share of the royalties from *One Day in the Life of Ivan Denisovich*, those who are 'saving' mankind from communism or those who are seeking to propagate communism in every part of the globe.

19. The Break-up of the *Novy Mir* Editorial Board

THE OFFICIAL PUBLICATION in 1962 of *One Day in the Life of Ivan Denisovich* was not a totally isolated event. It was the result of the trends in Soviet literature that had been growing up since the 20th and 22nd Party Congresses. It was no accident either that the story was published in *Novy Mir;* for the journal really did bring together the best writers in the country and was not afraid to discuss critical matters pertaining to literature and public life. Similarly, Solzhenitsyn's expulsion from the Writers' Union was not an isolated event. It was the consequence of changes permeating the whole political spectrum, the result of the attempt by some conservative circles to restrict the freedom of literature, to place literature and polemical journalism under the strictest ideological and political control. This process had begun back in 1963–4 under Khrushchev as a defensive reaction by the bureaucracy confronted with a body of critical literature which they found too sweeping in tone. Khruschev aspired to absolute rule in every aspect of social life and hence was unable to govern any particular department in a really organised or competent fashion. He made gross errors in his directives on agriculture, industry, foreign policy, education, the administration of the party structure, and the management of the economy of the country as a whole.

The life of our society proceeded by erratic leaps and bounds and there were incessant reorganisations in politics and economics. Some of these propelled the country forward, others acted as a powerful brake on development. There were similar volte-faces in literature. After the censure from the top of Dudintsev's novel *Not by Bread Alone* in 1957 and the all-out campaign against Boris Pasternak and his *Doctor Zhivago*, a period of literary stagnation ensued. Khrushchev abused both Dudintsev and Pasternak in speeches he made at gatherings of writers. In such circumstances, the publication of *Ivan Denisovich* came as a complete surprise. In 1954 Krushchev had personally presided over a meeting of the Secretariat of the

119

Central Committee of the Communist Party which had decided that Tvardovsky should be relieved of his post as editor of *Novy Mir*. The chief cause of Tvardovsky's dismissal was his satirical poem *Tyorkin in Paradise* which (*in its first version*) was judged anti-party and anti-Soviet. K. Simonov spoke against Tvardovsky at this meeting and was afterwards appointed editor of *Novy Mir*. In 1958 he too was removed, largely for having published the novel *Not by Bread Alone* and Tvardovsky was reappointed. In 1963 Khrushchev's assistant Lebedev arranged for the new – and far more pointed – version of *Tyorkin in Paradise* to be read to him at his Black Sea residence. Khrushchev liked the poem very much and asked Adzhubei, the editor of *Izvestiya*, to print it immediately. It was in impulsive decisions like this that Khruschev's so-called 'subjectivism' manifested itself. After his resignation the direction of literary matters passed into the hands of specialists in ideology and became more consistent and purposeful. It was the conservative elements in the bureaucracy and leaders in the apparatus of censorship that took over. Sholokhov's novel *They Fought for the Motherland*, which he had been working on for many years, contained a chapter in which one of the characters tells of illegal methods of investigation and of prison camps during the years 1937–40. He was ordered to eliminate the chapter. But it was an integral part of the story and should, moreover, have been perfectly acceptable from a party point of view since it showed a man who had endured torture and prison-camp life remaining true to the party and to all the ideals upon which Soviet society was based. But the censor had his instructions not to pass anything about the camps. As a member of the Plenum of the Central Committee Sholokhov sought an interview with L. I. Brezhnev, but was refused. Brezhnev could not see Sholokhov on a matter of this kind, for such decisions were no longer within the competence of the Secretary General. Sholokhov made several unsuccessful attempts to get round the censor's ban, then withdrew the chapter and replaced the tale of prison-camp tortures with a discussion about fishing techniques.

Differentiation of power had increased opportunities for ideological censorship, but the appointment and dismissal of editors of central journals still lay in the hands of the Secretariat or the Politburo of the Central Committtee. And although the ideological governors of literature were constantly irritated by the activities of Tvardovsky and the editorial board of *Novy Mir*, there were insufficient grounds for bringing Tvardovsky's name up in debate in the Secretariat of the Central Committee. In the difficult conditions of the day Tvardovsky and his authors' collective had found a *modus operandi* and the works published in *Novy Mir* were enthusiastically read by liberal sections of the intelligentsia. Conservative, bureaucratic figures in the leadership reacted with great displeasure to this activity and usually blocked the subsequent publication of the works in book form. The year 1969 saw the publication in *Novy Mir* of many unquestionably talented and truthful works, which at the same time made a social point. They included Natalia Baranskaya's *A Week like a Week* (*Nedelya Kak Nedelya*), Georgii Vladimov's *Three-minute Silence* (*Tri Minuty Molchaniya*), Vasil Bykov's *Kruglyanskii Bridge* (*Kruglyanskii Most*), Lev Ginzburg's *Meetings Beyond the Grave* (*Potustoronniye Vstrechi*), Efim Dorosh's *Country Dairy* (*Derevenskii Dnevnik*), Yury Trifonov's *The Exchange* (*Obmen*), Fyodor Abramov's *Pelageya*, and several others. The critics were ill-disposed to these works, but their readers were grateful to the journal. The number of people who took out a subscription in September 1969 was 40,000 higher than in the previous year.

At the beginning of 1969 Tvardovsky sent his new poem, *By Right of Memory* (*Po Pravu Pamyati*) to the type-setter; it was scheduled for publication in the April issue of the journal. The poem was withdrawn by the censor. In his capacity as editor Tvardovsky included it in the proofs of the May issue and once again it was banned. He then included it in the June issue and in addition ordered 20 proof copies which he intended to submit for discussion at a higher level. The 'higher level' refused to discuss the poem and the censor once more removed it from the proofs of the journal.

Alexander Tvardovsky had been working on *By Right of Memory* for some years. He had completed the first version in 1967 and sent it to the editorial board of the magazine *Yunost* (*Youth*). However, they declined to publish it and returned the author his typescript. On several occasions Tvardovsky read the poem to friends at his home but he did not give copies of

the text to anyone, fearing that it might circulate in *samizdat*.
At the beginning of 1969, during a visit to Tvardovsky's dacha
at Pakhra, near Moscow, my brother and I read the poem. In
June 1969 Tvardovsky made my brother a gift of a proof copy
of the final version of the poem which was far finer and fuller
than the one we had seen the year before.

The poem describes the fate of Tvardovsky's father and his
family, poor peasants who had obtained land only after the
October Revolution, worked their fingers to the bone, and
had then been dispossessed as 'kulaks' and deported to Siberia.
The author conveys his feelings at being branded as the 'son of
a kulak'. He gives too a general appraisal of the régime of
repression and lawlessness which prevailed under Stalin, and
reconsiders many of the attitudes he had expressed earlier in
his poem *The Land of Muravia* (*Strana Muravia*).

> O, years of hateful youth,
> Its cruel vexations.
> First my father, then all at once the enemy.
>
> You're here, my son, but you are not of this world,
> For what law can there be for you
> When your father's name has been
> Inscribed on that infernal list.
>
> ....in anguish deep
> He deserted hearth and home
> And, blind and savage, spurned a sentence
> In round figures.
>
> But in that place where all classes
> Were without exception equal,
> All men prison-camp brothers,
> Branded with the brand of treason. . . .

But one question he raises with particular clarity is the
writer's right to tell the whole truth about the past:

> They are mistaken who think
> That memory sets no store by itself,

That the waterweed of time will entangle
All the past,
All the pain.

That the earth revolves regardless,
Clocking up days and years,
And the poet will not be called to account
When he hides behind the phantom of prohibition
And says nothing about what is burning his soul . . .

No, duty calls upon him now to utter
All the unuttered omissions of the past.

It was clear that Tvardovsky would continue to press for publication of his poem. Furthermore, by circulating proof copies he had precipitated the *samizdat* process.

On 26 July 1969 the journal *Ogonyok* (No. 30) published a statement by eleven men of letters (Mikhail Alexeyev, Sergei Vikulov, Sergei Voronin, and others) entitled 'What Is *Novy Mir* Against?'. It was couched in exceptionally crude language and in a style reminiscent of a critical article of the late 40s, in which the Leningrad journals *Zvezda* and *Leningrad* had been the targets of attack. The authors of the statement alleged that *Novy Mir* was printing '. . . blasphemous material calling into question the heroic past of our people and of the Soviet Army . . .' 'The articles of criticism published in *Novy Mir* systematically and purposefully cultivate the tendency to take a sceptical view of the social and moral values of Soviet society, of its ideals and its achievements.'

The editorial board of *Novy Mir* published a fitting reply to this tirade (see *Novy Mir*, No. 7 1969, pp. 285–6), pointing out that all eleven signatures of the statement had at one time or another been seriously criticised by *Novy Mir* for the low artistic level of their works, their poor literary taste and the unoriginality of their writing.

But this reply was not merely *Novy Mir* getting its own back. The fact that these people had managed to publish their demagogy in an illustrated news magazine with a circulation of two million suggested the development of a large-scale campaign against *Novy Mir*.

The displeasure of conservative circles at Tvardovsky's attitude was not confined to his literary activities; for the poet's public activities too were becoming more and more those of the liberal activist. At the XXIII Party Congress he was not re-elected to the Plenum of the Central Committee. After the entry into Czechoslovakia by the armies of the Warsaw Pact, public party meetings were compulsorily convened in all Soviet organisations to express support for the actions taken by the government. At *Novy Mir* no meeting was convened until two warnings had been received from the District Party Committee. Tvardovsky did not attend the meeting. When the Board of the Soviet Writers' Union composed an address to the writers of Czechoslovakia, Tvardovsky refused to sign it. This led to a week's delay in the publication of the address: the Writers' Union leadership had demanded that all members of the Board sign. Tvardovsky was asked for an explanation. He wrote a letter to the Union stating briefly but plainly that he would have been willing to address his Czechoslovak colleagues before the armies of the Pact had been brought in, but he was not willing to do so after the event.

In the autumn of 1969 Tvardovsky was summoned to the appropriate department of an authoritative institution and shown in a recent issue of *Possev*. In it was his latest poem. Tvardovsky at once wrote a sharp protest which subsequently appeared in *Literaturnaya Gazeta*.

'The effrontery of this action', he wrote, 'which aims to discredit my work, is equalled by the brazen mendacity with which the poem has been supplied with the provocative title of "On Stalin's Ashes".'

Tvardovsky went on to say that the text of the poem as published by *Possev* was in many places corrupt. His protest remained unpublished for a long time; it did not appear in *Literaturnaya Gazeta* until 11 February 1970 (on page 9) and the date of its writing was altered. In the same issue the paper published an announcement that the editorial board of *Novy Mir* was being reorganised, so that the reader might come to the conclusion that there was a real connection between the two events.

The publication of the poem in *Possev* could not be explained by *samizdat*, since the version in *Possev* was the *old one*, dating from 1968, and very different from the version which had begun to circulate in April or May of 1969. The old version had not been passed around, but it had lain for a short time in the editorial office of *Yunost* magazine; a few of the poet's friends were familiar with it, but the typescript had not circulated. How it found its way to the émigré magazine remains a mystery.

Late in 1969 Voronkov, the Secretary of the Writers' Union, began insistently urging Tvardovsky to hand in his resignation 'for health reasons'. Tvardovsky refused, although he was simultaneously being offered a higher-ranking 'party appointment' as a Secretary of the Soviet Writers' Union.[1] But one could sense that the future of the journal had been decided. The staff of *Novy Mir* had ceased to feel any optimism. Visitors to *Novy Mir* at the end of 1969 usually asked 'Well, how are things?' to which the reply would be 'We're still in work *today* – touch wood.'

But all the same it was decided not to remove Tvardovsky by decree of the Central Committee Secretariat, and not to hold a discussion on the work of the journal. Tvardovsky must retire of his own accord, and a special plan was devised to this end. The Board of the Writers' Union does not have the authority to relieve the Editor-in-Chief of an important journal of his post. But it may sack and appoint members of the editorial staff. This is usually done on the recommendation or with the consent of the Editor-in-Chief. On this occasion the procedure was quite different. At the beginning of February 1970 a session of the *bureau* of the Board's Secretariat was held in Tvardovsky's absence to carry out a reorganisation of *Novy Mir*. I. I. Vinogradov, Deputy Editor A. I. Kondratovich, V. Ya. Lakshin and I. A. Sats – in fact the heads of the principle sections – were relieved of their responsibilities. D. G. Bolshov and O. I. Smirnov were appointed joint deputies for Tvardovsky, and three new people – V. A. Kosolapov, A. I. Ovcharenko and A. E. Rekemchuk – joined the editorial board. Tvardovsky immediately appealed against these changes in a statement to

[1] There are a great number of Secretaries on the Board of the Soviet Writers' Union but only some of these Secretaries are staff members of the Secretariat and receive official salaries. Tvardovsky was a Secretary, but in his capacity as editor of *Novy Mir*. Subject to his retirement he was being offered a permanent post as Secretary of the Writers' Union with a correspondingly high salary.

the Central Committee of the Party. But on 11 February 1970 the decision of the Bureau of the Writers' Union was given a brief mention in the 'Chronicle' section of *Literaturnaya Gazeta*. This meant that Tvardovsky's appeal had been rejected. Of course, Tvardovsky could not work with his new staff, and he sent in his resignation. This was soon followed by announcements from A. M. Maryamov, E. Ya. Dorosh and Chief Secretary M. N. Khitrov that they were leaving the editorial board. V. A. Kosolapov was appointed Editor-in-Chief of the journal although he was not even a writer or a member of the Writer's Union. (Prior to his appointment Kosolapov had been Director of a publishing house). First Deputy Editor Bolshov too could not have been called a writer, nor was he a member of the Writers' Union. Until his appointment to *Novy Mir* he had been head of one of the departments of Moscow Television. Thus *Novy Mir* had become a literary journal headed not by writers or poets or literary critics but by mere obedient administrators.

On 18 February 1970 *Literaturnaya Gazeta* published a reply from the leadership of the Soviet Writers' Union to a letter the Union had received from G. Vigorelli, Secretary General of the European Writers' Association, protesting against the persecution of Solzhenitsyn. The Soviet reply to Vigorelli was: 'Your attitude rules out the possibility of our further cooperation with you.' Thus it was that the Soviet Writers' Union decided to withdraw from the European Writers' Association. Moreover, the Soviet Vice-Chairman of the European Writers' Association was ordered to send in his resignation. Solzhenitsyn's case was of course merely a pretext for the Soviet withdrawal from the European union of writers. Cultural cooperation with Western Europe no longer figured in the plans for the further development of 'socialist realism'. Besides, the Soviet Vice-Chairman of the EWA was none other than Tvardovsky. In the past he had travelled abroad sometimes twice a year to participate in the work of the Council of the EWA. The time had now come to put an end to all this.

After handing over their affairs to the new editorial board, the old staff of *Novy Mir* gathered in March, in what had once been Tvardovsky's study, for a farewell photograph. *Novy Mir's* influence on Soviet literature was at an end.

20. The Difficult Summer of 1970

CONTRARY TO EXPECTATIONS, the breaking up of the *Novy Mir* editorial board provoked extraordinarily little public reaction in the Soviet Union. Only two written protests are known to have circulated in intellectual circles, and even they were anonymous. However, extensive comment appeared outside the Soviet Union on the suppression of the literary trend represented by *Novy Mir*.

In the wake of such an abrupt shift in policy, which destroyed the last remaining legal platform for a realistic liberal literature reflecting the political mood engendered by the 20th Party Congress, not only Solzhenitsyn but a considerable number of other writers could no longer hope for publication in their own country. Those who had introduced these new restrictions on the freedom of the press evidently also realised the possible spread of *samizdat*, which was increasing with the publication of *samizdat* works abroad, and various measures were introduced that aimed further to discredit authors who viewed the uncensored circulation of their works with indulgence.

Amongst them Solzhenitsyn was the most prominent. The role of chief critic of Solzhenitsyn was assumed by Sergei Mikhalkov, the children's poet. At various conferences and meetings of literary organisations he went almost as far as to accuse Solzhenitsyn of 'betrayal of the fatherland', ranking him among 'ideological speculators' and 'literary Vlasovites'[1] (see, for example, an article by Mikhalkov entitled 'The Artist's Position' in *Komsomolskaya Pravda*, 14 December 1969).

Naturally Mikhalkov's speeches were noted by his superiors. In the spring of 1970 he was made leader of the RSFSR Writers' Union and awarded the Lenin Prize for Literature; this was clearly dictated by political considerations. Sergei Mikhalkov is a very ordinary poet whose verses are frequently very crude in form and devoid of genuine merit.

[1] Andrei Vlasov was a Soviet general who surrendered to the Germans during the war and later commanded units of Russian ex-prisoners of war who fought with the Germans against the Soviet army.

Once again the old story of Solzhenitsyn's verse drama *Feast of the Victors* was used as the pretext to discredit him further. This play could not be seriously used against the author as long as it remained unpublished. In his letter to the Fourth Writers' Congress in 1967 Solzhenitsyn had warned that if publication of the play did take place it would be with the knowledge of the KGB since they had confiscated the *only copy*. The publication of the play abroad, though, would be a godsend for the anti-Solzhenitsyn campaign – they could always query whether the play had really only existed in a single copy, and furthermore, could thereafter 'analyse' it without the need to refer to an unpublished source – the special collection of the KGB.

At the beginning of 1970 it became known that secret emissaries were making attempts to place the play with some Western journal. The snag was that any publishing house which published the play would demonstrate its direct or indirect connection with the KGB.

However, the story of the advance publication of Svetlana Alliluyeva's book, which Victor Louis brought to the West, showed that commercial interest could overcome even this obstacle. The French Writers' Union, which had earlier sent a strong protest to the Soviet Writers' Union on the occasion of Solzhenitsyn's expulsion, once again rendered invaluable assistance by publishing the following statement in *Le Monde* on New Year's Eve:

We have learnt that a West European specialised organisation is at the present time offering to publishing houses the manuscript of a theatrical work by Solzhenitsyn [*Feast of the Victors*]. However, the work in question is one whose publication the author has forbidden, and which, circulated against his will, has served as grounds for bringing political charges against the author.

It is important that circles interested in the future publication of the work, whether publishers or readers, should be aware that its appearance in the West, on whatever pretext, and in present-day circumstances, would be promptly used as an argument for bringing charges against Alexander Solzhenitsyn, would conflict with both his intentions and his entitlement as author to copyright, and finally, could only be a new weapon in the hands of those people who are seeking to discredit a Soviet intellectual in the eyes of public opinion in his own country, and perhaps force him to leave it.

Solzhenitsyn for his part was also taking the necessary steps to prevent provocations of this kind and the arbitrary use of his works. He engaged a Swiss lawyer, Dr Fritz Heeb, entrusting him with the protection of his author's rights outside the Soviet Union. Dr Heeb published a statement dated 5 March 1970 in all the principal Western papers, forbidding any unauthorised publication of Solzhenitsyn's books. Henceforward application would be made to the appropriate courts in the event of any infringement of this ruling by private publications.

An account of Dr Heeb's statement was published even in the British communist paper *Morning Star* on 9 or 10 March, but this issue, like some other issues of communist papers containing information 'undesirable' for Soviet readers, was confiscated by the Soviet censorship.

In this new situation a publisher who decided to publish anything by Solzhenitsyn without his consent, or rather, without the consent of his representative Dr Heeb, risked incurring substantial damages and an injunction preventing him from publishing the pirate edition. It was made clear that these legal sanctions would in fact be applied, and they have proved effective. The émigré journal *Grani* succeeded in publishing Solzhenitsyn's play *Candle in the Wind* (*Svecha na Vetru*) in March 1970, but that was the last time the émigré press interfered in Solzhenitsyn's affairs. It was in this month that Dr Heeb's powers came into effect.

At the beginning of May 1970 Solzhenitsyn moved to his cottage 'Borzovka' for the summer to finish work on his novel *August 1914*. I visited him there on 3 May. By then it was known that a film of *One Day in the Life of Ivan Denisovich* was being made in Norway.

At the end of May, also apparently in connection with some general scheme to discredit authors of *samizdat*, I was myself the victim of unexpected measures of restraint.[2] Throughout this period of detention, Tvardovsky and Solzhenitsyn, together with

---

[2] See Zhores A. Medvedev and Roy A. Medvedev, *A Question of Madness.*

many other friends and colleagues, gave me great moral and practical support. When I came into the visitors' room at the Kaluga psychiatric hospital on 9 June and saw Alexander Tvardovsky, who embraced me, I found it very difficult to restrain my tears. Solzhenitsyn too had been ready to come to Kaluga at once, but my wife and brother dissuaded him. On 2 June Solzhenitsyn wrote a sharply-worded protest which he toned down slightly in the next few days on the advice of friends. But even in its modified version, published on 15 June in all the principal Western papers, the statement was applauded by public opinion as a powerful protest against the persecution of dissenters. When I was finally released after 19 days of illegal deprivation of freedom, I went to see Solzhenitsyn at his cottage to thank him for the help he had given me. He looked more cheerful than he had seemed in the spring. He had almost completed the first revision of his new novel, and it was to be the beginning, the '*First Knot*',[3] of a large-scale epic narrative about the First World War and its consequences.

In July I saw Tvardovsky. He seemed in poor health – positively ill in fact. He had just celebrated his sixtieth birthday. All the main papers had carried articles about the poet's work, some accompanied by a photograph. But these outward displays of recognition – which were inevitable since Tvardovsky's work had been part of Soviet literature curricula in schools and institutes for many years – contained a good deal of nonsense dictated from on high. An 'instruction' was issued that there was to be no reminder that Tvardovsky had been Editor of *Novy Mir*, nor any mention of the existence of the poem *Tyorkin in Paradise*. Newspapers and journals were forbidden to approach the poet for new poems or to ask him questions about his literary plans. This was in sharp contrast to the celebration, ten years before, of his fiftieth birthday, when he was besieged by editors of magazines and papers requesting some new poem or fragment.

Towards the end of the summer Tvardovsky had a stroke that left him partially paralysed. He was rushed to the Kremlin Hospital where acute pleurisy was also diagnosed. But this was a mistake on the part of the doctor, and as a result of it, the poet was prescribed cupping-glasses and poultices – treatment

[3] 'Uzel Pervyi' – the sub-title given to *August 1914* by Solzhenitsyn.

which was quite wrong for the illness from which Tvardovsky was really suffering. Only after two weeks did the doctor discover that the condition of his lungs had sharply deteriorated and decide to take an X-ray (which should have been done in the first place). The X-ray plate distinctly showed a cancerous tumour, already too large to operate. But even here politics intervened. The doctors were forbidden to mention the stroke. It was reported in the case history that there had been no thrombosis but that there had been a metastasis of a tumour on the brain. This conclusion was confirmed at a doctors' consultation. One leading literary figure, explaining to friends what had happened to Tvardovsky, particularly stressed that there had been no thrombosis. 'The word thrombosis should not be mentioned at all,' he said, 'people might connect a thrombosis with the *Novy Mir* business, but cancer – that's from God.'

But metastases to the brain meant that the case was utterly hopeless and the end would come soon. This was what the doctors told Tvardovsky's wife and relatives, giving him no more than a month to live. However, a month passed, the thrombosis was resolved, the paralysis vanished and the poet's speech was restored. His condition improved so much that he was discharged from the hospital and allowed to go home. He was well enough to read, receive visitors and chat. On the initiative of family and friends a group was formed to lend assistance and mobilise the finest medical advice available for the treatment of lung cancer. Even consultant oncologists from abroad were enlisted to advise on treatment. Great hopes were placed on new chemical methods of arresting the development of tumours.

21. The Nobel Prize for Literature

ON 8 OCTOBER 1970 I was in Moscow. In the afternoon I
called to see Veronica Turkina, a mutual friend of Solzhenitsyn.
At about 3 o'clock another mutual friend telephoned and told
Veronica the amazing news that Solzhenitsyn had been awarded
the Nobel Prize for Literature. We were both delighted and
asked our friend for details, but he knew no more than the bare
fact. He had been told of the award by a foreign correspondent
who had rung him and asked for Rostropovich's telephone
number – Solzhenitsyn was staying with him at the time. Of
course, the correspondent failed to obtain the number – Solzhenitsyn was not in the habit of giving interviews to foreign
correspondents and did not allow the telephone number of
Rostropovich's dacha to be given to anyone, fearing interrup-
tions to his work. What is more, Rostropovich's number is ex-
directory. About twenty minutes later our mutual friend phoned
again and said he was being besieged with calls from the correspondents of various foreign newspapers asking to be put in
touch with Solzhenitsyn and insisting that in view of the international importance of the event they had the right to put
questions to him. Our friend was afraid that if he did not grant
their request they would find the telephone number somehow
or other.

Realising that this was so, I advised him to give the number
to no one except representatives of the Swedish press. Since
the Nobel Prize is awarded by the Swedish Academy, Swedish
pressmen certainly have the right to be the first to inform the
prize-winner of the award and to communicate his reaction to
the press. I suggested that he might make contact with Per Egil
Hegge, who was Moscow correspondent of three Scandinavian
papers, Swedish, Norwegian and Danish. Apart from that Per
Egil Hegge spoke excellent Russian and was a great admirer of
Solzhenitsyn's work. Shortly afterwards Per Egil Hegge did
indeed ring and was given Solzhenitsyn's number.

I had been introduced to Per Egil Hegge at the end of June

1970 by an American historian whom I had known for many years, and who had visited the Soviet Union several times. He had returned in May, when we had several meetings, and talked at length; and later that month he learned how I had been deprived of my freedom in a quite original way.[1] He was most agitated and organised the publication of several statements of protest through foreign correspondents, in which Per Egil Hegge had assisted him. After my release the American historian arranged for a group of foreign correspondents to meet me; Hegge was among them. I subsequently saw him on two more occasions, feeling that meetings of this kind were useful and might prevent the repetition of experiments by those who, given the contradictory twists and turns of domestic and foreign policy, still harped on 'ideological unity'.

In the evening of 8 October I learned, this time from foreign radio broadcasts, that Hegge was the only foreign journalist to congratulate Solzhenitsyn on the award of the Nobel Prize and to gain a brief telephone interview with him. Solzhenitsyn thanked the Swedish Academy warmly for the honour they had done him and expressed his readiness to travel to Sweden for the traditional prize-giving ceremony (which takes place annually on 10 December, the birthday of Alfred Nobel, the founder of the Prize. Nobel Prizes in Literature and Science are awarded in Sweden, while the Nobel Peace Prize is awarded at a ceremony in Norway.)

The award of the Nobel Prize to Solzhenitsyn was hardly a surprise. He had been on the list of candidates since 1968. In 1968 and 1969, however, preference had been given to other candidates, and the Soviet authorities had evidently decided that the possibility of Solzhenitsyn getting it had virtually disappeared. Thereafter came Solzhenitsyn's hasty expulsion from the Writers' Union in November 1969, an event reported in *Literaturnaya Gazeta* only a week after the same paper had published a cordially-phrased article on Samuel Beckett, the 1969 Nobel Prize-winner, whose works were almost unknown in the Soviet Union.[2] In 1970, however, Solzhenitsyn's chances

[1] See *A Question of Madness*.
[2] See *Literaturnaya Gazeta*, No. 47, 19 November 1969, an article entitled 'Samuel Beckett – Nobel Laureate'. None of Beckett's major works has been translated into Russian. Only one of his plays, written in 1953, has been published by the journal *Inostrannaya Literatura* (*Foreign Literature*).

improved considerably with the Swedish publication early in the year of *Cancer Ward* and *The First Circle*, superbly translated by Hans Björkegren, who had worked for seven years as a correspondent in the Soviet Union.

It was obvious that official circles in the Soviet Union, and particularly the Writers' Union leadership, would view the Nobel award with extreme displeasure. Common sense, however, should have told them to express this displeasure by keeping quiet and attempting to ignore the Swedish Academy's decision. No one, after all, had ever seriously disputed the literary talent of the author of *One Day in the Life of Ivan Denisovich;* his contribution to the Russian language and literature was also obvious. This had been acknowledged by Soviet literary criticism when he was first published in 1962–3, and it was no accident that he was short-listed for the Lenin Prize. If his work had subsequently fallen out of favour, this was from non-literary considerations, the most important of which was Solzhenitsyn's refusal to handle his subject-matter in accordance with changing political directives. But this was a domestic quarrel and one which the Swedish Academy, judging Solzhenitsyn's work by the criteria of world literature, could not take into account. The decision of the Swedish Academy was a courageous one precisely because it was not determined by political factors. Therefore the Soviet press might continue to criticise Solzhenitsyn's writings from a party viewpoint, but ought not to have disputed the Swedish Academy's choice. The Academy was pledged to make its decision not in accordance with temporary 'party' standards but by criteria of universal significance.

However, common sense was precisely what was lacking in those who decided what the official reaction of the Soviet press to the Nobel Prize award should be. They also lacked self-possession and a sense of proportion. The evening issue of *Izvestiya* on 9 October managed to squeeze in a hasty paragraph 'An unseemly game. On the award of the Nobel Prize to A. Solzhenitsyn.' In the days that followed, this paragraph was reprinted in other central papers, which shows that it was in the nature of a directive. It said that an *Izvestiya* correspondent had received the following interpretation of the Nobel Prize award from the Secretariat of the Soviet Writers' Union:

As the public already knows, the works of this author, illegally sent abroad and published there, have long been used by reactionary circles in the West for anti-Soviet purposes .... Soviet authors expelled A. Solzhenitsyn from the ranks of their union. As we know, this decision was actively supported by the entire public of the country.

One can only regret that the Nobel Committee has allowed itself to be drawn into an unseemly game, undertaken by no means in the interests of the development of spiritual values and literary traditions, but dictated by speculative political considerations.

On 10 October Solzhenitsyn received an official telegram from the Swedish Academy and the Nobel Foundation. He telegraphed a reply expressing his gratitude and his intention of going to Stockholm.

The decision of the Swedish Academy was welcomed by the communist press in several Western countries. On the same day the papers *L'Humanité* and *L'Unità* published articles supporting the Nobel award to Solzhenitsyn.

From Soviet citizens there were only a modest number of telegrams of congratulations, about fifty in all, some signed anonymously 'a group of friends', 'a reader', 'a comrade-in-writing', and so on. It is possible that many of them simply did not arrive. It may also have had something to do with the fact that people who had sent telegrams to Solzhenitsyn congratulating him on his fiftieth birthday in 1968 had been subjected to various forms of criticism. I know of people living in the provinces who had sent Solzhenitsyn telegrams and who were summoned to the local party organisation or KGB branch for lengthy interviews.

I thought that the official Soviet reaction would be confined to the above-mentioned statement. There was no point in becoming embroiled in a serious argument with the Swedish Academy who would doubtless be supported by men of letters throughout the world. But I was mistaken, once again overestimating the capacity of Solzhenitsyn's adversaries for judicious restraint. On 12–13 October the 'public' press agency Novosti (APN) began to circulate to foreign correspondents in Moscow the text of an anonymously written article, 'Where

Does the Nobel Committee Seek Literary Talent and Repute?'
It was assumed that some of the Western papers would publish
the article. However, not even the Western communist press
would do so. On 17 October the anonymous article appeared in
Komsomolskaya Pravda and then in some other Soviet papers.
Strikingly crude in its phrasing, the text read like a declaration
and displayed the extreme literary ignorance of its authors:

> ... The trenchant analogies drawn by some so-called 'spec-
> ialists in Soviet literature' who place side by side the name of
> Solzhenitsyn and the names of Russian and Soviet creators
> of classical works known the world over, can only be
> described as sacrilege ... a man with an unhealthy high
> opinion of himself, Solzhenitsyn gave in easily to the flattery
> of people who have no scruples about the means they use
> when it is a question of fighting the Soviet system ... Solz-
> henitsyn has foregone his conscience and stooped to lies every
> time his Soviet fellow writers have shown their frank concern
> over his fate as a creative writer ... One can only regret that
> when the Nobel Committee cast their votes for Solzhenitsyn
> they did not ponder on what a mockery they made of the
> Prize. But perhaps we are making too high moral demands of
> some members of the literature section of the Nobel Com-
> mittee. There was after all the case of the 'laureate' André
> Gide, accursed by his own countrymen and by others for
> collaborating with Hitler's monsters. In cases such as those
> of Solzhenitsyn and André Gide, does the Nobel Prize
> Committee choose who should be crowned with laurels or is
> the committee itself carefully selected to play the role of
> false witness with a notorious reputation?

I could not understand why the article should so unjustly
abuse Gide. He was never 'accursed by his own countrymen
and by others' and he did not 'collaborate with Hitler's
monsters'. Volume Two of the *Short Literary Encyclopaedia*[3]
gives the following information about Gide:

> *Gide*, André Paul Guillaume, born 1869 ... development
> strongly influenced by Dostoyevsky ... works showed the

[3] *Kratkaya Literaturnaya Entsiklopediya* ed. A. A. Surkov, Moscow, Gos-
litizdat 1964.

decline of capitalist culture, desperate position of the younger generation ... In 1926 shows themes of criticism of colonialism ... In articles and speeches of the early 'thirties Gide declares himself an enemy of capitalism and expresses sympathy with the camp of socialism ... After visiting the USSR in 1936 publishes an anti-Soviet pamphlet ... During Second World War Gide emigrated from France to Tunis ... Awarded Nobel Prize in 1947 ...

Yes, Gide did express sympathy with the Soviet Union, but he was profoundly disillusioned by his visit to the USSR in 1936. Clearly he had no liking for the mass repression of innocent people which had just then begun. In 1937–8 he was indeed cursed by Stalin's propagandists who had previously been well-disposed towards him. Evidently it was these curses which had stuck in the memory of the author from the Novosti Press Agency. Gide had left France for Tunis in his old age – he was then 71 – to avoid living under German occupation. He did not participate in the Resistance movement, but he was a patriot.

Following on APN's attack *Literaturnaya Gazeta* launched a campaign against Solzhenitsyn by simultaneously publishing three articles about him in its issue for 21 October. The first of these, 'A Question of Priority', claimed that Solzhenitsyn had been nominated for the Nobel Prize by a White Guard Russian language journal, *Sentinel* (*Chasovoi*), published in Belgium and edited by people who had once been retained by Generals Wrangel and Kutepov, and had collaborated with them. This was utter nonsense, since the right to make nominations for the Nobel Prize belongs only to reputable literary and scientific institutions, previous prize-winners and authoritative experts selected by the Nobel Foundation.[4]

The two other articles published in *Literaturnaya Gazeta* were reprints from two foreign communist papers, the American *Daily World* and the Swedish *Norrskens Flamman*. The Swedish paper alleged that the CIA was behind the Swedish Academy and was stage-managing all the articles in the press concerning the recently awarded literature prize, and that

[4] In fact Solzhenitsyn was nominated for the Prize by the eminent French writer François Mauriac and some of his colleagues.

137

Stockholm had become a focal point for CIA agents and a centre for their operations in the first instance against the socialist countries ... By its choice the Swedish Academy consciously wished to worsen relations between Sweden and the Soviet Union and profit the interests of imperialism...'[5] *Literaturnaya Gazeta* did not, of course, explain that *Norrskens Flamman* is a small provincial paper published in the town of Luleå by a Stalinist faction of Swedish communists who have serious differences of opinion with the Swedish National Communist Party over their attitude to the Stalin personality cult.[6]

The next issue of *Literaturnaya Gazeta* carried two more articles reprinted from the 'foreign' press (the Bulgarian *Literaturen Front* and the East German *Wahrheit*).

At the end of October my brother Roy visited Tvardovsky, who had been moved from the Kremlin Hospital to his dacha at Pakhra. He was very ill; since his stroke he had had difficulty in speaking and he was still partially paralysed. But when Roy mentioned the subject of the Nobel Prize Tvardovsky became a little more animated.

'It's our prize too,' he said, clearly thinking of the old editorial board of *Novy Mir*.

[5] This is a translation from the Russian.

[6] *Literaturnaya Gazeta* published this article under the heading 'A Stockholm Paper Criticises the Swedish Academy's Decision'. The word 'Stockholm' was evidently an intentional falsification – a reference to a paper from the Swedish capital, after all, looked more serious. But it is possible that the staff of *Literaturnaya Gazeta* did not know where *Norrskens Flamman* was published and had never seen the paper. The Soviet report may have been given to *Literaturnaya Gazeta* in its final form for printing so that all the paper had to do was supply a title. Luleå, the town where *Norrskens Flamman* is published, is a comparatively small place in the North of Sweden, remote from Stockholm and other cultural centres. According to the *Large Soviet Encyclopaedia* (*Bolshaya Sovetskaya Entsiklopediya*) the town is situated in an iron-mining area and has a population of about 25,000.

22. Where will the Nobel Prize be Presented?

THE QUESTION OF whether Solzhenitsyn would be able to travel to Stockholm for the traditional Nobel Prize Ceremony became a familiar topic of conversation especially among the Moscow intellectuals. Most people who expressed an opinion thought it very unlikely that he would be given permission to make the trip to Sweden. Solzhenitsyn himself had initially been in favour of the trip, as his first letters to the Swedish Academy show. But towards the end of October his resolution wavered. There were several reasons for this. He was fairly sure that if he did ask for a passport and exit visa to Sweden he would be given the opportunity to make the journey; but it was on the cards that the trip would result in his becoming an exile.

Solzhenitsyn was troubled also by the complete silence of the Swedish Embassy. In the past when Nobel Prizes had been awarded to Soviet citizens (including several awards for scientific discoveries and one for literature, awarded to Sholokhov in 1965), the Swedish Embassy had immediately sent telegrams of congratulation to the prize-winners. When Sholokhov was awarded the Prize the Swedish Ambassador in Moscow, Gunnar Jarring, personally visited him at his Moscow apartment on the day of the announcement to congratulate him and then gave a banquet in his honour at the Embassy. Solzhenitsyn received no congratulations from the Embassy, and no one there, not even the cultural attaché, sent him even unofficial congratulations. Nor did the Embassy ask the prize-winner about his plans to go to Sweden. Had the Embassy expressed the wish to help him with the journey to Sweden (which would have been quite natural since the Nobel ceremony is a State occasion and the prizes are presented by the King of Sweden), this would automatically have guaranteed Solzhenitsyn a return visa. The Soviet Union would have had to give its assurances on that score, not to a private person but to the Embassy of a friendly country. Solzhenitsyn was also worried by the uncertainty of the Swedish Academy itself that there would be no incidents during his visit that might be used against him. In its first congratulatory telegram to Solzhenitsyn the Academy had said that it was not obligatory that he should be present in person at the prize-giving ceremony, and this was subsequently stressed in letters to him. At the beginning of November Solzhenitsyn received a registered packet from the Swedish Academy containing various forms, details of the order of proceedings at the ceremony, a request that he send his curriculum vitae and photographs, and also a letter from the administrator of the ceremony. The letter stated that to avoid the attentions of the large number of foreign correspondents who would be there, Solzhenitsyn would be lodged, not in the Grand Hotel with the other prize-winners (the prizes for physics, chemistry and medicine were being awarded at the same time), but in an apartment the location of which would be kept secret.

In the first week of November reports reached Solzhenitsyn that certain persons in authority had said at various meetings of the Central Committee that if he presented an application he would be allowed to make a private visit to Sweden, the arrangements for which would be made through the Soviet Department of Visas and Registrations (OVIR). But Solzhenitsyn had by now decided against it. In November he had written to the Swedish Academy giving the reasons for his decision. His letter was later published. He wrote that he had at first intended to come to Sweden:

> However, in recent weeks, the hostile attitude towards my prize, as expressed in the press of my country, and the fact that my books are still suppressed – for reading them, people are dismissed from work or expelled from university – compel me to assume that my trip to Stockholm would be used to cut me off from my native land, simply to prevent me from returning home.

He went on to make the following suggestion:

> ... I could, if it were acceptable to you, receive the Nobel diploma and medal in Moscow at any time convenient to your representatives and myself ...

Solzhenitsyn now had the idea that it would be simplest and most expedient for him to receive the prize in the Swedish

Embassy in Moscow. The territory of the Embassy is by diplomatic tradition a part, as it were, of the territory of Sweden. A presentation in Moscow would be, if anything, more convenient, because Solzhenitsyn would be able to invite his friends to the Embassy reception. He hoped that he might perhaps also be able to give his Nobel lecture at this reception. (Nobel Lectures are traditionally delivered in Stockholm on a theme of the speaker's own choice; scientists usually explain the substance of their research. The lectures are delivered in various halls on one of the days after the prize-giving ceremony. Solzhenitsyn contemplated a Moscow ceremony in January 1971.)

He needed, of course, to discuss the plan with the Swedish Embassy directly. To prepare the ground for a conversation on the subject with Ambassador Gunnar Jarring or the cultural attaché (Ambassador Jarring spent a good deal of time in New York or elsewhere carrying out his duties as UN mediator in the Arab-Israeli conflict), a competent go-between was needed. In this connection Per Egil Hegge willingly offered his assistance. I am not breaking a confidence by describing here the role played by Per Egil Hegge in Solzhenitsyn's negotiations with the Swedish Embassy. In March 1971 Hegge was deported from the USSR, and in October of that year published in Norway a short book entitled *Go-Between in Moscow* which contained a detailed account of his negotiations on Solzhenitsyn's behalf with Swedish diplomats. The book provoked widespread comment particularly in Sweden, and I shall return to it in describing the events that ensued.

In mid-November I told Per Hegge of Solzhenitsyn's plans and his intention of asking the Swedish Embassy to send the explanatory letter quoted above, together with the material, to the Swedish Academy – he was afraid that the package might vanish without trace if he sent it through the ordinary post – and that he wanted to discuss with the Embassy the possibility of his receiving the Prize at some kind of open ceremony. He felt that a secret presentation of the Nobel insignia would be undignified both for himself and for the Nobel Prize, and he believed that the Swedish officials in Moscow would share this view; after all the Swedes are rightly proud of having instituted the Nobel awards; no other prizes carry the prestige that these have enjoyed for almost seventy years. We agreed that Per

141

Hegge would go into all this with the Swedish Embassy and we arranged to meet again on 20 November over their proposals.

On the evening of 20 November I introduced Solzhenitsyn and Per Hegge to each other so that they could discuss a situation which was surely unique in the history of Nobel Prize-winners. It was already winter but the frost was not too severe. It was clear from the start that Solzhenitsyn trusted Hegge. The conversation was completely frank. However, the news Hegge brought was not good, and totally unexpected. The Swedish Embassy rejected the idea of a ceremony, and even more so the idea that the prize-winner should invite his friends to the Embassy. (Solzhenitsyn had a list of guests he proposed to invite in his pocket, but it was never needed.) The Embassy had also refused to accept the papers that Solzhenitsyn wished to have sent on to the Swedish Academy, and suggested that he send them by post.

With the Swedish diplomats taking such a cautious attitude to his Nobel award, Solzhenitsyn's visit to the Embassy had lost its point, but he still went there nonetheless on 27 November. The Ambassador and other Embassy staff received him politely but formally. Ambassador Jarring said he was willing to help Solzenhitsyn to receive the diploma and medal, but would not arrange any reception or ceremony for the purpose in the Embassy.

When on 10 December the prize-giving ceremony was held in Stockholm in the presence of the King of Sweden, I listened to it in a Swedish radio broadcast. (Several radio stations transmitted the ceremony live from Stockholm.) Although Solzhenitsyn was not there, the Secretary of the Swedish Academy, Karl Ragnar Gierow, delivered an official address on the reasons why he had been awarded the Nobel Prize. I noted down parts of the speech:

A literary work belongs to its time and its creator is a product of his social and political situation. This applies especially to this year's Nobel Prize-winner in Literature. We emphasise this because from all points of the compass not least the West, people are prone for various reasons to regard this year's Prizewinner as an exception ... Solzhenitsyn was born in 1918 in Kislovodsk and belongs to that generation of Soviet writers who grew up with and were shaped by the growth of the Soviet state ... He has himself said that he cannot contemplate living anywhere but in his native land ... His books can; they are already living all around the world. But their vitality springs not least from the feeling that roots his being to his country and its destiny. Here too Solzhenitsyn is of the incomparable Russian tradition ... The same background offsets the gigantic predecessors who have derived from Russia's suffering the compelling strength and inextinguishable love that permeate their work ... There is little room in their description for the prescribed idylls of programmed prognoses. But it would be a gross misunderstanding of their quest for the truth not to feel in this their profound, decisive identification with the country whose life provided their subject matter and for whose life their works are essential. The central figure in this powerful epic is the invincible Mother Russia. She appears in various guises under diverse names. One of them is Matryona, the main character in one of Solzhenitsyn's stories ...

When Solzhenitsyn's novel *One Day in the Life of Ivan Denisovich* first appeared eight years ago it was recognised at once in his own country and soon all over the world that a major new writer had entered the arena. As *Pravda* wrote: 'Solzhenitsyn's story at times calls to mind Tolstoy's artistic power. A writer gifted with a rare talent has come into our literature.' It would also be difficult to outdo *Pravda's* exposé of the power exercised by Solzhenitsyn's narrative art: 'Why is it that upon reading this remarkable story not only is one's heart wrung with grief but a light penetrates one's soul? It is because of his profound humanity, because people remained people even in an atmosphere of mockery ...'

After the solemn presentation of the Nobel Prizes the King of Sweden traditionally holds a banquet in honour of the Prize winners. At this banquet each prize-winner (and in 1970 there were seven or eight, as the prizes for Science were shared by two or three scientists) delivers a short speech lasting no more than two or three minutes. Solzhenitsyn was resolved not to break this tradition, and his speech was read at the banquet by Dr Gierow. The text, as received in Sweden, ran as follows:

Your Royal Highness! Ladies and Gentlemen! I hope that my involuntary absence will not cast a shadow over today's cermonies. I am expected, along with the other prize-winners, to make a short speech. I desire even less, however, that my words should cloud the festivities. Yet I cannot close my eyes to the remarkable fact that the day of the Nobel Prize presentation coincides with Human Rights Day. Nobel prize-winners cannot fail to feel a sense of responsibility in the face of this coincidence. No-one in the Stockholm City Hall can fail to see a symbol in it. Let us then at this richly laden table not forget the political prisoners who are on hunger strike today to assert their rights which have been belittled or completely trampled underfoot.

This brief speech was read out, but without the final sentence about the political prisoners on hunger strike. Evidently the organisers of the banquet felt that the image of starving men deprived of their rights was inappropriate, and would disturb the joyous solemnity of the sumptuous royal banquet.

23. Persecution of Friends and a New Wave of Criticism

ONE WOULD HAVE expected that after 10 December the storm of rage in the Soviet press over the Nobel award to Solzhenitsyn would begin to die down. The writer was currently engaged in work on a historical theme which official circles might view more calmly than they could his other writings. But it was by now too late to slow down the momentum of persecution. It seems likely that a special interdepartmental 'committee' had been set up to keep an eye on Solzhenitsyn's affairs. Its members had to have some work to do, and one thing they did was to attempt to create a vacuum around Solzhenitsyn by persecuting people who were friendly to him or took a favourable view of his writings. These officials wanted to deprive Solzhenitsyn of even limited public support. Their policy was implemented in various ways. A party member who had openly expressed his approval of Solzhenitsyn's works could expect speedy expulsion from the party, and without his 'personal file' being examined at a party meeting. Solzhenitsyn's close friend Lev Kopelev was expelled in this way. So, shortly afterwards, was the mother of Solzhenitsyn's second wife. The latter was herself dismissed from her job at a Moscow institute; this dismissal came almost immediately after the birth of her son, although the law forbids dismissal during maternity leave. Another victim of persecution was Mstislav Rostropovich who had made a flat available for Solzhenitsyn at his dacha. In November 1970 Rostropovich wrote an agitated letter to the Central Committee begging that the unjust treatment of Solzhenitsyn should cease, that he be given permission to receive the Nobel Prize, and that he should no longer be hounded in the press:

I am not talking about political or economic questions in our country [wrote Rostropovich]; there are people who understand these better than I. But will you please explain to me why in our literature and art people with no competence in

145

this field so often have the final word? Why are they given the right to discredit our art in the eyes of our people?

... Talents of which we are so proud must not be subjected to a battering in advance. I know many of the works of Solzhenitsyn, I love them, I consider that he has earned the right through his suffering to write the truth as he sees it, and I see no reason to hide my attitude towards him at a time when a campaign has been launched against him.

Rostropovich's letter spread rapidly in *samizdat* and was published abroad, whereupon the USSR Ministry of Culture cancelled a concert tour he was to have made in Finland and France. His concerts had already been announced in those countries but they never took place. Other tours Rostropovich was to have made abroad later were also cancelled.

These measures were announced directly by the Minister of Culture, Madame Furtseva, but action of this kind against Rostropovich could only stem from a decision made at a higher level. Eminent as he is Mstislav Rostropovich does not plan his tours abroad on his own initiative. They are arranged on the same principles as the tours of theatrical or ballet companies and the proceeds from the concerts, in whatever currency, go to the State. The artist does receive a certain percentage of the takings, but the main revenue goes into State reserves. Consequently the cancellation of a foreign tour by Rostropovich, who invariably plays to crowded halls, means a definite loss of foreign currency income. Furthermore, the cancellation of concerts already announced requires that compensation be paid. Since these payments are made in foreign currency, the operation is supervised not by the Ministry of Culture but by the Ministry of Finances. Any action that involves payments in foreign currency is carried out only with the knowledge and consent of the Currency Board in the Ministry of Finances, and they in turn will not consent to an action involving loss of foreign currency unless this has been approved from above, for instance by the USSR Council of Ministers, or an authority empowered to issue directives – such as the Central Committee.

The cancellation of Rostropovich's tour provoked widespread comment in the foreign press, underlining the senselessness of such action. Rostropovich's prestige is so great that his influence is felt in the musical life of all civilised countries. Audiences at the concerts of this genial musician feel not only delight and gratitude toward the performer, but also gratitude to the country that has reared and given to the world such a remarkable artist. When the Soviet government suddenly decided to discontinue his performances abroad, it was only the prestige of the government that suffered. Rostropovich profited by the cancellation of his foreign concert tours to undertake more intensive tours within the USSR. And everywhere he was received with redoubled warmth. He came unexpectedly to give a concert in Obninsk, where he was given an enthusiastic reception. My wife and I visited him afterwards in his dressing-room at the House of Culture where he was resting before leaving for Moscow in a mini-bus. He was deeply moved by the rapturous welcome he had received from the large audience – due entirely, of course, to his great artistry; but he was always acutely aware of his surroundings, and sensed that in some measure it was also a response to the stand he had taken in civic dispute. 'I can divide my musical activity into two periods now,' he said jokingly, '*before* my letter in defence of Solzhenitsyn, and after.' Shortly afterwards though, there were rumours that even Rostropovich's concert tours within the Soviet Union would be cut back.

Surveillance of all Solzhenitsyn's personal contacts increased sharply, especially of the people who were helping him to gather material for his work, and those who came to visit him and talk about the First World War. Although these people were in their seventies, even they were given no peace. Everything was done to make contact with Solzhenitsyn 'dangerous', to make fewer and fewer people inclined to come out in open support of the writer. At the same time press criticism of Solzhenitsyn became particularly crude. On 17 December 1970 *Pravda* printed a long article, 'The Poverty of Anti-Communism', by I. Alexandrov. 'I. Alexandrov' is a pseudonym which has appeared several times in recent years under *Pravda* articles based on directives from on high. For instance, 'I. Alexandrov' was the author of an article criticising the policies of the Czechoslovak leadership on the eve of the entry of the Warsaw Pact armies into the country. Alexandrov's latest article contained particularly scathing comments on Solzhenitsyn's work and activities

147

interspersed with the usual jumble of stereotyped threats and accusations:

... the imperialist gentlemen and their underlings do not scruple to resort to any means ... to the most impudent and cynical subversive actions, a tangled network of imperialist intelligence agents, venerable professors of misinformation and mercenary quill-drivers from the bourgeois press ... The activisation of anti-communist and in the first place anti-Soviet propaganda is obviously aimed at clouding and dulling the awareness of alarmed public opinion in the countries of the West, at trying to push it aside from the magnetic forces of progress and freedom ... Such are the aims of our ideological enemies. And what of their means? ... One of the American propaganda bosses once gave them away: 'in the ideological struggle with communism we need not truth but subversion – in a war like this we require all the cut throats and gangsters we can get, never mind how ...' As we see, the affairs of the adversaries of communism are in such a sorry state that to squeeze out any anti-Sovietism they have to resort to the services of criminal elements, an assortment of renegades, parasites, rascals and swindlers, and even people in whom only psychiatrists could take an interest ... Suffering a fiasco with rogues and schizophrenics of this kind, the heralds of anti-communism have decided to resort to provocation on a somewhat larger scale and to raise a hullabaloo around the name of A. Solzhenitsyn, with his tacit consent. Solzhenitsyn's lampoons on the Soviet people – *Feast of the Victors*, *The First Circle* and *Cancer Ward* – which blacken the feats and achievements of our homeland and the dignity of the Soviet people, have proved suitable material for the current anti-Soviet campaign being blown up in the West ... Spiritually an internal émigré, alien and hostile to the entire life of the Soviet people, Solzhenitsyn has been elevated to the office of a 'great' Russian writer by imperialist propaganda and was recently awarded the Nobel Prize. The Nobel Committee followed the lead of anti-socialist speculators who extolled Solzhenitsyn not for his talent but solely because he had been besmirching Soviet life ... Such is the pit of filth into which Solzhenitsyn has slid, expelled from the ranks of the Soviet Writers' Union and condemned by Soviet public opinion. . .

On 26 December a vituperative attack on Solzhenitsyn was published in the paper *Krasnaya Zveda* (*Red Star*), the organ of the Soviet Armed Forces: 'Solzhenitsyn is a renegade, the author of lampoons on the Soviet people . . .' and so on. In January 1971 the journal '*Kommunist Vooruzhyonykh Sil SSSR*' (*Communist of the USSR Armed Forces*) (No. 2) printed an article by Colonel V. Sapunov entitled 'Literature and Art – the Front-Line of the Ideological Struggle'. The article stated that Solzhenitsyn had been awarded the Nobel Prize as a 'mark of Cain for the betrayal of his people'. On 12 February 1971 *Pravda* published an attack on Solzhenitsyn by a Secretary of the Soviet Writers' Union, Georgii Markov.

Per Egil Hegge, who was still trying to ascertain through the Swedish Embassy the chances of Solzhenitsyn's receiving the Nobel Prize in Moscow, also became the target of special measures. Either from the articles he was then writing for Scandinavian papers, or because Swedish diplomats complained about his interference in Solzhenitsyn's affairs, Soviet officials found out a little about the role he was playing. The Soviet Ambassador in Norway lodged a verbal protest with the Norwegian Ministry of Internal Affairs against Hegge's 'anti-Soviet' publications. In Moscow Hegge was closely watched. His car was constantly trailed by an operational 'Volga', always with the same number plate, and Hegge could not get away from it. ('Operational' cars of this kind have extremely powerful engines and can reach higher speeds than ordinary Volgas. Also, operational cars can ignore traffic regulations, go through red lights, etc. A transistorised transmitter, so small as to be quite inconspicuous, is installed inside the car of the person who is being shadowed, and its signals enable the car to be easily traced if the driver succeeds in temporarily evading his pursuers).

After he had been continuously shadowed for several days Hegge published a statement in Western papers protesting at this interference with his work as an accredited correspondent. He even gave the number of the car that was trailing him. The statement was broadcast by foreign Russian language radio stations.

The publication of this statement was a mistake. After all, the shadowing of foreign correspondents is not new or illegal. A number of foreigners with diplomatic status in the USSR assume that they are being observed in one way or another. Soviet representatives in certain countries abroad may find themselves in the same situation. Per Hegge was favoured with a particularly crude kind of surveillance designed expressly to provoke a protest from him. It was a purely psychological tactic. Serious shadowing, in real life as well as in detective thrillers, aims to go unnoticed. Thus the signals of a transistorised radio transmitter concealed in the victim's car enable its position to be pinpointed anywhere in the city with the help of the listening devices available to police and security agencies in most of the world's capital cities. An operational car following its victim closely will not use the same number plate all the time. It always has a collection of different number plates in the boot.

I decided to warn Hegge not to make any further protests and to advise him not to enter into open conflict with the Soviet Ministry of Foreign Affairs which controls the work of foreign correspondents. I knew that Hegge was happy working in the Soviet Union and that he had no intention of asking his papers to give him another assignment. He apparently thought there were no legitimate grounds for the Soviet authorities to take extreme measures against him such as deportation, especially as accredited Soviet correspondents in Norway and Denmark might be expelled in retaliation. Under existing agreements a correspondent may not be deported from a country for the opinions he expresses in his articles or for being in touch with 'undesirable' citizens, but only for genuinely illegal activities such as collecting information about secret establishments, travelling to districts closed to foreigners, currency manipulations, etc. Per Hegge had a clean record; he had therefore decided to protest, hoping thereby to oblige the Soviet authorities to call off their exasperating surveillance. It was a naïve hope.

One day in February 1971 I had arranged to meet him to hear the outcome of the Swedish Academy's efforts to organise a proper ceremony of presentation of the Nobel Prize in Moscow. I was certain that Hegge would come to the rendezvous unaccompanied; it is not too difficult to evade surveillance, especially if one uses public transport – and in particular the underground – instead of one's own car. There are several simple ways of shaking off a 'tail' and the resourceful person can think up a dozen new ones based on his knowledge of the city. The Russian revolutionaries, from the members of 'Narodnaya Volya'[1] in the mid-nineteenth century down to the Bolsheviks, made it a strict rule to come to a rendezvous only without a 'tail'. If this was impossible there was no rendezvous. But there have been no illegal revolutionary organisations in Norway for centuries now and Norwegians are evidently unfamiliar with these traditions. They are also used to travelling in their own cars. Although it was no distance at all from the foreigners' 'ghetto' in Kutuzovsky Prospect where he lived to the café where we had arranged to meet, Hegge came by car. He arrived a little late in a state of great agitation. 'They've already thrown me out,' he said as soon as he'd sat down. 'Yesterday I was summoned to the Press Department at the Ministry of Foreign Affairs and ordered to leave the USSR by the end of the week. They follow me everywhere, that's why I'm late, but I still haven't shaken them off. You see that man sitting by the door there – he's from the car that was following me.'

I asked Hegge why he was being deported: the order must have been based on some real charges. Hegge said that he had been accused of two illegal acts, but that both charges were false. A Soviet journalist whom he knew had stated that Hegge had sold him a Swedish record-player at an inflated price (the charge was one of speculation or currency manipulation). This was a lie. The Soviet journalist had often visited Hegge's flat, and begged him to sell him his record-player. Hegge felt he could not refuse his friend and sold him the player, but strictly at the price he had paid for it, which was far less than the second-hand price of a similar player in the Soviet Union. The second allegation had been made by the elderly father of a Jew who for some reason had been arrested accusing Hegge of having a bad influence on his son. This too was a lie: obviously the man had been told that his son would be in trouble if he

[1] Narodnaya Volya, or 'People's Will', a revolutionary terrorist secret society responsible for the bomb attack which killed Tsar Alexander II in March 1881. (Translator's note.)

didn't play along. At that time, early in 1971, Soviet Jews who had applied to emigrate to Israel were being persecuted in various ways. As a result, they sought meetings with foreign correspondents on their own initiative, and almost every accredited correspondent in Moscow had had such meetings. Per Hegge was far less involved than other correspondents in the so-called 'Jewish question', since he represented Scandinavian papers that were comparatively little known. But even if plausible, the charges were too minor to justify deportation. Other correspondents involved in similar activities, such as the sale of second-hand cars, were given a 'warning'. Even protests in the Soviet press by groups of Soviet citizens against foreign journalists, articles on the 'Jewish question' accompanied by demands for their expulsion from the Soviet Union, have never really led to anything. It was clear to both Hegge and myself that the sanction had been imposed because of his intervention in the matter of the Nobel Prize. I asked Hegge not to insist that the Norwegian Ministry of Internal Affairs take reciprocal action and not to demand the deportation of any Soviet correspondent from Norway, so as to avoid providing further provocations for Solzhenitsyn's adversaries. Hegge promised to pass this advice on to his papers; but he said that in the autumn he would certainly publish a long article or a book describing in detail his part in the attempt to organise a Nobel Prize presentation, and the attitude taken by Swedish diplomats to the affair. 'The Swedish diplomats', he said, 'have asked me not to write anything about all this, but I promised them only that I would not divulge the information until I came to write my memoirs. It's customary for a journalist who has been expelled from a country to publish his memoirs; the Soviet Ministry of Internal Affairs has done the Swedish Embassy a very bad turn.' A few months later I realised the truth of these words. The questions raised in Per Hegge's book which came out in the autumn of 1971 provoked a stormy debate in the Swedish parliament and the Swedish Prime Minister, Olof Palme's, explanations satisfied no one.

Hegge was about to take his leave of me, perhaps for ever; a correspondent who has been thrown out of the Soviet Union can never hope to obtain even a tourist visa. But my mind was on other things. In a moment Per Hegge would drive away while I might well be detained and questioned as to my identity. Since Hegge had been charged with certain offences, there were legal grounds for interrogating his contacts, especially those of the last few days. I had absolutely no desire to be a detainee. I explained this to Per Hegge and we decided that I would go with him and jump out of his car somewhere along the way, after which he would try to shake off the Volga trailing us. We drove through the city centre towards Gorky street, then turned off into one of the boulevards and then into the darkness of narrow side-streets. Hegge drove beautifully, dodging in and out of side-streets. The KGB car was still on our tail. But it had to brake at a cross roads where there was no traffic light in order to avoid colliding with a lorry which had passed us in the other direction. Hegge at once turned into another side-road and then we came out on to the Sadovoye Ring. There was no-one behind us. We were passing Mayakovskaya underground station. I said goodbye to Hegge, leapt out of the car and joined the crowd going into the station. After a few stops it was clear that I was not being followed.

24. A New Novel – *August 1914*

AMID ALL THE complex and stormy events of 1968–70, Solzhenitsyn yet managed to abstract himself from life's unpleasantnesses to write a new, large-scale novel which was to be the beginning of a sweeping, epic narrative that its author had dreamed of in his youth and which still remained his ultimate literary ambition. Solzhenitsyn had completed the second stage of revising the novel in the autumn of 1970, before the award of the Nobel Prize. He had also taken special steps to ensure that the novel did not become the property of *samizdat* or the plunder of pirate publishers abroad.

He then sent special letters to seven Soviet literary journals and publishing houses informing them that he had completed a novel, *August 1914*. At that time he only had one copy of the typescript and a few carbon copies. Publishers always ask the author for a top copy and carbon, and Solzhenitsyn was prepared to send the two copies immediately to any publishing house or journal which agreed simply to take a preliminary look at the novel without necessarily promising publication. But none of them replied. I heard that the Leningrad journal *Zvezda* (*Star*) had wanted to reply to Solzhenitsyn's letter merely to have the opportunity of reading his new novel, but in the end the Editor-in-Chief could not even get permission to correspond with Solzhenitsyn.

Solzhenitsyn now had three choices. First, he could put the novel away and hope for better times. Second, he could hand typescripts around for unrestricted reading, and they would be picked up by *samizdat* with the further risk of a copy finding its way abroad and being published in *Grani*, *Possev* or somewhere else. Third, he could sign a standard contract with some solid publishing house through his lawyer, thereby safeguarding his copyright and ensuring that translations into other languages would be executed by reputable translators who would strive to convey the original text adequately rather than to produce a rush edition.

154

The first choice was unacceptable: a writer needs readers; moreover, the better times might not come within the lifetime of this generation. The second choice too was not suitable to a work such as *August 1914*. It would be wrong to allow it to fall into the hands of hasty, irresponsible translators. A Russian language edition published abroad by some independent publisher might circulate to a certain extent in the Soviet Union, whereas an edition published by *Grani* or *Possev* could prove dangerous to any Soviet citizen who managed to obtain it; he would certainly not place it on his bookshelves for all to see. There remained the third possibility, which Solzhenitsyn finally opted for.

Dr Fritz Heeb signed a contract for world rights with a West German publisher, Luchterhand Verlag, and, for the Russian edition abroad, with a small independent publisher in Paris, the YMCA Press. Rights for an English edition were offered to the Bodley Head. No translations were to appear before 1972. The Russian version published by the YMCA Press came out in an edition of 20,000 copies in June 1971. It was sold out very quickly, and by the end of 1971 a second edition was ready.

There are about six or seven million Russians living outside the Soviet Union. Apart from that, copies of the book were sometimes brought into Russia by tourists or Soviet citizens returning from business trips abroad. Solzhenitsyn had given me a typescript copy in June after the news that the Russian edition had come out in France. At the beginning of July I got hold of the YMCA version also. From the end of July *August 1914* began to circulate in *samizdat* too, but the fact that the author owned the copyright of the Russian edition and any translations acted as a bar to any pirate editions abroad.

Solzhenitsyn saw another advantage in publishing *August 1914* abroad. The book was only the beginning of a series of novels about the First World War. The gathering of material relating to Russia at that time was presenting considerable difficulties. There were many people in the Russian emigration of 1917–22 whose papers and memories might prove extremely valuable to Solzhenitsyn. By publishing the first book abroad, he hoped to attract this material; the Postscript contains a request for material to be sent to the publishers and indicates geographical areas to be used in subsequent projected volumes.

Reading *August 1914* made a very deep impression on me, but one that could not be compared to the special, emotionally exhilarating effects of Solzhenitsyn's earlier works. They had been devoted to events which still call up a vivid and direct response in the minds of readers in middle life and older; events that revive smouldering memories, stimulate a complex mixture of feelings and emotional experiences, resurrecting for some people the events of their own life, and forcing others to remember the fate of their fathers, brothers, sisters, husbands, wives and friends. Such is the history of our country that I do not know anybody who would not identify the fate of Solzhenitsyn's heroes with the fate of his nearest and dearest. Many people read his books several times over trying to comprehend the significance of the events and mentally experiencing them so acutely that they have failed to notice, or ignored, the subtlety of style, the linguistic innovations and the vivid imagery. Everything was swallowed up in the awareness of an important truth told, and it is left to the critics to explain to us afterwards in specialised articles what, in the intensity of our emotional perception, we had overlooked.

August 1914 could arouse vivid memories only in the minds of people now in their late seventies. Younger people could read the novel more slowly and with greater equanimity, as a historical work. And the novel's sweeping range, calm and minutely detailed flow, multitude of characters, artistic expressiveness, novelty of style, and wealth of literary allusions, meant that it could be appreciated first and foremost as a work of art by a writer of unquestionable stature.

Since I am neither a literary scholar nor a critic, even in the amateur sense, a specialised critique of a work of the nature of *August 1914* is beyond my powers. I can speak only on the basis of personal impressions, and my own judgement would carry no weight with the professional critics; but I have discussed the novel with friends far more competent to appreciate the problems of literary art than myself, and have made notes of some of their opinions. I quote them here, incompletely, but objectively; I would not want to conceal the fact that some are critical.

A. You experience a joyful awareness of contact with real

Russian history. We've forgotten what literature is like – we're fed on substitutes ... The richness of language, the philologists will be studying it for decades, that new possibilities it reveals in the Russian language, and how much that had been forgotten is revived again ... When other writers write it's like bricklaying, they assemble it bit by bit. But Solzhenitsyn moulds his phrases and images in red-hot plastic material; when he's shaped a phrase or an expression you feel it's absolutely right ...

B. A wonderfully conscientious study of the military strategy behind the battles in East Prussia ... But there are too many characters, especially generals, it's difficult to keep track of them all ... He writes with an unexpected warmth about the Germans and East Prussia ... His picture of the social-democrat defeatist is too negative ... On the other hand Vorotyntsev has too many positive qualities ... Samsonov is the most successful portrayal ... The descriptive passages make you see and feel everything – nature, surroundings, people – in three dimensions ...

C. I read a hundred pages and got bogged down – you're always coming up against quite unnecessary new words and anachronisms. Little symbols you're supposed to pay attention to and which you forget about straightaway ... For some reason there are 'film-scenario' passages, 'wide-screen' – why this hybrid of prose and film-scripts? ... He overdoes his striving to draw attention to the form – the reader ought to be engrossed by the action, the content of the novel ...

D. It was like a visit to the Russian Museum ... I must go through it again and have a closer look at everything ...

E. The best thing about the novel is the language – extraordinarily vivid, condensed, full of surprises, new word-formations, which enrich our literature and go to make up Solzhenitsyn's unique style. Some of the new words make you stop and think about them. Of course, there are some unsuccessful ones, but only a few. Whatever else you may say about the novel, Solzhenitsyn takes the Russian language further forward than any other writer has managed to do this century. It was certainly no accident that he was awarded the Nobel Prize . . . The novel requires not only reviews and commentaries but study in depth, in all its aspects; it has the hallmark of a tremendously powerful literary talent . . .

F. Solzhenitsyn's novel gives a cross-section of Russian society in 1914. He depicts the peasants, the soldiers, the intelligentsia, with love. The Russian officers are portrayed as positive figures, even the entrepreneurs, Tomchak, for instance. But there are no workers in the novel. No one from the working class. The revolutionaries are portrayed negatively. There is a strong note of indignation in the way most of the generals are depicted, and especially the members of the Tsar's family and the government leaders – undistinguished, stupid nonentities . . .

G. Lenartovich in the novel is a social-democrat and defeatist. But in that war it was only the Bolsheviks who were defeatists. Lenartovich is the only coward among the officers. But the Bolshevik slogan of defeatism didn't mean cowardice at the front-line. The front-line Bolsheviks had different instructions; they were supposed to gain the sympathy of the soldiers by their courage and battle-skill in order to bring about a transformation of the war from an imperialist war to a civil war. Lenin's general thesis of defeat was one thing, but the specific situation at the front was quite another. In the conversation between Lenartovich and the doctor, the social-democrat is utterly unsympathetic towards the soldiers' sufferings. But a real social-democrat cannot have such a callous attitude to the fate of ordinary people.

H. There are evidently several mouthpieces for the author's ideas and thoughts in the book . . . You can tell this from the sympathetic way they're drawn. But they have no worthy opponents in the dialogues, they argue either with children or with fools . . . If only he'd pitted them against veterans of the revolutionary movement, real theoreticians or polemicists, brilliant people like Plekhanov, Martov, Krasin or Lunacharsky. The dialogue would have been more interesting then

... In the beginning the revolutionaries influenced the masses by words, by the art of oratory. Terror only came into use much later ...

I. The military scenes are splendidly and grandly done, with absolute confidence that what is being depicted corresponds exactly to the events as they really happened. It would be difficult to hope for a better description of a strategical and tactical situation, even from a professor of military science...

J. Solzhenitsyn may disapprove of the destructive tendencies of revolution. He sees society's strength as the preservation of traditions, of continuity, of the cultural heritage of the past. But like a great artist he has shown the inevitability of the revolution in Russia and the total destruction of the monarchy and the entire social élite ... He has shown the vast potential of the people, ignorant, illiterate, oppressed and religious though they be. The social stratum with which the author apparently sympathises, the engineers, the literate officers, the teachers, even the entrepreneurs profiting by the achievements of technology, this stratum is too thin, weak and unorganised. These people, the repositories of culture and economic development, will obviously be unable to restrain the people and the soldiers when they unite in anger against a monarchy rotten to the core ...

K. For years Russian history has been falsified and tendentiously altered, by writers as well as historians. And although Solzhenitsyn has written a novel about the distant past he'll be criticised if only because he was determined to depict history truthfully and realistically. There are so many brutal and merciless acts of violence in the past that we've been told to forget ...

L. The comparison with Tolstoy's *War and Peace* inevitably arises. As epics, bearing in mind what Solzhenitsyn intends to write as a continuation of *August 1914*, we shall be able to place them side by side as two distinct, but equal works ... always remembering, of course, the difference between the epochs in which the authors wrote ... Tolstoy was, I think, more subjective in his manner of depicting events, less concerned with historical authenticity. His portrayal of Kutuzov, and particularly of Napoleon, bears absolutely no resemblance to the historical character ... And one mustn't forget, either, that Tolstoy worked on his own spacious estate or in his Moscow mansion, whereas Solzhenitsyn has been hiding in other people's flats to write and barred from archives ...

I could go on to quote many more opinions.

August 1914 was unconditionally acknowledged as an outstanding work and an indication that the author's talent was reaching to still greater heights. By a strange irony of fate it was on 14 August, but in 1971, while holidaying on the Baltic quite near the area which was once East Prussia and is described in the novel, that I heard a foreign radio station report that Solzhenitsyn had protested violently at a raid on his summer cottage. It had been carried out by a squad of policemen, or perhaps representatives of some other authority; they had beaten up a friend of Solzhenitsyn's, Gorlov, who had gone to the cottage in Solzhenitsyn's absence. Solzhenitsyn had sent his protest to Andropov, the Chairman of the KGB.

25. The Death of Alexander Tvardovsky

IN THE AUTUMN of 1970 the doctors had given up Tvardovsky's case as hopeless; but he hung on for over a year. In the spring and summer of 1971 Solzhenitsyn paid him several visits and left him the text of *August 1914* to read. In November his condition deteriorated and he was readmitted to the Kremlin Hospital. He died on the night of 18 December. The news was broadcast first by foreign, then by Soviet radio stations, and although it was hardly unexpected, his friends experienced an acute sense of loss. Tvardovsky's death marked the end of an era. He had been sincerely and passionately loved by all who shared his ideas, respected by those who took a different stand in literature, and even appreciated by his adversaries. Tvardovsky was a remarkable poet, but that was not his only virtue. He was an uncompromising defender of true literature who supported and promoted many new talents; Solzhenitsyn was his brightest, but by no means his only star. He was profoundly convinced that true communism could be combined with freedom of thought, and with a diversity of opinions, and that the literary trends which both the people and the party needed could only develop by means of competition, and the interchange of ideas, and with the help of genuine criticism and discussion, not under the pressure of a secret, faceless censorship.

'What we need is not the kind of freedom of the press you see in the West,' he once said to me, 'but simply the freedom of creativity we had in our own country in the twenties.' Tvardovsky had a rare, almost unique awareness of his responsibility, not only to the living – to those around him, *to the people*, as the idea is commonly expressed, as opposed to the egoism of the individual or of the group or party – but responsibility also to the dead, to those who perished, who died a martyr's death for ideals still unrealised. This acute awareness is most powerfully expressed in his last poem, *By Right of*

161

Memory (*Po pravu pamyati*), in the introduction with which the author begins his confession:

> Compounding the lessons of age,
> Involuntarily the idea comes
> Of appealing to all who travelled the road with me,
> The living and the dead alike.
> It comes not for the first time,
> To give the word a double force:
>
> Where the living perhaps keep silence,
> The dead will break it: 'Surely
> In the light of what has been in the past,
> You have no right to act against your conscience,
> For we have paid for this past
> The greatest price of all.'
>
> And I – I'm getting on in years,
> I have no right to grant myself
> Deferment.
>   A weight off my mind—
>
> If I lost no time, if I had the time
> To put my mute anguish into words.

But Tvardovsky did not live to complete his task. He had hardly embarked upon the new stage of his career as a poet which this banned poem represented, when he was overtaken by illness and death.

The obituary that appeared in the papers was signed by all the members of the Politburo, the members of the Board of the Writers' Union, and leaders of other artistic unions. It gave Tvardovsky his due as poet, public figure, and Editor-in-Chief of *Novy Mir*. Other articles written in the memory of the poet, even those published in *Literaturnaya Gazeta* and *Literaturnaya Rossiya*, said nothing about his public activities and did not mention his work as Editor of *Novy Mir*. Even Chingiz Aitmatov, a talented writer who was greatly indebted to Tvardovsky, having worked with him for several years on the editorial board of *Novy Mir*, wrote only about Tvardovsky the poet in his article 'I Bow My Head'. This could not have happened by chance. The censor had no means of altering the official obituary, but he could place restrictions upon the display of feelings by particular writers. No one mentioned the poem *Tyorkin in Paradise* either, although it was much discussed in private. And none of the notices in any of the papers gave any indication of where or when the funeral, leavetaking and burial would take place.[1] It had evidently been decided to avoid attracting too big a crowd.

I found out from friends that the funeral and leavetaking would be held at the Central House of Writers on Herzen Street. I was told that the funeral ceremony would begin at midday on 21 December but that it would be best to come earlier because by midday there would be no seats left in the hall. At eleven o'clock my wife and I arrived at the House of Writers. The public were being allowed to pay their last respects to Tvardovsky, but only members of the Soviet Writers' Union were to be admitted to the funeral and leavetaking. The cloakroom at the House of Writers was only serving people who produced their cards, and vigilantes in attendance at the end of each row of seats in the hall ordered people in their outdoor clothes to leave. For the rest, we were only allowed to file past the coffin in a general stream. It was the right way to organise it, of course, for there were many thousand people and the hall where the meeting was to take place could only seat six hundred. As we filed past the flower-strewn coffin for the second time, we came across some friends who helped us to divest ourselves of our coats. Among the first people to arrive had been the members of the old *Novy Mir* editorial board and former editorial assistants. They stood in a huddle near the exit and the stream of people paying their respects to Tvardovsky filed past them also.

Solzhenitsyn too had come to the House of Writers long

---

[1] In the U.S.S.R., as elsewhere, the funerals of ordinary people have a private character, but important people are given state funerals. The organisation where the deceased worked forms a 'funeral committee' which organises everything and pays the expenses. Some prominent people are buried near the Kremlin Wall, others in the Novodevichy Monastery on the banks of the Moscow River. The Novodevichy Monastery is now a state museum of art and architecture.

before most other people, when the hall was still almost empty. Friends escorted him to a room where he left his sheepskin coat. Once he reached the hall, Tvardovsky's wife and daughter invited him to sit next to them in the front row.

For two hours people filed past the coffin to the sound of funeral music. Then the hall doors were closed and the meeting began. It was opened by S. S. Narovchatov, a Secretary of the Moscow branch of the Writers' Union. Of all the speakers at the brief gathering, not one had been a really close friend of Tvardovsky's. All the speeches had been prepared in advance and had passed through the filter of censorship, so that there should be no mention of the last ten years of the poet's life, of his journal, his polemical writing, his civic courage, and of *Tyorkin in Paradise*. The orators acknowledged only Tvardovsky the poet and even then only as the author of a restricted list of works. When Narovchatov declared the funeral assembly over, and requested everyone except the dead man's family and close friends to leave the hall, a young woman in the middle of the hall suddenly rose to her feet.

'Why are you closing the meeting so soon?' she cried, so that everyone could hear her. 'Is it possible that no-one is going to say that we are burying our civic conscience here? That Tvardovsky was forcibly removed from his work, that he was compelled to leave *Novy Mir*, that his last poem was not published? That they shut his mouth before he shut it of his own accord?' This short speech was followed by the noisy shouting of vigilantes trying to drown whatever the woman might say next. But she was already pushing her way towards the exit, a scarf thrown over her head. Soon she was lost in the crowd filing out of the hall. Nobody stopped her. Evidently she got away from the House of Writers without being detained – and none of Tvardovsky's friends ever managed to discover her name.

The hall emptied, and Solzhenitsyn and Tvardovsky's family were left alone with the coffin. They, and a handful of relatives of the dead man, set out on the journey to the cemetery at Novodevichy Monastery.[2] Buses had been laid on for members of the Writers' Union who wished to go to the cemetery. There was a heavy frost and I persuaded my wife, who had a cold, to

[2] See below, page 163, footnote.

go back home, while I boarded a trolley-bus which went near Novodevichy cemetery. As the bus approached the stop a number of the people got up from their seats. Obviously they too were going to the poet's burial. But the bus drove straight past the stop without slowing down. The passengers began shouting loudly for the bus to stop, but the driver said through his loudspeaker: 'Don't worry comrades. The cemetery stop is temporarily out of use today, there's some burial or other.' 'But that's just where we're going,' the passengers shouted indignantly, 'at least you can stop the bus somewhere near the monastery.' But the bus proceeded without stopping and the doors were not opened until we had reached the Luzhniki stadium. From here it was about fifteen minutes walk back to the cemetery. But when we got there we found all the approaches to the monastery and the cemetery cordoned off with portable barriers, and large squads of policemen in attendance. On the other side of the street the entrance to the cemetery from the underground station was barred by a row of soldiers, a whole company at least, I should think. I tried to approach one of the barriers where there was a narrow way through, guarded by a squad of police. I was immediately stopped and asked to produce my Writers' Union card. I showed the policeman my passport. 'We're not interested in that,' retorted a police lieutenant, 'we've been instructed only to let through people with Writers' or Journalists' Union cards.' I answered indignantly, 'What nonsense is this? The funeral of a poet ought to be public. Tvardovsky is my friend; and I have known him for almost ten years.' My protests were to no avail. By now I had become angry, and I walked straight past the lieutenant towards the cemetery gate, ignoring the shouts from behind me ordering me back. Some men rushed up to me, grabbed my arms and escorted me back to the other side of the barrier uttering threats. By now there was a crowd of about fifty behind the barrier; they had all come for the funeral. There were young people shouting that they were from the philological faculty of the University and that Tvardovsky was a 'national poet'.

An elderly gentleman was pleading with the lieutenant to let him go through, assuring him that he had known Tvardovsky ever since the Second World War. 'This is outrageous! Even worse than Pushkin's funeral!' somebody shouted. 'You were there, then, were you?' a policeman replied coolly.

Convinced that I would never get through here, I crossed to the opposite side of the street and stood some way away from the cordon of soldiers. Only organised groups arriving in buses were being allowed through the gates of the cemetery. Suddenly I saw a group of about thirty schoolchildren with their teacher walking up to the gate. Tvardovsky's poetry is studied in Soviet literature courses in senior forms, and so the funeral organisers had seen to it that a class of schoolchildren came to the cemetery. I quickly ran across the street and mingled with the group of teenagers. The police guarding the entrance did not stop me. When I got to the graveside, the brief ceremony of leavetaking was already over and the coffin was being nailed up. About two hundred or two hundred and fifty people stood around the freshly-dug grave. It was impossible to get near the graveside and throw on a handful of earth as is the Russian custom. A man I did not know, carrying earth in a plastic bag, was trying to persuade the people in front of him to let him through to the grave. The crowd made way for him. I asked him what he was carrying. 'It's Tvardovsky's native soil, earth from Smolensk, from the hill over the communal grave of the men who fell in the liberation of Smolensk. They call it the "hill of heroes".' And he went on pushing his way forward to sprinkle this native soil over the coffin.

In Russia it is traditional to hold a wake after the burial and on the ninth day after the death. On the fortieth day after the death, relatives and close friends visit the graveside and pay their respects to the memory of the deceased. For the ninth day Solzhenitsyn composed a prose elegy which circulated rapidly in typescript and was published in many newspapers and journals abroad.

There are many ways of killing a poet.[3] The method chosen for Tvardovsky was to take away his offspring, his passion, his journal.

The sixteen years of insults meekly endured by this hero were as nothing so long as his journal survived, so long as literature was not stopped, so long as people could be

[3] Translated by Michael Scammell in *The Observer*, 9 January 1972.

166

printed in it, so long as people could go on reading it. But then they heaped the coals of disbandment, destruction and mortification upon him, and within six months these coals had consumed him. Within six months he took to his deathbed, and only his characteristic fortitude sustained him till now, to the last drop of consciousness, of suffering.

For the third day now the portrait hangs over the coffin – there the dead man is still only forty, his brow unfurrowed by the sweetly bitter burdens of his journal, radiant with that childishly luminescent trust that he managed to carry with him throughout his mortal life and that returned to him even when already doomed.

To the best of all music they bear the wreaths, bear the wreaths ... 'From Soviet soldiers'.... And with reason. I remember how the lads at the front to one man preferred the marvel of his trusty 'Tyorkin' to all other wartime books. But let us remember too how army libraries were forbidden to subscribe to *Novy Mir*, and how not so long ago its readers were hauled before the CO for questioning.

And now the whole body from the Writers' Secretariat has flopped on to the scene. The guard of honour comprises that same flabby crowd that hunted him down with unholy shrieks and cries. It's an old, old custom of ours; it started with Pushkin. It is precisely into the hands of his enemies that the dead poet falls. And they hastily dispose of the body, covering up with breezy speeches.

They crowd round the coffin in a solid ring and they think they have fenced it off. Just as they destroyed our only journal and they think they have won.

But you need to be deaf and blind to the last century of Russia's history to regard this as a victory and not an irreparable blunder.

[Blinkered fools!] When the voices of the young resound, keen-edged, how you will miss this patient critic, whose gentle, admonitory voice was heeded by all. Then you will be set to tear the earth with your hands for the sake of returning Trifonich.[4] But then it will be too late.

[4] Trifonich is an affectionate form of Tvardovsky's patronymic.

On the fortieth day after Tvardovsky's death I happened to be in Moscow and decided to visit the poet's grave. I bought a bunch of flowers outside the monastery and went to the farthest corner of the cemetery where Alexander Tvardovsky lay buried. Near his grave there was another one also freshly dug and still awaiting a tombstone – Nikita Sergeyevich Khrushchev's. Khrushchev's ex-assistant V. S. Lebedev, who had once read *One Day in the Life of Ivan Denisovich* to him, was also buried somewhere here. He had died at a relatively early age, not long after Khrushchev's retirement. Tvardovsky's grave was a mound of faded wreaths heaped as high as two men. Beside his portrait lay fresh flowers shrivelled by the frost: The poet's family had evidently been there in the morning. I stood by the graveside for about ten minutes going over the unforgettable and all too infrequent conversations, and then turned to leave. I saw figures approaching whom I recognised as members of the staff of *Novy Mir*, or rather, of the old *Novy Mir*. There were three of them. They came up, placed flowers on the grave and greeted me in silence. A few moments later several more people arrived, all of them former *Novy Mir* staff. Then five or six other people appeared bearing flowers and talking in undertones. I did not know them. As we left the cemetery we introduced ourselves – they were well-known authors who had written for *Novy Mir*, some of the wonderful writers Tvardovsky had attracted to the journal. One of the ex-members of staff, the oldest among them, invited us to a funeral wake in memory of Tvardovsky and his journal. And so fifteen of us found ourselves at an impromptu table in a small room. I was the only one who had no connection with belles-lettres, so I shall not attempt to describe what was said at that table in memory of Tvardovsky. I leave it to someone better able than I to do so.

Once, in the quite recent past, Tvardovsky had brought all these talented people into the orbit of a journal which was the pride of Russian literature. Now that journal was controlled by Kosolapov and Taurin, and Tvardovsky's glorious galaxy of friends were scattered about various editorial offices and institutions. Two of our gathering had been pensioned off. As our melancholy conversation drew to a close, one very well-loved writer rose to his feet, to add: 'And how profoundly Alexander Trifonovich foresaw everything . . . Do you remember that meeting of the editorial board when it was clear already that the storm-clouds were gathering, and he said: "They want to put out our fire. But it's too bright to be blown out or quenched with water. If they're going to put it out they'll certainly have to scatter all the smouldering, red-hot pieces to the four winds. Then it will be extinguished."'

26. *Literaturnaya Gazeta* Launches an 'International' Campaign

THE PUBLICATION OF *August 1914* soon after the award of the Nobel Prize greatly enhanced Solzhenitsyn's literary standing. This was why the decision was taken somewhere 'at the top' to intensify criticism and 'expose' his new work by fair means or foul. Furthermore, speakers at various propagandist meetings and private lectures began to accuse Solzhenitsyn of immoral behaviour, giving a distorted account of the break with his first wife Natalia Reshetovskaya. (Solzhenitsyn had come up against what were clearly deliberate obstructions in his divorce proceedings. Again as a result of directives from above, every possible obstacle was put in the way of his new marriage despite the fact that a genuine family had been established and a son had been born. Evidently the intention was to prevent Solzhenitsyn from moving to Moscow, which was where his second wife, Natalia D. Svetlova, lived.) At these meetings extracts from *Feast of the Victors* were read all over again. At the end of 1971 the KGB carried out a series of searches at the homes of intellectuals in Moscow, Leningrad and Kiev. At these searches all *samizdat* copies of works by Solzhenitsyn were confiscated along with other material. When my old friend S. Myuge was searched, two copies of *August 1914* were seized. In October 1971 a search was made without any legal justification at my brother's flat. His personal papers and a number of typescripts were confiscated, among them a copy of Solzhenitsyn's play *The Love-Girl and the Innocent* (*Olen i Shalashovka*). This play had been in rehearsal at a Moscow theatre in 1962 but was never actually produced. The confiscation of works by Solzhenitsyn at these searches was no accident. It indicated that the KGB, or the Public Prosecutor's Office, were seeking an opportunity to implicate the writer in some 'political' case. In January 1972 the prosecutor at the trial of Vladimir Bukovsky declared that Solzhenitsyn was 'an inspirer' of anti-Soviet activity.

In November 1971 it transpired that the West German magazine *Stern* had published a long article on *August 1914* together with an account of Solzhenitsyn's family background and the circumstances of his father and mother, his aunt, his forefathers and so on.[1] The information about Solzhenitsyn's family had supposedly been obtained by a correspondent of *Stern* when he talked with the writer's aged aunt whom he had met during a visit to Georgievsk, a town in the Northern Caucasus. Solzhenitsyn was very much annoyed by this article and when I met him on New Year's Eve he said he was quite sure it had been published in West Germany solely so that *Literaturnaya Gazeta* might reprint it as an example of Western press comment and be able to blame the German magazine for the distortions and fabrications. Moreover when an article was reprinted from a foreign publication one could include the sort of details that Soviet journalists do not normally publish in their own articles.

Solzhenitsyn's forebodings were justified. On 12 January 1972 page 13 of *Literaturnaya Gazeta* carried a big article with a banner headline which read:

STERN MAGAZINE ON SOLZHENITSYN'S FAMILY

'They were a family of boors,' says Irina, aunt of the Nobel Prize-winner Solzhenitsyn, of his family, who were once the wealthiest of landowners . . .

So begins the 'translation' of the *Stern* article. (I put the word translation in inverted commas because the German original begins quite differently, with the words of one of the characters from *August 1914* who is angered by the stupidity of autocracy: 'Russia has to be governed by fools,' he exclaimed, 'Russia cannot do otherwise.' *Stern's* few favourable comments on *August 1914* – which had by then already appeared in a German translation – were 'abridged' in the Russian version of the article.[2]

According to the *Stern* article and the comments in *Literaturnaya Gazeta*, the Moscow correspondent of *Stern*, Dieter

---

[1] *Stern*, 21 November 1971.

[2] I am referring here to the German translation of the novel made by Alexander Kempfe and published by Langen-Müller without the author's permission. The publishing house Luchterhand Verlag, who owned the official translation rights of the novel, later succeeded in obtaining an injunction against the sale of the pirated version.

Steiner, had discovered the wife of Solzhenitsyn's mother's brother, Irina Ivanova Shcherbak, living in Georgievsk. She was 82 years old and half-blind. Steiner had visited her and she had given him an interview. She also gave him the manuscript of her 'memoirs' about the Solzhenitsyn family and photographs of relatives, on the basis of which Dieter Steiner had constructed a long article in which he identified some of the characters in *August 1914* with relatives of Solzhenitsyn. The main point of the article was to show that Solzhenitsyn's grandfather on his mother's side had been a rich landowner in the Rostov region. But even this was not enough for *Literaturnaya Gazeta*. The paper supplemented the *Stern* article with an account of how a special correspondent of its own had been sent to the Northern Caucasus to gather information about Solzhenitsyn's family on his father's side. This correspondent 'brought to light' the fact that Solzhenitsyn's grandfather, Semyon Efimovich Solzhenitsyn, had lived in the village of Sablya and had also been a very wealthy man. He had a large flock of sheep, owned two farm estates and had a bank account . . . etc. *Literaturnaya Gazeta* even printed a photograph purporting to show the two-storey house in which Solzhenitsyn's grandfather had lived. The insinuation was that the reason why Solzhenitsyn was dissatisfied with the existing order was that it had deprived his forefathers of their family possessions.

There were many distortions, inaccuracies and fabrications in *Literaturnaya Gazeta*'s comments, but responsibility for these could always be laid at the door of the German correspondent. And Steiner himself could put blame for everything on old Irina Shcherbak who at the age of 82 might well have got it all muddled up. And anyway, compared to her diminutive room and her state pension of ten roubles a month (though the reference to this was cut by *Literaturnaya Gazeta*), she would doubtless think back to whatever she had had in the old days as fabulous riches. There was, though, one question which begged for an answer: how had Steiner, a foreigner, discovered the existence of Irina Shcherbak and her whereabouts? Who had given him permission to visit Georgievsk which, like all small provincial towns, is closed to foreign correspondents? And who accompanied him on his trip?

The reputation of *Stern* magazine which is published in

Hamburg is not at all good, and there are facts which suggest that the magazine has special links with semi-official information sources in the USSR. It was *Stern* which first published the 'Memoirs' of Stalin's daughter Svetlana Alliluyeva, conveyed abroad in 1967 by Victor Louis.

The article about Solzhenitsyn's ancestors, as it was reprinted in *Literaturnaya Gazeta*, became the subject of much amusement in Moscow's literary circles; for the ancestors of several leading members of the Writers' Union Secretariat had not been proletarians either. This was especially true of Solzhenitsyn's chief adversaries, A. Chakovsky, the Editor of *Literaturnaya Gazeta*, A. Sofronov, Editor of *Ogonyok* magazine, and Sergei Mikhalkov, Chairman of the RSFSR Writers' Union. One extremely elderly member of the Writers' Union revealed that among the grandfathers of these writers had figured a gendarme, the proprietor of a flour-mill, and a landowner. This latter had once owned the village of Mikhalkovo, which was named after him and still bears his name. Furthermore, the famous house that belonged to Lenin's family in Ulyanovsk, was considerably larger than Solzhenitsyn's grandfather's house in Sablya, while Lenin's mother, M. A. Blank, was a blood relation of the exceedingly wealthy Blank family.

However, while the article in *Literaturnaya Gazeta* gave rise to much discussion, it provoked no open protests either in the USSR or abroad. This allowed the paper to pursue its aim of acquainting the Soviet public with foreign press comment on Solzhenitsyn's new novel. On 23 February 1972, again on page 13, *Literaturnaya Gazeta* reprinted two articles about *August 1914* from the foreign press. The paper added an editorial introduction which read as follows:

The appearance of A. Solzhenitsyn's novel *August 1914* in the West, after the author himself had sent abroad the manuscript, served as the starting-signal for a clamorous anti-Soviet campaign. The bourgeois press continues to extol this new work of Solzhenitsyn's.

What has provoked this sensational stir of publicity? What does *August 1914* in reality represent? The answers to these questions can be found in the two articles we reprinted here in slightly abridged form, one by the eminent Finnish writer Martti Larni first published in the Swedish paper *Norrskens Flamman*, and one by literary critic Marina Stutz which appeared in the West German *Deutsche Volkszeitung*.

The article by Larni was entitled 'When History Is Put In The Corner', and the piece by Marina Stutz had an equally pointed title 'In A Distorting Mirror'. Both authors, however, displayed remarkable ignorance of the history of Russia and an even more deplorable ignorance of the novel they were reviewing.

I have already mentioned *Norrskens Flamman* previously and its outburst on the occasion of the Nobel Prize award to Solzhenitsyn; it is a small communist paper published in the Swedish town of Luleå by a conservative faction in the Swedish communist party. *Deutsche Volkszeitung* is the organ of the German communists, but since their party is banned in West Germany it is unlikely that the paper is printed in that country.

Martti Larni's article was particularly thin; he talked of the novel in such general terms that one had the impression that he had not even read it but was judging it from somebody else who had. But where both articles fell into absurdity was when their writers tried to accuse Solzhenitsyn of anti-Soviet tendencies, anti-patriotism, and a negative attitude to the October Revolution, even though the novel's action was strictly confined to the month of August 1914 and there was not so much as an allusion to the events that followed. While criticising the novel Martti Larni takes care to speak of its author too in the most unflattering terms. In his opinion Solzhenitsyn is '. . . an egocentric, bilious and asocial man who, in a paroxysm of self-conceit, cannot see beyond his own navel . . .'[3]

The aim of the 'international' campaign initiated by *Literaturnaya Gazeta* was clear. By publishing a few articles by foreign critics, no doubt at the suggestion of someone at the top, the paper's editors could then elicit a number of indignant

[3] Martti Larni is known to Soviet readers as the author of a satirical novel *The Fourth Vertebra, or The Reluctant Rogue,* published in 1959–60. In 1964 Larni was Chairman of the Finnish Writers' Union. The Soviet *Short Literary Encyclopaedia* (volume 4) tells us that 'devices of hyperbole and caricature' are 'typical' of Larni's style. The encyclopaedia clearly used these terms as a polite cover-up for Larni's tendency to fantastic exaggeration and falsification, and also towards demagogy.

letters from Soviet readers. There were rumours that a selection of these letters had already been collected in the editorial office, and they included demands from Soviet writers and the general public for drastic measures to put a stop to Solzhenitsyn's anti-Soviet activities.

Then I received a letter from Per Egil Hegge in Norway. He felt that Solzhenitsyn and his friends should know about an interview Martti Larni had given to a correspondent of the Finnish paper *Uusi Suomi*, which had been published in Helsinki on 26 February, three days after Larni's article appeared, translated from Swedish, in *Literaturnaya Gazeta*. This interview had been accompanied by a report by the Moscow correspondent of *Uusi Suomi* on the publication of Larni's article in *Literaturnaya Gazeta*.

The interview had been given the title 'Larni Has A Different View'. What Larni said to *Uusi Suomi* was that he did not know the paper *Norrskens Flamman* and that he had never written an article for it. *Literaturnaya Gazeta* had asked him to comment on a review of *August 1914* by Anatole Shub, a correspondent of the *Washington Post*. That had been several months earlier, and he had been expecting his response to Shub to be published late in 1971. Larni stressed that he had been commenting only on Shub's review, not on the novel itself, since he had not read *August 1914* either at the time the article was written, or later.

Per Egil Hegge added that he thought Larni was telling the truth when he said that he had not written an article for the Swedish paper. He could neither read nor write Swedish.

27. The Cancellation of the Nobel Prize Ceremony in Moscow

IN LATE 1971 correspondence was resumed between Solzhenitsyn and Dr Karl Ragnar Gierow, Secretary of the Swedish Academy, about the possibility of a presentation of the Nobel Prize Diploma and Gold Medal in Moscow. (The prize money had been put into a bank account in Solzhenitsyn's name and could be used by the prize-winner through his Swiss lawyer.) The correspondence was revived by the publication of Per Hegge's book; the Swedish Academy wanted to solve the problem as quickly as possible. Meanwhile Swedish diplomatic representatives in Moscow were still willing to deliver the Nobel insignia in Moscow but without a ceremony worthy of the name. On 4 December 1971 Solzhenitsyn sent Dr Gierow a letter with a new proposal, and this was accepted by the Academy. The letter was not confidential; Gierow informed correspondents of its contents, and therefore I too feel I can quote an excerpt from the letter. After repeating what he thought of the attitude of the Swedish Embassy, Solzhenitsyn went on:

> ... since I know of no public or cooperative organisation in Moscow which would agree to place premises at your disposal for the purpose, may I take the liberty of suggesting an alternative – that the entire ceremony be held in a private flat in Moscow, more precisely, at the address to which you have been sending my letters. True, the flat is hardly as spacious as the Swedish Embassy, but it can easily accommodate – by Russian standards, that is – forty or fifty people. The ceremony may lose a little in the way of official dignity, but it will gain in domestic warmth ...

The proposal was accepted by Gierow who wrote to Solzhenitsyn telling him that for personal reasons he would not be able to come to Moscow to present the prize until April 1972.

Solzhenitsyn was in no hurry, and the date was fixed for 9 April. Solzhenitsyn planned a daytime ceremony and for the convenience of his guests, who were to be openly invited, chose a Sunday. It was to be at the flat of his second wife Natalia Svetlova. Solzhenitsyn wanted to ask about fifty friends and a few foreign and Soviet correspondents. He planned to send invitations to two Soviet papers, *Selskaya Zhizn* (*Agricultural Life*) and *Trud* (*Labour*). Neither had published attacks on him.

He realised that everything possible would be done to obstruct the ceremony, and its gathering of eminent representatives of Soviet literature, music, theatre and science. In mid-March it became reliably known that *Literaturnaya Gazeta* were preparing a series of articles attacking Solzhenitsyn and accusing him of anti-Soviet activity. These would probably be followed up with articles in which certain citizens would demand that Solzhenitsyn be called to account or expelled from the USSR. The possibility of expelling Solzhenitsyn from the Soviet Union had been discussed at various propaganda meetings ever since 1971.

To counter these plans Solzhenitsyn decided to reply to his critics, by giving an interview to the correspondents of the *New York Times* and the *Washington Post* – Hedrick Smith and Robert Kaiser. Both men, like many other foreign corrrespondents in Moscow, had long expressed their desire to meet Solzhenitsyn, but in the past he had always refused to give interviews.

Solzhenitsyn's talk with Hedrick Smith and Robert Kaiser took place in Natalia Svetlova's flat on 30 March 1972, and lasted several hours. The interview was published in somewhat abbreviated form in both papers on 3 April. Shortened versions appeared the same day in many other European and American papers, and were also broadcast by Russian-language radio stations abroad.

Solzhenitsyn told of his work on the new novel *October 1916*, and of the difficulties he was having in collecting material. He also described the various ways in which he was being victimised, and the slanders that were being spread about him at closed meetings and in the press. In particular he replied to the articles *Stern* and *Literaturnaya Gazeta* had published about

177

his family. In a Russian version of the interview which circulated later in *samizdat* (having been pieced together by a group of friends in part from a tape recording of the interview, and in part from Solzhenitsyn's preliminary notes and from translations of the version in the American papers) Solzhenitsyn went on record with the following statement:

And as for what *Literaturnaya Gazeta* and *Stern* wrote about my ancestors, it's all ridiculous nonsense, but there are deliberate and calculated lies there too ... The Editor-in-Chief of *Stern* insists that it was his correspondent, Steiner, a German, who visited my aunt in September. But that is not true. They came in August, not September, and they were three Soviet citizens speaking perfect Russian – I don't think Steiner even speaks it – and they visited my aunt five times, they weren't in any hurry. They were simply delighted with her life story and asked if they could borrow her jottings to read for a few hours – and they never came back, they stole them.

Literaturnaya Gazeta and *Stern* claim that my grandfathers were both landowners in the Northern Caucasus. *Literaturnaya Gazeta* ought to be ashamed of being so ignorant of the history of our country. Apart from the few cossack generals whom everyone knows about, there were never any landowners – members of the landowning gentry that is – in the Northern Caucasus. All the lands belonged to the Tersk and the Kuban cossack frontier troops. Right up to the 20th century much of the area was uninhabited ... but the cossack host was willing to lease out as much land as anyone wanted at extremely low rates. My grandfathers were neither of them cossacks – they were *muzhiks* (peasants).

It so happens that there is documentary evidence of the peasant stock of the Solzhenitsyns as far back as 1698, when an ancestor of mine, Filipp, was a victim of the wrath of Peter I (The Great) – the story was published in the paper *Voronezhskaya Kommuna* (*Voronezh Commune*) on 9 March 1969, in an article on the town of Bobrovo. And a great-great-grandfather of mine was exiled from the Voronezh province to the lands of the Caucasian host after an uprising ... The Solzhenitsyns were ordinary Stavropol peasants: in pre-revolutionary Stavropol a few bullocks and horses, a dozen cows and two hundred sheep were not regarded as a fortune by any means. It was a big family and they all worked with their hands. And I remember there was a simple clay-and-gravel dug-out on the farm. But they had to take a 'class line' to vindicate their 'progressive theory', so they invented some bank or other, added a few noughts to the value of the property, conjured up fifty farm labourers, and printed a picture of the Shcherbaks' dacha in Kislovodsk, where I was born, calling it the 'country estate of the Solzhenitsyns'. Any fool can see it's not a cossack's house . . .

The two journalists asked Solzhenitsyn if he thought there was a possibility that the authorities might refuse to grant Dr Gierow a Soviet entry visa to prevent the Nobel Prize ceremony from taking place. Solzhenitsyn replied:

. . . It can't be ruled out in theory, and in practice it would be very easy to do, it doesn't require much manpower, or wit. But I can't see it happening, it would be a shameful absurdity.

At the beginning of April I received my invitation card from Solzhenitsyn. It was a sheet of stiff paper, folded, and inside was a diagram showing the entrance to the house, and how to find the flat (the house where the ceremony was to take place had several courtyards and about twenty entrances), and to the right of the diagram Solzhenitsyn had written:

Dear Zhores,
I invite you to attend the Nobel ceremony on 9 April 1972, at 12 o'clock noon. Guests will assemble from 11.30 to 11.50.
A. Solzhenitsyn.

Similar invitations went out to about fifty friends and nearly all of them accepted. The one or two people who declined had entirely valid reasons for doing so. It appears that what worried the authorities most was that Solzhenitsyn would be host to a large gathering of representatives of the intelligentsia who were very well known both in the USSR and abroad. There would certainly be foreign correspondents at the ceremony, and so a detailed account of proceedings would become widely known outside the Soviet Union. The flat was now

179

being watched continuously, although Solzhenitsyn was not there at the beginning of April. I called there one day to discuss a few matters with Solzhenitsyn's wife; when I left I noticed that I was being followed by two plain-clothes men, and a car was trailing me winking its left indicator, although the only turning in the vicinity was a right-hand one. I decided it was their way of signalling that they had me under observation. One of the men was a young lad wearing a conspicuous cloth cap. I reached the Lenin Library and decided to turn in by the entrance to the scientific reading-rooms. The young lad could have no possible business there, but when I came out some time later, there he was hiding behind a column waiting for me. His mate was not far off. I had to spend half an hour riding around in the underground so as to reach home without an escort.

Karl Ragnar Gierow had applied at the Soviet Embassy in Stockholm for a visa to travel to the Soviet Union, about a month in advance of the proposed ceremony. Sweden is a friendly country which has always observed strict neutrality. No one in the Swedish Ministry of Foreign Affairs could recall an instance of an official Swedish representative being refused a visa for Moscow, and accordingly Swedish diplomats in Moscow received instructions to meet Gierow at the airport and book a room for him at the Rossiya Hotel. Particular correspondents were assigned to accompany Gierow, and they discussed procedural details with the prize-winner. It was clear that the Swedish Embassy in Moscow saw Gierow's arrival as a certainty and therefore did not wish to disregard the formalities completely.

However, on 4 April it was announced in an evening news bulletin from London, and by other radio stations, that the Soviet Ministry of Foreign Affairs had refused to issue Dr Gierow a visa. In Sweden the reaction to this decision was one of bewilderment and indignation.

Solzhenitsyn informed everyone he had invited to the ceremony of its cancellation. Only the papers *Trud* (*Labour*) and *Selskaya Zhizn* (*Agricultural Life*) were not notified, since the invitations he had sent them had not been in any particular name. At exactly 11.50 on 9 April there was a ring at the door of Solzhenitsyn's wife's flat. It was a sole arrival, and he showed his invitation card signed by Solzhenitsyn, and his identity card as correspondent of *Selskaya Zhizn*. The *Trud* correspondent did not show up. But that was understandable, for the paper had only two days earlier, on 7 April, published a long, two-page article attacking Solzhenitsyn and his novel *August 1914*. (This time the article was presented as a translation from the Polish, the original of which had appeared in a Catholic weekly by the mysterious name of *WTK*.)[1]

The correspondent from *Selskaya Zhizn* was invited in by Solzhenitsyn's wife and gave his name as Valentine Sukhanov. He said he had been given the invitation card by the Editor-in-Chief of *Selskaya Zhizn*. Natalia Svetlova told him there would not be any ceremony but that Solzhenitsyn would be glad to talk to him. The correspondent began to back out, excusing himself and saying that he had no time. 'But you came for the ceremony,' said Natalia, 'so you must have reckoned on spending quite some time here with us'. But Sukhanov was already outside the door. Evidently whoever had given him the invitation card had not approved a private talk with Solzhenitsyn. Next day Natalia Svetlova telephoned *Selskaya Zhizn* to ask for Sukhanov's number. She was told by the paper's enquiry desk that there was no one by the name of Sukhanov on the staff.

[1] *Wroclawski Tygodnik Katolików*. (Translator's note.)

28. Who Calls the Tune and Who Plays the Music?

ACCORDING TO AN editorial footnote in *Trud*, the Polish Catholic weekly *WTK* had published the article '*August 1914* by Alexander Solzhenitsyn or The Truth about the Book and the Myth' on 26 March 1972. The Russian translation appeared on 7 April in the Soviet weekly paper *Literaturnaya Rossiya* as well as in *Trud;* the translations were identical. So, with one exception, were all the 'editorial' footnotes, although the staff were quite different. This indicated that they had been supervised by the same boss. The author of the article was one Jerzy Romanowski, a totally obscure name in Polish literature (and one which I could not find in the catalogue of Polish books in the Lenin Library), and what he had written was an utterly unscrupulous review of *August 1914*, clearly intended for those who could not read the novel for themselves. Speaking as someone who has read the novel twice over, I find it positively embarrassing to argue with Romanowski's article. He writes, for instance,

> If these painful pages of history arouse the profound sorrow and anger of every Slav who sympathises with Russia, for Solzhenitsyn they are a chance to mock at all the Russian people ... Russian soldiers and officers are portrayed in the book as a gang of marauders ... The book abounds in calculated insults levelled at Russia and the Slavic people ...

And so on. So that the reader who is unfamiliar with the novel may appreciate the full absurdity of Romanowski's allegations, I shall now quote from sources which are accessible to everyone. For example, when Martti Larni reviewed the novel which he had never read in *Litteraturnaya Gazeta* on 23 February, he reproached the author for showing that 'tsarist Russia was a simply ideal state'. Marina Stutz's article reprinted in the same issue of *Litteraturnaya Gazeta* claimed that Solzhenitsyn portrayed the Russian people as '... backward, but endowed with latent energy and a common sense which it derived from profound religious feeling'.

Romanowski's article made a heavy-handed attempt to quibble with Solzhenitsyn over the details of the 1914 campaign in East Prussia. Romanowski quoted from quite rare works by Russian military historians. Apart from this, his article was full of Soviet journalistic jargon and it was immediately clear that it had been written originally in Russian, not Polish. So I thought it would be interesting to find out what the Polish text in *WTK* looked like, and something about this Catholic journal which debated a topic so far removed from the Catholic religion – a topic, moreover, on which the Polish reader could form no proper opinion, since there was no Polish edition of *August 1914*.

I had been unable to find the Catholic *WTK* in the Lenin Library – the most important library in the Soviet Union did not subscribe to religious periodicals from other countries – so I decided to call in at the offices of *Trud*, assuming that they would have a copy of the Polish original. When I asked the secretary of the literature and art section, she replied in a somewhat alarmed tone, 'We haven't got the Polish paper here. We only received the Russian text with instructions to publish it.'

'But you ought at least to have checked the quotations from the sources mentioned,' I said. 'After all, that's the rule with any article published in the central press. And anyway, the article has footnotes by your editors.'

The secretary realised that she had said too much. 'Please, go and ask the section head,' she said, indicating the other end of the room, 'I'm sure he'll explain everything to you.'

The section head, Yu. I. Skvortsov, listened to my request (I wanted to know the exact title of the Catholic weekly paper or at least the name of the town where it was published, since I intended, or so I said, to write a letter to the editor of the journal). Skvortsov said he did not have the *WTK* magazine in his section but if I waited he would find out. Twenty minutes later he came back. 'I'm afraid the editorial files are closed at the moment. Let me take your telephone number and when the person in charge of the files comes in I'll find out and give you a ring. Tell me your name, please.' And he pulled out a pen to note down my particulars, evidently for the same authority that had sent the article to *Trud* 'with instructions to publish'. I gave him my name, address and telephone number. (And although I sent him two reminders, he never wrote to me about the Polish weekly *WTK*. A month and a half later I sent him details about the journal and its editor.)

Five days after the *Trud* article, *Literaturnaya Gazeta* published a page of readers' responses, prepared long ago, to the articles by Martti Larni and Marina Stutz (once again on page 13). They were introduced in the following way:

> ... the editors of *Literaturnaya Gazeta* have received a big response to the articles by M. Larni and M. Stutz. Our readers provided a suitable rebuke to the slanderous fabrications contained in A. Solzhenitsyn's 'historical' work. Today we publish what is only a small part of our readers' responses.

The words 'a small part' were a warning that the paper might continue the anti-Solzhenitsyn campaign in its next issues. Most of page 13 was taken up with an article by a Byelorussian writer, Leonid Proksha, entitled 'Which Russia is Solzhenitsyn Weeping Over?'. It was the usual kind of demagogy, and Proksha made an attempt to link Solzhenitsyn with the émigré organisations that had published *Cancer Ward* in 1968. To add a little more spice Proksha revealed details of the past of some of the directors of *Possev*. Proksha had not read the novel but based his review on the words of Martti Larni, who, as we have seen, had not read it either but had based his comments on a *Washington Post* review. Proksha's article descended to the very depths of absurdity. He confused the First and Second World Wars, and talked of certain 'blasphemous insinuations' made by the author from which he drew the conclusion that 'the author would not have been averse to seeing a German victory'. (In fact the novel reflects the mood prevalent at the beginning of the war and takes a distinctly patriotic attitude. Only the social-democrat is portrayed as a defeatist in the novel, and this accords with the tactics of the social-democrats at that time. In an article written in September 1914 and entitled 'The Mission of the Revolutionary Social-Democrat in the European War',[1] Lenin wrote:

---

[1] See *Collected Works*, 5th Edition, Vol. 26, p. 6.

From the point of view of the working class and the toiling masses of all the peoples of Russia, defeat of the Tsarist monarchy and its forces would be the least evil . . .

Lenin formulated this thesis even more clearly in a specialised article, 'On the Defeat of our own Government in the Imperialist War',[2] and in many other documents dating from that period.)

Leonid Proksha's article was supplemented with an article by an Azerbaidzhani writer, Dzhalal Mamedov, called 'The Sources of Bitterness'; another, called 'A Fitting Rebuke' by an Armenian literary critic, M. Mkryan; another by a Kirghiz writer N. Zharkambayev, as well as extracts from irate letters from workers, labourers, engineers, a transport controller, a teacher, a headmaster, and an engine-driver who was a Hero of Socialist Labour. The final paragraph of this tastefully chosen collection of programmed human automata was penned by an engineer, Yakshin, who exclaimed about the author of *August 1914*: 'But what kind of Soviet author is he when he rummages in cesspits and slanders his own country?'

Naturally I opened the next issue of *Literaturnaya Gazeta* (19 April) on page 13. On the left-hand side there was an article entitled 'In Harness with the Enemies' signed by five Byelorussian writers (Maksim Tank, Ivan Melezh, and others), but it was only further comment on the 'reviews' by Larni and Stutz, and just as silly as all the rest. On the right I saw a long article by Eusebio Ferrari, 'Who Calls the Tune?', which the paper presented as a translation from the April issue of an Italian journal *Calendario del Popolo*. It was not Solzhenitsyn's new novel that Eusebio Ferrari was discussing. For some reason he gave an account of Solzhenitsyn's play *Feast of the Victors*, the only copy of which had been confiscated by the KGB in 1965. How could the Italian writer have got to know what it was about? According to Ferrari, he had talked to people who had read the play. He displayed a more practical approach to the matter than had his predecessors. Precisely, and point by point, he expounded the charges being levelled against Solzhenitsyn:

[2] *Ibid.* pp. 286–291.
185

In Moscow concrete charges are being brought against Solzhenitsyn, and they amount to roughly these: an attempt to undermine the social and political bases of the Soviet system with the aim of replacing the principles on which that system is founded ... with other principles; propagation of this attitude by means of his literary works, appeals, addresses, and suchlike; and the use, for this purpose, of mass information media abroad (papers, publishing-houses and radio-stations) which are known to be taking a stand against Soviet society.

Ferrari went on to try and prove that these 'concrete charges' were justified and 'answered the logic of the struggle of the proletariat for the victory of communism'.

Eusebio Ferrari, who was presented to readers of *Literaturnaya Gazeta* as an Italian, was in effect expounding the Criminal Code of the Russian Federation, and in particular, article 70, which deals with 'anti-Soviet agitation and propaganda'. This article runs as follows:

Agitation or propaganda carried on for the purpose of subverting or weakening Soviet power ... or circulating for the same purpose slanderous fabrications which defame the Soviet state and social system, or circulating or preparing or keeping, for the same purpose, literature of such content, shall be punished by deprivation of freedom for a term of six months to seven years and by exile for a term of two to five years ...

In legal terms 'preparing' includes 'composing'. It was under this article that Sinyavsky and Daniel were convicted in 1966.

The discussion of Solzhenitsyn's works initiated by *Literaturnaya Gazeta* in January had clearly almost reached its end. After Eusebio Ferrari's article it seemed probable that the paper would publish articles by representatives of the proletariat calling for the writer to stand trial. The Italian journal had based its charges on an article of the Soviet Criminal Code, but it would have to be the author's compatriots who demanded that justice be done. The 'discussion' could logically be steered on to a legal course in the May issue of *Literaturnaya Gazeta*. But May 1972 was not a particularly convenient month for administration justice of this kind, for it was then that President

Nixon was planning to come to Moscow. An agreement was expected, amongst many others, on cultural and scientific cooperation, and reprisals against Solzhenitsyn would not sound quite the right harmonious note. Nevertheless the Novosti Press Agency did put in some spade-work, so that the foreign guests would be prepared even for reprisals, were they to happen. At the beginning of May APN organised a rapid translation into French and English of all the critical articles on Solzhenitsyn that had appeared in the Soviet press (from the article in *Literaturnaya Gazeta* in June 1968 to the piece by Eusebio Ferrari) and published them under the same covers, giving the anthology the title of *Press Comment on Solzhenitsyn*. This anthology was distributed in the press-centre, for the benefit of the American delegation in Moscow, and also abroad.

Meanwhile I had written to several literary figures in Poland, and also to the Warsaw Institute of Literature, asking them to send me a copy of the Catholic weekly *WTK* for 26 March. The Italian journal *Calendario del Popolo* was openly available in the Lenin Library, but at the beginning of May the April issue had not arrived from Italy. Looking at other issues I discovered that it was a small illustrated communist journal published in Milan. I have a good friend in Milan, and accordingly I wrote and asked him to send me the April issue of the journal and to find out as quickly as he could who Eusebio Ferrari was.

At the end of May I received a registered packet from Milan containing the April issue of *Calendario del Popolo* and a letter from my friend. The article by Eusebio Ferrari had appeared under the title 'Questions for Solzhenitsyn' (and not 'Who Calls the Tune?') but the content was roughly the same as that of the Russian version in *Literaturnaya Gazeta*. But there was an editorial note to say that Eusebio Ferrari lived in Moscow. There were no further details of his address. My friend had little to say on the subject of Eusebio Ferrari. 'I cannot tell you much about the author of the article,' he wrote, 'for the simple reason that no one here has heard of him. But he is *certainly not a writer or a critic . . .*'

The April number of *Calendario del Popolo* did not appear in Moscow libraries until 20–21 May. This showed that when

Literaturnaya Gazeta had published its 'translation' of the article on 19 April it undoubtedly had the text before the Italian journal came out in Milan.

Early in June I received two copies of *WTK* for 26 March 1972 from Poland. It was a weekly newspaper. Its full title was *Wroclawski Tygodnik Katolików (Warszawa)*. The article by Jerzy Romanowski on August 1914 was a double-page spread (pp. 4–5 of the paper). A simple comparison of the Russian with the Polish version showed that it was the *Russian* which had been the original. The article contained a number of quotations from extremely rare sources. In the Russian version there was in every instance a numbered footnote giving bibliographical details of the source and also a page reference for each quotation. The Polish version had no bibliographical footnotes.

But it was my Polish literary friends who provided the main proof of the prior existence of the Russian text. The article contained may quotations from the American historian Barbara Tuchman's book, *The Guns of August*. The English spelling of Tuchman does not change in Polish transcript since Polish uses the Latin alphabet, and retains the original spelling of English names. Mrs Tuchman's book has, moreover, been published in Polish with the original spelling of the name retained. In the Polish version of Romanowski's article the name consistently appears as *Takman*, that is to say the author uses a re-transcription from the *Russian* phonetic spelling of the name. This error could only arise in a translation from Russian, and, moreover, a translation done by a Pole unfamiliar with the book. What is more, in the Russian version of the article, all the quotations from Mrs Tuchman's book are given from the English edition *as it would have been translated into Russian*. In the Polish version of the article these quotations do not appear as quotations from the English original. They are a translation of the Russian translation of the English text.

My Polish friends also told me a thing or two about the weekly paper *WTK* and its editor. *WTK* is published by a particular faction of so-called 'independent' Catholics, unrecognised by the Polish Catholic Church. The head of this group and the editor of *WTK* is Piasecki, who is well known in Poland as a reactionary. In 1945 he was arrested by the NKVD but was soon released. He then began publishing *WTK*, first in Wroclaw (formerly Breslau), then in Warsaw. Jerzy Romanowski is unknown in Poland as a journalist or a writer; evidently this is a pseudonym. Thus the enigma of the appearance of Romanowski's article in *WTK* was solved.

29. The Nobel Lecture

NOBEL PRIZE-WINNERS MAY, while in Stockholm, deliver the traditional Nobel Lecture, a public address which is then published in the Nobel Yearbook and may also later be reprinted in other publications and in other languages (publication in the *Nobel Yearbook* is in the original language). The lectures delivered by scientists are usually reprinted in international scientific journals such as *Nature* and *Science*. The lecture is, however, a voluntary gesture, and the prize-winner may decide not to give it. In 1965, for instance, Mikhail Sholokhov gave a press-conference instead which made a very bad impression in Sweden.

In the autumn of 1970 Solzhenitsyn had intended to take up the Swedish Academy's invitation to prepare a lecture, but when he later gave up his attempts to travel to Sweden the question of the lecture became somewhat less pressing. The Nobel Foundation, however, expressed great interest in it, and Solzhenitsyn began to ponder the matter in earnest when discussions started about the procedure of delivering the prize in Moscow. He thought to read the lecture at the ceremony of presentation of the Nobel medal and diploma. It was decided to publish it in the *Nobel Yearbook* for 1971, in other words, a year late. The *Yearbook* would not appear until the summer of 1972 and so, if the ceremony had taken place, the guests invited to the presentation at the flat of Solzhenitsyn's wife would have heard the lecture for the first time from the laureate's lips. Neither I nor any of Solzhenitsyn's friends whom I knew, had seen the text of the lecture, and we were awaiting its delivery at the ceremony with enormous interest. But there was to be no ceremony, no delivery.

The *Nobel Yearbook* came out at the end of August 1972 and Solzhenitsyn's lecture immediately acquired worldwide significance and attracted the attention of the press everywhere, with the exception, of course, of the USSR, China, Korea and a handful of other countries. Leading newspapers and journals published extensive excerpts from the lecture accompanied by commentaries pointing to the great dignity of the author, his humanity, the importance of the ideas he had expressed on the tasks of literature and art, as a whole, and the concentrated stylistic brilliance of the lecture. The Russian text of the lecture was broadcast several times by Russian-language stations in the west, and after I had listened to two of these broadcasts I was joyfully convinced that the lecture was indeed deeply impressive, that it expressed with amazing clarity the universal, 'supra-party' role of literature and the priority of moral and ethical ideas over materialist ones; this, I thought must inevitably make the lecture an important document. Shortly afterwards I received from Sweden a photocopy of the published text of the lecture. It took up twelve pages in the *Nobel Yearbook*[1] but those twelve pages, as I later discovered, had doubled the number of copies printed in comparison with previous years. I will not quote the full text of the lecture here – it will be familiar to many people already – but I will give a few quotations which, I feel, echo some of the arguments of this book:

To get to this platform for the Nobel lectures – a platform that is offered to but a few writers and then only once in a lifetime – to get to this platform I have climbed not the usual portable flight of three or four steps, but hundreds and even thousands of them, daunting, steep and covered with ice, from out of the darkness and cold where it was fated for me to survive, while others, perhaps more gifted and stronger than I, there perished. I met only a few of them myself in the Gulag Archipelago,[2] strung out in a multitude of scattered islands – and under the millstone of surveillance and mistrust there were few I managed to speak to, others I only heard of and yet others I could only guess at. Those with literary reputations when they sank down into the abyss are at least known to us, but how many more went unrecognised and never once achieved public recognition! And hardly any of them came back alive. A whole national literature remained there, buried not only without a grave but even without any underwear, with only a token tied to their toes.

[1] *Les Prix Nobel en 1971*, Stockholm, Imprimerie Royale, Norstedt & Sönef, pp. 129–40.
[2] *Gulag* is an acronym for 'State Administration of Labour Camps'.

191

Not for a moment did Russian literature cease to exist, yet from outside it looked like a desert! Instead of the abundant forest that might have grown up there, all that remained after the harvest were a handful of forgotten trees.

And how can I today, accompanied by the shades of the fallen and with bowed head ceding this platform to others who were worthy before me – how can I divine and express what *they* would have wanted to say?

... Who can create for mankind a single system of evaluation – for good deeds and evil deeds, the tolerable and the intolerable, for where the line between them should be drawn today? Who will enlighten mankind as to what is genuinely oppressive and intolerable and what only rubs us the wrong way because it is close at hand – and will direct our anger at what is truly appalling and not at the closest target? Who is capable of impressing stubborn, insular man with the remote joys and sorrows of others, with an understanding of dimensions and blunders that he himself has never experienced? Propaganda, compulsion and scientific proof are all powerless here. Happily, however, a means does exist – and that is art, literature.

Art is capable of the following miracle: it can overcome man's characteristic weakness of learning only from his own experience, so that the experience of others is wasted on him. From man to man, augmenting his brief span on earth, art can convey the whole burden of another's long life experience, with its cares, colours and flavour, can re-create in the flesh the experience of other men and enable us to assimilate them as our own.

But there is more, much more to it, than that. Countries and even whole continents repeat each other's mistakes at a later date, sometimes even centuries later when, as you might think, everything is so plain and obvious. But no, things that have already been experienced, considered and rejected by certain peoples are suddenly seen by others to be the very last word. And here too, the sole substitute for experience we haven't had ourselves is art, literature.

Art is endowed with the miraculous capability of transferring experience – in spite of all the differences in language, customs and social structure – from one whole nation to another, experience which has never belonged to the recipient and is the painful fruit of many decades of national history, and which in fortunate cases can save a whole nation from following a pointless, erroneous or even disastrous path, thereby somewhat straightening the tortuous twists of human history.

... And there is another priceless direction in which literature can tranfer condensed, irrefutable experience – from generation to generation. In this way it becomes the living memory of nations. In this way it cherishes and nourishes within itself the nation's lost history in a form not susceptible to distortion and slander. And thereby, together with language, it preserves the national soul.

... But woe betide the nation whose literature is interrupted by force. This is not simply a violation of 'the freedom of the press', it is the incarceration of the nation's heart, the amputation of the nation's memory. The nation can no longer remember itself, the nation is deprived of its spiritual unity, and despite what seems like their common language, the members of that nation suddenly cease to understand one another. Mute generations languish and die without giving an account of themselves either for their own sake or for generations to come. If such master writers as Akhmatova and Zamyatin are immured alive throughout their natural life, condemned to create in silence until the grave, deprived of any response to what they have written, this is not merely a personal misfortune for them, but a tragedy for the whole nation, a threat to the whole nation. And in some instances a threat to the whole of mankind too, when the whole of *history* ceases to be understood as the result of such a silence.

... They will say to us: what can literature do against the remorseless onslaught of open violence? Ah, but let us not forget that violence does not and cannot exist on its own, it is inextricably bound up with the *lie*. The link between them is fundamental and entirely natural and organic: violence has nothing to cover itself with except the lie, and the lie has no way of maintaining itself except by violence. Anyone who once proclaims violence as his *method* is inexorably bound to choose the lie as his *principle*. At the time of its birth, violence operates openly and is even proud of itself. But no sooner has it affirmed and established itself than it feels the air around it growing thinner and cannot continue to exist without surrounding itself with a smokescreen of lies and hiding behind their honeyed sounds. Violence does not always and of necessity come right out and throttle you: more often than not it simply demands of its subjects that they subscribe to the lie or participate in it.

And the simple course of the simple brave man is not to participate in the lie and not to support lying actions. Even if *that* comes into the world and reigns in the world, let it not be through me. But writers and artists are capable of more: they can *conquer the lie!* For in the struggle with the lie, art has always conquered and always will conquer – visibly and irrefutably for all to see. The lie can withstand much in this world, but never art. . . .

That is why, my friends, I think we are able to help the world in its hour of need.[3]

[3] Translated by Michael Scammell in *Index* Vol. 1, nos 3–4, 1972. Copyright in the original Russian 'The Nobel Foundation 1972'.

30. Ten Years

IT IS NOW ten years since the publication of *One Day in the Life of Ivan Denisovich* in *Novy Mir*. In the course of those ten years I have read and re-read the story many times, and Ivan Denisovich and everything that happens to him on that particular day is deeply imprinted in my memory and will remain there for ever, perhaps more vividly and in more detail than any day from my own life. Such is the power of art. Ivan Denisovich also had ten years to serve, three thousand six hundred and fifty-three days, all alike. The ten years we have lived through in this book, however, have not all been alike. But the changes we have traced have not been changes simply in the life of the main protagonist but changes in society as a whole, in the world as a whole. Ten years ago the author of *Ivan Denisovich* made his sudden, triumphant début, and it was the triumph of truth. The enthusiasm with which the new writer was first greeted was not just an expression of delight at contact with genuine art. It was a delight above all that the time had come when the *whole* truth could be told, when the terrible, but so memorable, so bitter events of the recent past, which had cast a cloud over the life of the majority of people, were laid bare for merciless analysis. It was delight that art could conquer violence and the lie. Solzhenitsyn had painted a picture of hell, but everyone could see that he had done so in order that this hell should not be repeated. What he had shown in *One Day in the Life of Ivan Denisovich* had not been the most fearful circle of hell. It had been Kazakhstan, not Kolyma – construction sites and not copper mines – places where people lived for years at a time and did not die within a year or two as a result of vitamin deficiencies and exhaustion, as they did in the terrible camps inside the Arctic Circle, where the husband of Lidia Chukovskaya died, where my own father died, and the fathers of several of my friends and many millions of our compatriots.

Of all the writings of Solzhenitsyn known to us, *Ivan Denisovich* was the most astonishing. In *The First Circle* the protagonists live an easier life. They do not have to think of their daily bread ration; they are engaged in scientific research, and they can even love. The only thing they lack is their freedom. In *Cancer Ward* the author takes his readers outside the confines of hell, into ordinary life, full of fresh hopes and the gradual blossoming of justice. In *August 1914*, Solzenitsyn goes beyond the harrowing framework of the present time and depicts a world of events for which hardly anyone alive today bears direct responsibility. In these ten years Solzhenitsyn has shown that his talent has not only not declined, but has gained a new strength, a new maturity. Why did *One Day in the Life of Ivan Denisovich* sell millions of copies in our country – and why was it greeted with enthusiasm by the majority of its readers, of literary critics and of the country's leadership, while *August 1914* was never published, never read by any one of our publishing houses, never submitted to the verdict of the reading public, and was greeted with the dagger-thrusts of mercenary critics, many of them hiding behind the suspect mask of pseudonyms? Is it possible that we are approaching another reign of violence and terror? Is it possible that art, which flashed all too briefly before our eyes and revealed some – but by no means all – of the colours of the rainbow, must now once again take on a solitary hue?

I have a close friend, the oldest of all the former *Novy Mir* staff, a man who remembers the Revolution and the Civil War, during which he served in the legendary Shchors division. He once answered this question very simply:

'Many people think that we had a democracy under Khrushchev,' he said. 'That is nonsense. There was no democracy. There was *occasional* liberalism, but in the conditions in which we live, that does not mean very much. It's a humane form of arbitrariness. And in any case, as we see, it's a temporary phenomenon. There can only be stable justice when there is genuine, stable democracy.'

November 1971 – November 1972.

Epilogue

ALTHOUGH only four months have passed since December 1973, when the first English edition of this book was published, so many important and dramatic events have occurred in the life of the hero of our narrative, and in the fate of his work, that one could write a new book about them. Since late December 1973, when the Russian edition of the first two parts of *The Gulag Archipelago* were published in the West, provoking a sensation, the whole world has anxiously followed the fate of its author. With his book Solzhenitsyn challenged the authoritarian régime, based on terror, which between 1918 and 1955 had destroyed tens of millions of innocent people. He questioned the system of total censorship, which even today prohibits writing and speaking the truth about the past. And he dispelled the illusion that classifying archives as secret, or destroying them, can save those guilty of past crimes from the full exposure of their harshness.

Previously, many books, documentary studies and reminiscences had been written about the Stalinist and pre-Stalinist camps and terror. Experts, historians, eyewitnesses and victims of the terror had told a great deal. All these books, accounts and sketches were bullets which had made small holes in the concrete wall of silence – holes through which very little light came. And those holes could be rapidly closed up. *One Day in the Life of Ivan Denisovich* opened a large breach in that wall – one that the builders of the wall have not succeeded in sealing even today. Written by only one man (whose voice, nevertheless, was strengthened by the cries of millions of dead), *The Gulag Archipelago* was merely in its first two parts an artillery shell which destroyed such a large part of that wall that now it will never be restored. And when, having brought down malicious abuse on the author through the organs of the state and Party press, the authorities realized their impotence, a dramatic dénouement occurred – one that had undoubtedly been thought out in detail. Solzhenitsyn was arrested and charged with high treason. But even before the world was able to express its angry protest, the arrest was transformed into deportation to the West.

The unprecedented sensation produced by this event; the perplexity of Solzhenitsyn, who a few hours after being in a prison cell was surrounded by hundreds of reporters, newspaper photographers and television cameras; his feverish search for quiet isolation, which at this writing he has still not been able to find; and the recent surfacing of his *Letter to the Leaders of the Soviet Union,* written in September 1973 under the apparent influence of a temporary pessimism by a practitioner of art unversed in international politics – all these things combined to make the national tragedy end in a way that could only gladden those who for many years have combatted reforms and freedom of creativity in the Soviet Union.

On the evening of February 12, 1974, Lydia Chukovskaya, a close friend of Solzhenitsyn, wrote the following statement upon returning home from the apartment where he had been arrested a few hours earlier:

The fifth act of the drama has begun.

Shame on a country that allows its greatness and glory to be outraged.

Woe to that country whose tongue is torn out by tongs.

Ill fortune to a nation that is deceived.

Blessings and support for the man who right now, crudely separated from his family and friends and slandered before his own people – right now, this very minute – is waging silent single combat against illegal violence.

This 'single combat against illegal violence' has not ended, even though Solzhenitsyn is in Switzerland. In the past, Western public opinion has been the writer's ally in that combat. Now, being in the West, he may prove, paradoxically, to be much more alone. And such was the design of those who organized this deportation.

My book was completed in 1972, and was published in order to support the new, fresh current in Soviet literature and social life engendered by *One Day in the Life of Ivan*

Denisovich. The book had a final chapter, but it was not an Epilogue. Now the events of the past few months have become the book's real Epilogue. But in order to show that in the USSR the struggle for truth is far from having ended in defeat – that it is still too soon to celebrate even the temporary victory of violence – I have set down this brief account of the most important events of 1973 and 1974, events which led to such a conclusion.

For Solzhenitsyn, 1973 began rather quietly, and even with signs of improvement. In April of that year he left the hospitable home of M. Rostropovich and settled in Moscow in the apartment of his wife, Natalia Svetlova. Their third son was born that same month.

Although Solzhenitsyn had not received official permission to live in Moscow, the authorities for a time tried not to notice his existence. The Soviet press even discontinued criticism of his works and statements. The lengthy interview that Solzhenitsyn granted, in late August, to correspondents of *Le Monde* and the Associated Press received broad coverage in Western newspapers. And his statement on 'Peace and Violence', published in early September in the Norwegian newspaper *Aftenposten,* which contained several comments on the hypocrisy and weakness of the Western democracies, was the subject of criticism in several Western papers. His name was mentioned several times in the sharp attacks on Academician Andrei D. Sakharov which were widely reported in the Soviet press in September.

In the interview with the two foreign correspondents, translations of which appeared in Western papers on August 28, Solzhenitsyn noted that the persecutions of himself and members of his family were taking on the new forms of threats of physical reprisals sent through the mail.

But [said Solzhenitsyn] even if these threats are carried out, my death will not please those who are counting on it to put an end to my literary activity. Immediately after my death or disappearance, or any form of my imprisonment, my literary testament will enter into force irreversibly. And publication of the main part of my works, something from which I have abstained all these years, will begin.

The organs of state security knew which of those works Solzhenitsyn had foremost in view. The title of his *Gulag Archipelago* had been known since 1968, and it was sufficiently eloquent. Many people were aware of the existence of the book, rumored to consist of several volumes, but not even his close friends had read it. In 1969 several foreign newspapers and magazines published items about the book – and there was even a report that a copy was somewhere in the West. But the rumor died down, and talk about the book ceased. Solzhenitsyn himself did not want the manuscript to be discussed, and asked that his friends not even confirm the fact of its existence. One American publishing house, however, announced that it owned the rights to the book, and that preparations were being made to translate it into English and other languages. But the book was not published, and the question as to whether it actually existed remained unsettled. Nevertheless, Solzhenitsyn hinted in the 1973 interview that there was such a book, and that he considered it the most important of his works.

Meantime, agents of the KGB had not halted their search for the *Archipelago*. This organization had undoubtedly been hunting for the book for many years, but had not succeeded in tracing the manuscript. In September the KGB managed to learn that Elizaveta Voronyanskaya had retyped the work. According to a statement by Solzhenitsyn published in the Western newspapers, after five days of continuous interrogation Elizaveta Voronyanskaya told the investigators where one copy of the manuscript was being kept; when she came home, Voronyanskaya committed suicide. This tragic episode compelled Solzhenitsyn to lift his ban on the publication of *Gulag Archipelago*. The Russian text of the first two parts was published in Paris in late December, and translated excerpts in German, English and French began to appear in January 1974.

From these two sections, which constitute a thick volume, one can comprehend the author's over-all design and realize that Solzhenitsyn has in fact created a document of tremendous political and artistic force. With unusual frankness he has shown the development, in the USSR, of an apparatus of violence and terror ranging from the first, almost amateur revolutionary tribunals of the civil war period (which destroyed thousands of people, often without any trial), to the huge

GULag[1] archipelago, consisting of thousands of individual islands: prisons, transfer points and concentration camps. He showed the unprecedented size of the human meat-grinder of the GPU and NKVD,[2] which functioned continuously for decades, chewing up the millions of human beings who passed through it. Solzhenitsyn dealt with several topics which had not been discussed previously even in the *samizdat* literature on repressions. Foremost among them were two topics: the beginning of the terror, encouraged by Lenin during the first years of the Soviet régime; and the fate of several hundred thousand former Soviet POWs who, driven to desperation in the Fascist prison camps, agreed to serve in special Russian units in the German Army. After the war, when Solzhenitsyn himself was in a labor camp, those same former POWs, the 'Vlasovites',[3] who had received sentences of twenty-five years, constituted, together with ordinary POWs, sentenced to ten years, the majority of the population of the 'special' political labor camps. By that time most of the prewar prisoners had died.

In particular, it was the matter of the 'Vlasovites' that was utilized by the Soviet press, which now launched an anti-Solzhenitsyn campaign so virulent that it could not even be compared to the prewar hysterics in the press against the 'enemies of the people'. In those days, only the Soviet press was used – even against the chief 'enemies'. But now articles against Solzhenitsyn were published in many countries – not only in such countries as Poland, Bulgaria and Czechoslovakia, and not only in the Communist press of France, Italy and Sweden, but even in such newspapers as the *New York Times,* the *Christian Science Monitor,* and others, in which, owing to the sensational interest in the book and the figure of Solzhenitsyn, the Novosti Press Agency was able to place specially-commissioned critical (and sometimes simply libelous) articles. More-

[1] This is the correct form of the acronym, which stands for *Glavnoye Upravleniye (Ispravitelno-Trudovykh) Lagerei* (Main Administration of [Corrective Labor] Camps. Elsewhere I have used the form 'Gulag', which by now has become conventional in references to the book. (Translator's note.)

[2] Respectively, the State Political Administration and the People's Commissariat of Internal Affairs: forerunners of the KGB. (Translator's note.)

[3] After General Vlasov, commander of the Soviet defectors. (Translator's note.)

over, the world press published items about critical articles in the Soviet press, often without any commentary. The Western media also printed statements in support of Solzhenitsyn by several members of the Soviet intelligentsia. Those which attracted most attention were the statements of Andrei Sakharov and Lydia Chukovskaya, and the review of *The Gulag Archipelago* by Roy Medvedev, a detailed account of which was published on February 7 in the *New York Times* and the Washington *Post*. As a historian known in the West for *Let History Judge,* his volume on the genesis and consequences of Stalinism, Roy Medvedev, while noting certain inaccuracies inevitable in such a large-scale study, stated that *The Gulag Archipelago* did in fact fairly reflect events in Soviet history, and that this book could not be compared with any other in Russian or world literature.

The sharp attacks in the Soviet press were supplemented by critical radio broadcasts from Moscow in the basic languages of the world. Beginning on January 4, the Bulletin of the British Broadcasting Corporation, which publishes daily summaries of world radio transmissions, was obliged to set up a special category, 'Attacks on Solzhenitsyn', in which (for example) on January 5 alone it gave an account of six different anti-Solzhenitsyn broadcasts from Moscow in the English language for Britain, Ireland and the US and mentioned similar programs in German, Italian, French, Czech and many other languages. From almost all of these texts it was evident that their authors had not in fact read Solzhenitsyn's book. Nor had the book been read by the majority of writers of anti-Solzhenitsyn articles in the Soviet press.

It would be senseless to try to expound any argumentation from this hysterical campaign. The titles of the articles are sufficiently characteristic: 'The Path of a Traitor', 'Damned by the People', 'A Corrupt, Petty Soul', 'Opposing the People', 'The Lot of a Traitor', 'A Slanderer Unmasks Himself', 'The Utmost Limit of Degradation', 'Rebuff to a Literary Vlasovite', etc. A big placard about 'The Works of Solzhenitsyn' was posted on Gorky Street not far from the building where Solzhenitsyn and his family were living. Displayed on the placard were the verses of some poetaster, branding Solzhenitsyn a traitor.

202

This campaign meant only one thing: that its organizers had in fact the most serious intentions. In and of themselves, all these threats in the newspapers and on the radio and television placed the lives of Solzhenitsyn and his family in real danger of reprisals. Friends of Solzhenitsyn reported that in the streets there were people ready to go and 'finish off that traitor'. One writer who, like Solzhenitsyn, has a beard, was attacked by a drunken young man who pursued him with a knife, shouting, 'I know you're Solzhenitsyn!'

On February 8 a police officer brought to Solzhenitsyn's apartment a summons to the public prosecutor's office. Mrs. Solzhenitsyn refused to accept the paper, since it bore no registration number and did not indicate the case in connection with which Solzhenitsyn was being summoned. On February 11, the same police officer brought a new summons and served it on Solzhenitsyn personally. Solzhenitsyn, however, returned it with a statement in which he refused to appear at the prosecutor's office, since under the law as he understood it he did not believe he could be legally interrogated.

The refusal to appear at the prosecutor's office in answer to the summons meant that the person summoned could be brought in for interrogation 'under compulsory procedure'. On the morning of February 12, a number of KGB agents in civilian clothes appeared outside the building where Solzhenitsyn was living. Some foreign correspondents also were present, but they were asked to leave. Later in the day, when Solzhenitsyn's mother-in-law had taken the children for an outing in a nearby park, two police vehicles drew up to the entrance of the building. The group which was to 'deliver' the writer to the prosecutor's office consisted of seven persons. A few hours later Mrs. Solzhenitsyn received a telephone call from the prosecutor's office and was informed that her husband was under arrest.

The circumstances of the interrogation and arrest are still unknown. Nothing was published in the Soviet press about the Solzhenitsyn 'case'. But for the Bulgarian newspaper *Rabotrichesko Delo* the Novosti Press Agency prepared a special article, 'A. I. Solzhenitsyn: Case #3-47-74', which was published on February 19. The authors, Boris Korolev and Vitaly Pomaznev, had interviewed the USSR Deputy General Prosecutor, Mikhail Malyarov, who had interrogated Solzhenitsyn on February 12 and 13. According to Malyarov, Solzhenitsyn was indicted under Article 64 of the RSFSR Criminal Code. He was charged with 'high treason'. Punishment under this article ranges from ten years' imprisonment to death. Judging even from this tendentious item, there was not any actual interrogation, since the 'accused' apparently refused to answer the prosecutor's questions.

Article 64 of the RSFSR Criminal Code, the first in that section of the Code titled 'Especially Dangerous Anti-State Crimes', could in no way have been applied to the Solzhenitsyn 'case'. Like many articles in the Code, however, this one is susceptible to the broadest interpretations. Thus together with 'espionage', 'betraying military secrets', and 'plotting with a view to overthrowing the régime', this article includes such vaguely-defined acts as 'assisting a foreign state in carrying on inimical activity against the USSR'. Apparently, foreign publication of *The Gulag Archipelago* was found to fall into this category.

Solzhenitsyn spent the night in the Lefortovo Prison. The next day, instead of continuing the 'interrogation', Malyarov informed Solzhenitsyn of the decree of the Presidium of the USSR Supreme Soviet, in accordance with which Solzhenitsyn was deprived of Soviet citizenship 'for the systematic commission of acts incompatible with Soviet citizenship and damaging to the Union of Soviet Socialist Republics'. That same day, under guard in an Aeroflot plane, Solzhenitsyn was sent to West Germany. He was deported to Frankfurt most probably because it is a center of anti-Soviet activities. But Solzhenitsyn left Germany very quickly.

On February 12, after Solzhenitsyn's arrest, many of his friends assembled at the apartment, where his family remained: among them were A. Sakharov, L. Chukovskaya, Yu. Daniel, V. Kornilov, Yu. Shafarevich, L. Kopelev and others. The telephone rang. The caller, speaking English, represented himself as a Western correspondent. Sakharov quickly composed a statement of protest, which was translated into English, and the correspondent was asked to take it down. The protest was signed by eight persons. It was brief but sharp. Sakharov said that Solzhenitsyn's arrest was vengeance for his *Archi-*

pelago; that it was an insult not only to Russian literature but to those millions of dead persons to whom the book was dedicated. The 'correspondent' took it down; but not a word of the protest ever appeared in the press. It is still unclear whether this 'correspondent' was genuine.

Since February 13 Solzhenitsyn has lived outside his own country; and it would be superfluous to describe his first weeks in alien surroundings. But the persecution of Russian literature has not ended with the expulsion of Solzhenitsyn. It has been reported that Vladimir Voinovich, a fine prose writer, has been expelled from the Writers' Union, and that Victor Nekrasov, author of *In the Trenches of Stalingrad,* the best book about World War II in our literature, has had his home searched and his files confiscated.

In his statement on these persecutions, Nekrasov asked whose interests were served by forcibly ousting some people, compelling others to leave and preventing others from returning to their homeland.

Who needs this? The country? The state? The people?

Have we not been too free-handed in squandering people we should be proud of? . . . Solzhenitsyn was *thrown out* . . . The artist Chagall, the composer Stravinsky, the aircraft designer Sikorsky, the writer Nabokov, became the property of other cultures. With whom are we going to stop? After all, KGB agents will not paint pictures for us, or write books or symphonies.

April 1, 1974
(Translated from the Russian by Guy Daniels)

205

Appendix

Solzhenitsyn's open letter to the Fourth[1] Soviet Writers' Congress

To the Presidium and the delegates to the Congress, to members of the Soviet Writers' Union, and to the editors of literary newspapers and magazines:

Not having access to the platform at this Congress, I ask that the Congress discuss:

1. The no longer tolerable oppression, in the form of censorship, which our literature has endured for decades, and which the Union of Writers can no longer accept.

Under the obfuscating label of GLAVLIT, this censorship – which is not provided for in the Constitution and is therefore illegal, and which is nowhere publicly labelled as such – imposes a yoke on our literature and gives people unversed in literature arbitrary control over writers. A survival of the Middle Ages, the censorship has managed, Methuselah-like, to drag out its existence almost to the twenty-first century. Of fleeting significance, it attempts to appropriate to itself the role of unfleeting time – of separating good books from bad.

Our writers are not supposed to have the right, are not endowed with the right, to express their cautionary judgements about the moral life of man and society, or to explain in their own way the social problems and historical experience that have been so deeply felt in our country. Works that might express the mature thinking of the people, that might have a timely and salutary influence on the realm of the spirit or on the development of a social conscience, are proscribed or distorted by censorship on the basis of considerations that are petty, egotistical, and – from the national point of view – shortsighted.

[1] English translation, *Solzhenitsyn: A Documentary Record*, edited by Leopold Labedz, pp. 106–12 (Allen Lane, the Penguin Press 1970).

Outstanding manuscripts by young authors, as yet entirely unknown, are nowadays rejected by editors solely on the ground that they 'will not pass'. Many members of the [Writers'] Union, and even many of the delegates at this Congress, know how they themselves have bowed to the pressures of the censorship and made concessions in the structure and concept of their books – changing chapters, pages, paragraphs, or sentences, giving them innocuous titles – just for the sake of seeing them finally in print even if it meant distorting them irremediably. It is an understood quality of literature that gifted works suffer [most] disastrously from all these distortions, while untalented works are not affected by them. Indeed, it is the best of our literature that is published in mutilated form.

Meanwhile, the most censorious labels – 'ideologically harmful', 'depraved', and so forth – are proving short-lived and fluid, [in fact] are changing before our very eyes. Even Dostoyevsky, the pride of world literature, was at one time not published in our country (still today his works are not published in full); he was excluded from the school curriculum, made unacceptable for reading, and reviled. For how many years was Yesenin considered 'counter-revolutionary'? – he was even subjected to a prison term because of his books. Wasn't Mayakovsky called 'an anarchistic political hooligan'? For decades the immortal poetry of Akhamatova was considered anti-Soviet. The first timid printing of the dazzling Tsvetayeva ten years ago was declared a 'gross political error'. Only after a delay of twenty or thirty years were Bunin, Bulgakov, and Platonov returned to us. Inevitably Mandelshtam, Voloshin, Gumilev and Klyuev will follow in that line – not to mention the recognition, at some time or other, of even Zamyatin and Remizov.

A decisive moment [in this process] comes with the death of a troublesome writer. Sooner or later after that, he is returned to us with an 'explanation of [his] errors'. For a long time the name of Pasternak could not be pronounced out loud; but then he died, and since then his books have appeared and his verse is even quoted at ceremonies.

Pushkin's words are really coming true: 'They are capable of loving only the dead.'

But the belated publication of books and 'authorization'

[rehabilitation] of names does not make up for either the social or the artistic losses suffered by our people as a consequence of these monstrous delays and the suppression of artistic conscience. (In fact, there were writers in the 1920s – Pilnyak, Platonov, Mandelshtam – who called attention at a very early stage to the beginnings of the cult [of personality] and the peculiar traits of Stalin's character; but these writers were silenced and destroyed instead of being listened to.) Literature cannot develop in between the categories of 'permitted' and 'not permitted', 'about this you may write' and 'about this you may not'. Literature that is not the breath of contemporary society, that dares not transmit the pains and fears of that society, that does not warn in time against threatening moral and social dangers – such literature does not deserve the name of literature; it is only a façade. Such literature loses the confidence of its own people, and its published works are used as wastepaper instead of being read.

Our literature has lost the leading role it played at the end of the last century and the beginning of this one, and it has lost the brilliance of experimentation that distinguished it in the 1920s. To the entire world the literary life of our country now appears immeasurably more colourless, trivial and inferior than it actually is – [or] than it would be if it were not confined and hemmed in. The losers are both our country – in world public opinion – and world literature itself. If the world had access to all the uninhibited fruits of our literature, if it were enriched by our own spiritual experience, the whole artistic evolution of the world would move along in a different way, acquiring a new stability and attaining even a new artistic threshold.

I propose that the Congress adopt a resolution which would demand and ensure the abolition of all censorship, open or hidden, of all fictional writing, and which would release publishing houses from the obligation to obtain authorization for the publication of every printed page.

2. The duties of the Union towards its members.

These duties are not clearly formulated in the statutes of the Soviet Writers' Union (under 'Protection of copyrights' and 'Measures for the protection of other rights of writers'), and it is sad to find that for a third of a century the Union has not

208

defended either the 'other' rights or even the copyrights of persecuted writers.

Many writers have been subjected during their lifetime to abuse and slander in the press and from rostrums without being afforded the physical possibility of replying. More than that, they have been exposed to violence and personal persecution (Bulgakov, Akhmatova, Tsvetayeva, Pasternak, Zoshchenko, Platonov, Alexander Grin, Vassily Grossman). The Writers' Union not only did not make its own publications available to these writers for purposes of reply and justification, not only did not come out in their defence, but through its leadership was always first among the persecutors. Names that adorned our poetry of the twentieth century found themselves on the list of those expelled from the Union or not even admitted to it in the first place. The leadership of the Union cravenly abandoned to their distress those for whom persecution ended in exile, labour camps, and death (Pavel Vasilev, Mandelshtam, Artem Vesely, Pilnyak, Babel, Tabidze, Zabolotsky, and others). The list must be cut off at 'and others'. We learned after the Twentieth Party Congress that there were more than 600 writers whom the Union had obediently handed over to their fate in prisons and camps. However, the roll is even longer, and its curled-up ends cannot and will not ever be read by our eyes. It contains the names of young prose-writers and poets whom we may have known only accidentally through personal encounters and whose talents were crushed in camps before being able to blossom, whose writings never got further than the offices of the state security service in the days of Yagoda, Yezhov, Beria and Abakumov.

There is no historical necessity for the newly-elected leadership of the Union to share with its predecessors the responsibility for the past.

I propose that all guarantees for the defence of Union members subjected to slander and unjust persecution be clearly formulated in Paragraph 22 of the Union statutes, so that past illegalities will not be repeated.

If the Congress does not remain indifferent to what I have said, I also ask that it consider the interdictions and persecution to which I myself have been subjected.

(1) It will soon be two years since the state security authorities took away from me my novel, *The First Circle* (comprising thirty-five author's sheets [*avtorskie listy*],[2] thus preventing it from being submitted to publishers. Instead, in my own lifetime, against my will and even without my knowledge, this novel has been 'published' in an unnatural 'closed' edition for reading by an unidentified select circle. My novel has [thus] become available to literary officials but is being concealed from most writers. I have been unable to obtain open discussion of the novel within writers' associations and to prevent misuse and plagiarism.

(2) Together with this novel, my literary papers dating back fifteen to twenty years, things that were not intended for publication, were taken away from me. Now, tendentious excerpts from these papers have also been covertly 'published' and are being circulated within the same circles. The play, *Feast of the Victors*, which I composed in verse from memory in camp, where I went by a four-digit number – and where, condemned to death by starvation, we were forgotten by society, and no one outside the camps spoke out against [such] repressions – this play, now left far behind, is being ascribed to me as my very latest work.

(3) For three years now, an irresponsible campaign of slander has been conducted against me, who fought all through the war as a battery commander and received military decorations. It is being said that I served time as a criminal, or surrendered to the enemy (I was never a prisoner-of-war), that I 'betrayed' my country and 'served the Germans'. That is the interpretation being put now on the eleven years I spent in camps and in exile for having criticised Stalin. This slander is being spread in secret instructions and meetings by people holding official positions. I vainly tried to stop the slander by appealing to the Board of the Writers' Union of the RSFSR and to the press. The Board did not even react, and not a single paper printed my reply to the slanderers. On the contrary, slander against me from rostrums has intensified and become more vicious within the last year, making use of distorted material from my confiscated papers, and I have no way of replying.

---

[2] 'Author's sheets' are printed pages, each containing 40,000 typographical characters, used in the Soviet Union for computing the author's fee.

(4) My novel *Cancer Ward* (comprising twenty-five author's sheets), the first part of which was approved for publication by the prose department of the Moscow writers' organisation, cannot be published either by chapters – rejected by five magazines, or in its entirety – rejected by *Novy Mir*, *Zvezda* and *Prostor*.

(5) The play, *The Tenderfoot and the Tramp*, accepted in 1962 by the Sovremennik Theatre, has thus far not been approved for performance.

(6) The screen play, *The Tanks Know the Truth*; the stage play, *The light That is in You*; a short story entitled *The Right Hand*; the series, *Miniature Stories* – [all these] cannot find either a producer or a publisher.

(7) My stories published in *Novy Mir* have never been reprinted in book form, having been rejected everywhere – by the 'Soviet Writer' Publishers, the State literary Publishing House, and the 'Ogonyok' Library. They thus remain inaccessible to the general reading public.

(8) I have also been prevented from having any other contacts with readers [either] through public readings of my works (in November 1966, nine out of eleven scheduled meetings were cancelled at the last moment) or through readings over the radio. Even the simple act of giving a manuscript away for 'reading and copying' has now become a criminal act (ancient Russian scribes were permitted to do this five centuries ago). Thus my work has been finally smothered, gagged and slandered.

In view of such flagrant infringements of my copyright and 'other' rights, will the Fourth Congress defend me – yes or no? It seems to me that the choice is also not without importance for the literary future of several of the delegates.

I am of course confident that I will fulfil my duty as a writer in all circumstances – from the grave even more successfully and more irrefutably than in my lifetime. No one can bar the road to truth, and to advance its cause I am prepared to accept even death. But may it be that repeated lessons will finally teach us not to stop the writer's pen during his lifetime?

At no time has this ennobled our history.

A. I. SOLZHENITSYN

16 May 1967

Zhores A. Medvedev is the Soviet biochemist whose own conflict with the Soviet government culminated in his politically forced committal to a mental hospital, from which he was released only after an international storm of protest. He has described his experience in *A Question of Madness,* written in collaboration with his brother, the historian Roy A. Medvedev. He currently lives in England, where he is continuing his scientific investigations at the National Institute for Medical Research. His passport was recently confiscated by the Soviet authorities—barring his return to the Soviet Union.